Economic Cooperation in the Asia-Pacific Region

Economic Cooperation in the Asia-Pacific Region

EDITED BY
John P. Hardt and
Young C. Kim

Westview Press
BOULDER, SAN FRANCISCO, & OXFORD

This Westview softcover edition is printed on acid-free paper and bound in library-quality, coated covers that carry the highest rating of the National Association of State Textbook Administrators, in consultation with the Association of American Publishers and the Book Manufacturers' Institute.

All rights reserved. No part of this publication may be reproduced or transmitted in any form or by any means, electronic or mechanical, including photocopy, recording, or any information storage and retrieval system, without permission in writing from the publisher.

Copyright © 1990 by Westview Press, Inc.

Published in 1990 in the United States of America by Westview Press, Inc., 5500 Central Avenue, Boulder, Colorado 80301, and in the United Kingdom by Westview Press, 36 Lonsdale Road, Summertown, Oxford OX2 7EW

Library of Congress Cataloging-in-Publication Data
Economic cooperation in the Asia-Pacific region/edited by John P.
  Hardt and Young C. Kim.
    p. cm.
  "Outgrowth of a series of meetings held in Washington, D.C., in the spring and summer of 1989 under the auspices of The American Council on Asian and Pacific Affairs, Inc. (ACAPA)"—P. vii.
  ISBN 0-8133-7941-5
  1. Asia—Economic policy—Congresses. 2. Pacific Area—Economic policy—Congresses. 3. Asian cooperation—Congresses. 4. Asia—Foreign economic relations—Congresses. 5. Pacific Area—Foreign economic relations—Congresses. I. Hardt, John Pearce. II. Kim, Young C.
HC412.E215 1990
337.5—dc20   90-38668
                                                                      CIP

Printed and bound in the United States of America

∞ The paper used in this publication meets the requirements of the American National Standard for Permanence of Paper for Printed Library Materials Z39.48-1984.

10   9   8   7   6   5   4   3   2

Contents

Acknowledgments   vii

    Introduction, *John P. Hardt*   1

1. Soviet Global Integration Prospects, *John P. Hardt*   3
2. Japan's Role in Asia-Pacific Cooperation: Dimensions, Prospects, and Problems, *Edward J. Lincoln*   21
3. Asia-Pacific Economic Cooperation and U.S.-Japan Relations, *Dick K. Nanto*   46
4. Trade, Policy, and Korea-U.S. Relations, *Paul W. Kuznets*   69
5. Korea's Perspectives on Asia-Pacific Economic Cooperation, *Bon Ho Koo*   89
6. China and Asia-Pacific Economic Cooperation, *Nicholas R. Lardy*   101
7. Economic Cooperation in the Asia-Pacific Region: The Southeast Asia Dimension, *Anthony C. Albrecht*   109
8. Taiwan's Future Role in International and Regional Economic Cooperation, *Yuan-li Wu*   123
9. The Future Role of Hong Kong in the International and Regional Economy, *Yuan-li Wu*   141
10. U.S. Economic Policy in a World of Regional Trading Blocs, *Richard S. Belous*   161
11. Technology Transfer in the Pacific Basin: Issues and Policies, *Charles T. Stewart, Jr.*   177
12. The European Community: A Looming Challenge, *William H. Lewis*   199

About the Editors and Contributors   211
Index   213

Acknowledgments

This volume is an outgrowth of a series of meetings held in Washington, D.C., in the spring and summer of 1989 under the auspices of The American Council on Asian and Pacific Affairs, Inc. (ACAPA). It contains the expanded versions of the papers presented at the final conference and therefore incorporates comments made by specialists from various academic research institutes and governmental agencies who attended the meetings. I would like to take this opportunity to express my appreciation to all the participants for their insightful analyses and stimulating discussions.

I would also like to express my gratitude to the Japan Economic Foundation for providing the research grant that partially supported this ACAPA program. Finally, I would like to thank the Ministry of International Trade and Industry of Japan for sharing the findings of the interim report of the Asia-Pacific Trade and Development Study Group, "Toward New Asia-Pacific Cooperation: Promotion of Multilevel Gradually Advancing Cooperation on a Consensus Basis" (June 1988); the Council for the Promotion of Asia-Pacific Cooperation (Japan) for sharing the findings of their report on "Toward an Era of Development Through Outward-Looking Cooperation" (June 1989); and the Study Group on a Japan-U.S. Free Trade Agreement (Japan) for sharing their report on "A Double-Track Approach Aimed at a Japan-U.S. Economic Cooperation Charter" (June 1989).

Young C. Kim

Introduction

John P. Hardt

Under the best of circumstances, the Asia-Pacific region may well become the engine of global economic growth as we move into the twenty-first century. The Asian market-oriented economies, following the Japanese example, have modernized their domestic economies, raised living standards, and competed vigorously in the global market economy. Indeed, South Korea, Taiwan, and Hong Kong have emerged as global leaders in economic performance in recent years. The most populous country of Asia, the People's Republic of China, embraced the general principles of Western economic success in the post-Mao period by keying its plans toward modernization. The countries of Southeast Asia have also been pulled toward growth and improved economic health, primarily by Japan and the Newly Industrializing Countries (NICs).

The region has had no major military conflicts since Vietnam, and the prospects for resolution of differences by peaceful means and reduction in military burdens in most of the major Asia-Pacific countries are good to excellent. Even the Soviet Union may move away from its militarily driven Asia policy toward reconciliation and economic cooperation. Indeed, the global East-West confrontation is moderating and settlements of arms issues and conflicts between regional powers, Great Powers, and East-West are more likely than at any other time since the World War II settlements.

However, this favorable economic picture is clouded by troublesome problems that, if not resolved, could reverse the favorable prospects. On the global scene, Japanese economic competition may have replaced the Soviet military threat in the psychology of the European Community and North America. Moreover, some Asian countries, while benefiting from Japanese economic assistance and cooperation, still have a fear of economic domination that reflects their earlier concerns about military domination in the pre–World War II period. Although the European Community 92 and the North American Free Trade Zone are not solely regional economic alliances to counter the perceived economic threat of Japan, there is at least an element of protective competitiveness in the policies of these regional groupings. Major U.S. deficits and Japanese surpluses in trade accounts and investable funds are evidence of a realignment of economic power. And yet the policy adjustments in international institutions and in the global market structure have yet to be made. Japan has not yet taken or been accorded the institutional recognition and responsibility commensurate with its economic power and command of investable funds.

The integration of the Communist economies into the global market has proceeded more in rhetoric than in fact. The East European economies and the Soviet Union are tied to Western industrial economies more through economic policies of aid than through improved competition. The People's Republic of China has receded from political and economic modernization and may be moving back to the policy of self-sufficiency and control that was so dominant in its former ideology.

Prospects for resolving the political-military sources of instability in Southeast Asia—namely, in Cambodia; in northern Asia, with the continued confrontational division of the Korean peninsula; in the disputed Northern Territories; and in the Soviet Union, which still has substantial military buildups—are all troublesome. Each appears to be on the agenda of regional powers and Great Powers and is potentially resolvable in the years ahead. However, regression on any or all of these areas would have serious impacts on political security and economic growth and cooperation in Asia.

Thus a theme that runs through the individual assessments in this book is that under the best of scenarios the region may pull itself and the global economy toward higher levels of performance through structural change and competitive trade. Indeed, the region may live up to its name as a "pacific" area of the world. However, in order to bring about this favorable scenario, decision makers in Tokyo, Washington, Brussels, Moscow, Beijing, and elsewhere will have to take steps to ameliorate the serious economic and political problems threatening growth and stability. If they do not, the engine of growth and stability may work in reverse. Instead of becoming a leader in economic progress and a major contributor to a liberal global market, the Asia-Pacific region may face economic and political confrontation and instability. The contributors to this book do not make prescriptions to those who gather in Asia-Pacific policy councils, the economic summits of major Western economic powers, East-West summits, or the myriad of bilateral meetings, but those decision makers and other readers will gain insights on the issues that are likely to influence the search for solutions.

1

Soviet Global Integration Prospects

John P. Hardt

GLOBAL TRENDS AND THE ASIA-PACIFIC BASIN

Regionalism and the Liberal Global Regime

The increasing popularity of the concepts of globalism and the liberal commercial regime and the emphasis on development investment over defense allocations provides a favorable climate for increased efficiency and competitiveness, commerce and growth. This increasing acceptance *in principle* of developing a global economy based on universally accepted principles of openness and competition rekindles the spirit of those who projected a liberal world economic order to grow from the ashes of World War II. This new international economic order was to be an open, universal system that allowed for the development of a growing yet stable global economy that would assure improved living standards and reduce the prospects of conflict. Prosperity and peace were set out as the twin visions for the postwar world—visions that have largely been sustained through the 1980s.

The United States and Japan are likely to continue to dominate the commerce and investment of the Asia-Pacific region. Each has apprehensions about the future. A fear of the United States is that without changes in the factors leading to the trade deficit, Japan might own and control too large a share of U.S. assets by the end of the century. A Japanese concern is that external pressure to force open the Japanese markets in agriculture and other sectors too quickly might create strong negative political reactions in their country.

While reduction in the U.S. domestic deficit would help reduce U.S. current assets and merchandise trade deficits, as would a flexible exchange rate policy, and more resources to raise domestic investment and productivity could help raise the competitive position of the United States in Asian markets, without these favorable developments pressures working against a liberal regime may mount. A shift in domestic policies in Japan and the Asian Newly Industrializing Countries (NICs) toward domestic priorities, such as housing and a further reduction in institutional barriers to domestic markets, would further liberalize trade.

U.S. attention to the debt reduction problem in developing countries would also be essential to preserving liberal markets. Foreign aid and cooperation in addressing the debt issue is one of the top priorities in current Japanese economic policies. In 1988, Japan's official development aid passed the $10 billion level, exceeding the $8.8 billion of the United States. This made Japan the world's largest source of official development aid. A comprehensive conception and implementation of the Brady Plan, with Japan and the World Bank playing key roles, is another indication that U.S. economic hegemony is waning and roles are changing.

Japan and the Newly Industrializing Countries of Asia might be especially helpful in encouraging the integration of the People's Republic of China and Soviet Siberian regions into the rules-based multilateral economic system. All Western countries, especially the United States and Japan, may facilitate this integration in a global context, with regional affiliations reinforcing rather than countervailing global openness.

Soviet Domestic Reform Economies and Integration into the World Economy

While the West can take significant steps toward facilitating the integration of the Soviet Union into the global economy, the primary precondition for successful integration is domestic economic reform in the Soviet Union. Especially pertinent are the issues involving monetization in order to create a domestic market system and reduction of defense spending to facilitate modernization and political acceptance into the Western system. Without successful market-oriented reforms to cope with pressing problems of monetary overhang and extreme weakness in necessary economic infrastructures, and without effective steps toward relief of hard currency shortages and progress toward convertibility, effective integration is not likely. Market-driven economies at home are a precondition for effective integration of socialist economies into the global market system.[1]

Price reform, scheduled to begin in the early 1990s, is a process whereby prices that were formerly set by administrative procedures are allowed to "float freely" as determined by the market forces of supply and demand. The implications of price reform are substantial: Consumer and wholesale price reform would essentially create a market-oriented, decentralized economy. Specifically, implementation of price reform would lay the foundation for guidance planning; economic decision making based on objective criteria (e.g., efficiency, rate of return, and comparative advantage); competitive performance standards; mechanisms of accountability; a freely convertible exchange rate; and a rational tariff structure. Still, price reform presents policymakers with an inherent dilemma: While it is an absolute precondition for monetization and decentralization of the economy, it carries with it high short-term costs. Undertaking price reform in an economy like the Soviet Union with excess demand and heavily subsidized consumer sectors, the leadership faces unbridled inflation and negative social consequences.[2] Questions of equity—particularly for those workers on regular salaries whose living standard will fall rapidly as consumer prices increase—have left doubts as to the best way to proceed with consumer price reform, further delaying price reform until after 1991.

Dealing with the excess purchasing power in the system—that is, the monetary overhang—is clearly the first-order problem facing Soviet policymakers. Minister of Finance Boris Gostev[3] proposed the following strategy for dealing with the acknowledged 100 billion-ruble overhang:

1. Discipline the economic mechanism by tying wages to productivity and requiring enterprises to end deficits. Wages rose last year by 12 percent, productivity by 5 percent; one out of ten enterprises had a deficit. The "hard budget constraint" restricts loans to failing enterprises in order to end the "evil of freeloading."
2. Increase revenues by placing additional taxes on incomes and profits, especially the "unearned incomes" of some cooperatives. Also, sharply reduce capital investments and cut defense spending by 14 percent.
3. Absorb purchasing power through a 12 billion-ruble increase in domestic production of consumer goods, including some imports, and reduce supplies to nonmarket consumers (a euphemism for cutting special privileges to members of the party and government bureaucracy).
4. Increase savings and personal investments through the sale of housing and property claims on farms, enterprises, and cooperatives.

Nikolai Shmelev, who estimates a much larger overhang, would reverse alcoholic prohibition and instead introduce a heavy tax abstinence policy and import on credit of up to $15 billion worth of consumer goods in one year and $3.5 billion on a continuing basis.

The defense "burden" issue[4] came to the public agenda in 1988 with critical discussion of defense spending; conversion of military-industrial plants; the necessity of the current military draft; and a public debate on allocation issues. The primacy-of-defense claim has been politically challenged and the burden of defense generally acknowledged. Instead, investment for civilian restructuring over military programs would place perestroika in conflict with the more traditional view of the requirements of military security. In 1989, for the first time in Soviet planning history, the "guns versus butter" argument appears to be moving in favor of butter. So far, several proposals have been advanced to commission new plant and equipment for modernizing industry and agriculture; to delay new resource allocation for upgrading models of tanks, aircraft, and artillery; to reduce the draft of eighteen-year-olds for military service and instead release them to pursue advanced education or to become gainfully employed in the industrial or agricultural labor force. New military force planning may shift from offensive to defensive capabilities requiring smaller forces and fewer officers. Reduced foreign policy roles for military sales and aid may require less military production and claims on hardware inventories.

Nevertheless, the last Soviet leader to challenge the military budget, Nikita S. Khrushchev, was widely opposed by the military and was eventually removed from power. The Soviet reformers must therefore find the "proper" balance; they must prove the validity of reform to the average Soviet citizen by showing positive results without losing the military bureaucracy to reactionary forces.

Shifting to market forces in management and incomes policy is a daunting task in any centrally controlled economy.[5] Proceeding directly to consumer price reform, say in the early 1990s, would create high short-term economic and political costs. Perhaps the most critical initial requirement is to manage demand by bringing the money supply into line with the supply of goods and services. While all elements of fiscal policy may be employed to reduce monetary overhang, improvement in the quality of goods supplied, together with rising real income for the productive workers, may allow for the inevitable increase in prices without the consequences of severe austerity.

The labor surplus created by improving productivity in the service sector could be redirected into new cooperatives. This policy could provide significant short-term improvements in the quality of life. The growing attention given to cooperatives suggests their important role not only in improving the quality of life but also in creating jobs. Thus, hundreds of thousands of cooperatives formed in 1987-1988 have served the dual role of providing more products and services for the population and providing a new source of productive employment. Still, in response to the official perception that cooperatives have led to "unearned" price increases (despite improved services and products), a sharp control of activities and profits of cooperatives was set down in December 1988, and a new regulatory decree on cooperatives has dampened the development of cooperatives in 1990.

Intervention by the center represents a major setback in progress toward reform: As long as members of the old bureaucracy trained in the thinking and decision making associated with central planning continue to intervene, local decision makers may continue to base decisions more on the interests of government bureaucrats and less on market forces. In addition, private producers, without the benefits of being inside the "old system," may find it very difficult to compete on an uneven playing field. Eventually reform begins to be suffocated at its root—the enterprise. These dynamics effectively undermine newly implemented reform measures, bolstering instead the very structure meant to be transformed.

Step-by-step approaches may be critical to minimizing the highly negative social consequences of price reform and avoiding the inflation/intervention cycle. Transition toward market forces could take place through the use of short- and medium-term strategies. In the short term, any shift in prices alone might result in overt or concealed inflation; only an increase in supply may dampen the wage-price pressure and cushion the impact of reductions in income that would result from increasing sensitive prices such as meat and rent. In the interim, effective incentive systems may bring about an increased availability of "hard goods" such as quality food products, home appliances, and services. Output in agriculture may be less an obstacle to improving food supplies than the infrastructure that "preserves the harvest and crop" from field to table. Thus, direct attention to losses in quality and volume in harvesting and transport may lead to substantial improvements where it counts—on the consumer's table.[6]

A transitional phase during which a "simulated market" was created would allow price ranges to be created for goods, which would lead toward a rational price structure but would also meet the political and equity concerns of the leadership. Movement of producer and consumer goods toward market clearing levels would both provide useful price indicators for management and restrict the role of the second economy. For example, both housing and meat are currently heavily subsidized. During the transitional period, higher relative price ranges could be set for housing and goods production, which would eventually stabilize at a market clearing price. The point would be to move in the direction of a rational price structure in steps.

During the transitional period, before a fully rational price structure is established and objective criteria for policy-making set forth, problems of inefficiency, corruption, and inflation will most likely persist. These negative aspects of a staged approach may, however, be mitigated by a strong emphasis on increasing supply—through growth of both social and private production. This approach would help to keep down the worst aspects of inflation and may broaden the influence of the market and weaken the control of central bureaucratic managers. While Western economists agree that it is only through comprehensive price reform that other aspects of reform can be successful, political economists might be more inclined to emphasize the transitional approach, taking into account the short-term politico-economic benefits of maintaining a staged approach.

Other countries share with Soviet leaders the desire to avert the negative social consequences of inflationary pressure. In the initial stages of the transition, Soviet efforts to produce rising real income through an increase in the quantity of agricultural products may draw on Western experience in managing the farm-to-market food system and service industries. Development of cooperatives, coupled with investment in the farm-to-market infrastructure, which would facilitate marketing from cooperatives and family units as well as state and collective farms, would promote an increase in real income. The United States, the Scandinavian countries, and Western Europe have developed experience in agricultural cooperatives, as Lenin was aware when he wrote his famous article on cooperatives, referred to in the seventieth anniversary speech of General Secretary Mikhail S. Gorbachev. Western techniques regarding food storage, transportation, and processing of perishable products, if successfully adopted by the Soviet Union, and marketing techniques in Western economies, such as in the United States and the European Community, are especially relevant for Soviet economists and businesspeople.

Interdependence entails the establishment of an effective interrelationship between domestic and foreign markets whereby external economic relations are based on calculations of comparative advantage rather than ideology. Gorbachev's conception of interdependence and globalism appear to go far beyond the strictly economic; it embraces the political as it bears on arms control, the environment, the sharing of world resources, problems in overpopulation—in brief, a whole range of interaction in our experience today.[7]

Soviet New Thinking and the Reasonable Sufficiency Security Policy

The application of the New Thinking to regional issues has led to the withdrawal of Soviet troops from Afghanistan, a cease-fire in the Persian Gulf, and new withdrawal negotiations in South Africa and Southeast Asia. The formula suggested by Soviet diplomats for settling regional crises is the Afghanistan formula. The prime areas not influenced in the 1980s by this New Thinking are Northeast Asia—the Northern Territories and Divided Korea—and Central America. The former is a major impediment in moving toward a peace treaty and a summit with Japanese leadership, which the Soviets project for the early 1990s. Divided Korea is a dominant issue for South Korea and for stability in Asia. In the view of the United States, Central American intervention by the Soviet Union and Cuba restricts U.S.-USSR normalization in that region.

The unilateral and proposed symmetrical reductions in Conventional Forces Europe (CAFE) have led to considerable expectations of deep cuts in Europe. These have not been reflected in comparable Asian military negotiations and reductions.

On New Thinking, leading Soviet foreign policy advisers aver that progress toward the settlement of the Northern Territories, a precondition for a Tokyo Summit, is possible.[8] In reassessing the status of the Kurile Islands, one possibility that has been mentioned is to institute a transitional mode preceding their return under which Japan could lease some facilities on the four islands. Were Gorbachev to include a stop in Seoul as part of his trip to Japan, some Soviet formula for negotiation of relations between the two Koreas might be explored.

On force reductions, the NATO proposal of General Andrew Goodpaster of a mid-term goal of a 50 percent cut with balanced forces might be applied to China border forces, and unilateral cuts in the Trans Baikal district might be explored.[9] These symmetrical Soviet changes in regional and security policy would reduce the threat and open the prospects of commercial normalization.

Prospects and Options for Integrating the Soviet Union into the Asian and Global Market System

Western developed economies could reinforce the rules-driven liberal market system in the global economy by further integrating the economies of the Common Market in Europe past 1992; further integrating the leading Asian economies, such as Japan and the Newly Industrializing Countries of Asia (South Korea, Taiwan, Hong Kong, Singapore); and further integrating the North American economies into the global system, especially the United States and Canada.

In addition, measures should be pursued through the Uruguay Round of Multilateral Trade Negotiations under GATT and other means to facilitate integration of the developing countries into the global system through improved policies dealing with the debt of Less Developed Countries (LDCs).

Domestic reform, or sustainable perestroika, in the Soviet Union would provide an economic and institutional domestic basis for effective integration of the Soviet economy into the global market. In time, progress toward joining the Bretton Woods institutions of GATT, the IMF, and the World Bank could be facilitated.

THE SOVIET UNION IN ASIA: ALTERNATIVE FUTURES

Status Quo: Defense-Dominant, Slow Commercial Development

The Soviet domestic policy of perestroika has very little to offer Siberian development—especially investment in East Siberia and the Far East. The era of the big projects, such as the Baikal-Amur Magistral (BAM), is over;

driving the golden spike to complete the rail line in 1984 was the last Siberian hurrah for some time from Moscow. Investment under Gorbachev is not for new large-scale Siberian projects but for renovation of hundreds of old European plants to bring about a Second Industrial Revolution. The Soviet "rust belt" has won out for the time being over the development of the Siberian frontier. Likewise, consumer goods and modernization have an edge over military outlays. So the two legs of Brezhnev's policy east of Baikal—BAM (the Project of the Century) and buildup of the Trans Baikal military district—have been deferred and may be reversed. Still, although Gorbachev has taken his new military leaders from their posts in this area—Marshals Dimitri Yazov and Nikolai Moiseyev—he may continue on the policy course set in motion by his antecedents. While the "Far Eastern Comprehensive Economic Development Plan to the Year 2000" was announced in August 1987 with a promise for investment to exceed 230 billion rubles, I expect this to be a largely empty promise along with the undeveloped part of BAM. The railroad and regional development may be the Project of the Century, but from current indications the century referred to will not be the current one. So an economic status quo in East Siberia and the Far East is likely unless a new environment permits substantially expanded commercial relations with Japan, South Korea, the PRC, and the United States. Continuity or the status quo would mean that the defense-dominant, economic deferral policy would continue.

New Global Integration Policy: Commercial-Dominant, Defense-Threat Reduction[10]

Soviet commercial relations with its Asian neighbors—the People's Republic of China, Japan, South Korea, and others—have been modest to date. "Soviet-Chinese commerce has increased from a relatively low level during recent periods of normalization and may be expected to increase at an accelerated rate."[11] Although the relative change in recent years is impressive, the absolute level is modest. Soviet shares of the markets in the PRC, Japan, and South Korea are likely to be quite small under present conditions. A major change in these relations may occur if the political, military, and economic constraints controlled by the Soviet Union are relaxed or removed. Gorbachev has indicated an interest in developing a new environment in the Pacific. Initiatives open to the Soviet Union to reduce the territorial, military, and economic constraints on trade would be consistent with policies Gorbachev has adopted for other regions, including Europe, South Asia and Southeast Asia, and with the domestic reform policy of perestroika.[12]

Japanese and South Korean authorities have indicated that if political constraints on improved relations were removed and the Soviet Union provided an environment for profitable business, then commerce and investment would increase.

Soviet commercial relations with the People's Republic of China may be facilitated by further improvement in the "three conditions" (settlements in Afghanistan, Cambodia, and a reduced military threat on the Soviet-Chinese Border). Resource-oriented joint ventures with developed Asian industrial economies and improvement in infrastructure-associated Special Economic Zones, such as Nakhodka, would improve prospects for profitable Soviet-PRC commerce.

In Soviet policy, a precedent for removal of political and security constraints on trade in Europe has been set through discussions of a "European House" and acceptance of deep verification and inspection in arms control. The Soviet Union has especially removed political constraints and improved prospects of profit for the Federal Republic of Germany. This application of European-style New Thinking in foreign policy and a new foreign economic strategy has been promised for Asia. There are some signs that the Soviet leader will continue to pursue this conducive environment for commerce.

Prospects for an Improved Political-Military Climate

If political and security constraints to normal relations are significantly reduced, the positive steps toward normal commercial relations will thereafter be facilitated in Soviet relations with Japan, South Korea, and the PRC. The criteria for serious progress in each case could involve engagement in an agreed upon step-by-step process:

Northern Territories. A leading specialist on the Soviet Union, Hiroshi Kimura, has suggested what he calls the "Hong Kong formula," i.e., "the combination of return of two islands upon the conclusion of a peace treaty and return of the remaining two by a definite deadline, say 1999—would also be good enough for Japan."[13] This formula might become attractive to the Soviet Union if no other nonnegotiable claims are made or opened for future negotiation and if the Soviet government and citizens are given a graceful exit. Kimura further noted that:

> Japan could sign a long-term economic cooperation agreement with the USSR—following the example set by many West European countries—to facilitate more active trade and economic intercourse. The Japanese Export-Import Bank, a semi-governmental bank, could agree to loan huge amounts of long-term bank credit at low interest rates. With the official blessing of the Japanese government, private business in Japan could positively participate in joint ventures with the Soviets. Taken together, the chances are that Soviet-Japanese economic relations could be improved to the level of Sino-Japanese relations,

which are now (in terms of the total trade in US dollars) three times bigger than the former.[14]

Korean Peninsula. Soviet and East European recognition of South Korea informally by the USSR and diplomatically by Hungary would help raise prospects of stability. Provision of the good offices of the Soviet Union for developing a peaceful Korean dialogue would also be helpful.[15]

Three Obstacles. Progress on withdrawal from Afghanistan, peaceful return of Cambodia to domestic rule, and reduction of military forces on the China border are all under way. Serious negotiations on major troop reductions could be a further step. This could parallel Soviet European policy—an Asian version of the European conventional arms reduction talks (Conventional Forces Asia—CAFA to mirror CAFE).

A NEW SOVIET COMMERCIAL STRATEGY FOR ASIA

The response of Western Europe, especially the FRG, to perestroika and to new Soviet military policy, including deep arms reductions and a new regional policy opening up relations between Eastern and Western Europe, has been to develop new, more normalized commercial relations.

The treaty between the Federal Republic of Germany and the USSR concerning commercial promotion and joint guarantee of capital investment signed at the Bonn Summit in June 1989 set a favorable environment for profitability of Western partners. Specifically, it provides for,

> Comprehensive transfer, in convertible currency, of all existing payments relating to capital investment. This comprises without exception all revenue (profits, dividends, interest, licensing and other fees) as well as loan repayments, proceeds from liquidation and also appropriation compensation. Payments are to be made no later than three months after application and at the rate of exchange prevailing on the day of transfer.

That is, all rubles made on the domestic market can, upon demand of the German investor, be exchanged and transferred in any freely convertible currency. Furthermore, the same is true if assets are expropriated or nationalized.[16]

The European Community is providing attractive bilateral agreements, beginning with Hungary, to normalize relations. Some East European countries, such as Poland and Hungary, are even interested in joining the European Community, or European Free Trade Area (EFTA). First in this queue is probably neutral Austria.

Asian countries also seem prepared to offer the Soviet Union more normalized commercial relations with comparable political and security changes made. Still, even with an improved political climate, it should be underlined that commercial exchange must also be profitable to Western and Eastern partners alike to justify substantially expanded commerce and investment. The new Soviet commercial strategy must also facilitate and draw from domestic economic progress in perestroika. As noted above, this is a priority concern. Soviet policies reducing the protectionist trade system are now beginning to meet some of the commercial requirements of Asian partners. The new Soviet commercial strategy draws lessons from the successful export-oriented Asian models of Japan and the Newly Industrializing Countries of Asia.

The negative model of the past is Brezhnev's commercial détente: import substitution of materials and food, turnkey technology for large-scale projects, and no reform in the domestic industrial and agricultural systems. Gorbachev reformers refer to habitual reliance on import substitution, e.g., grain imports to meet domestic shortfalls, as analogous to a "drug habit"; the inefficient supply system of Soviet agriculture was perpetuated through grain imports because they sustained the illusion of adequacy. Likewise, technological imports without reform in the system brought some modest improvements in domestic products—e.g., the Soviet Fiat model car, the LADA, was an improvement in domestic transport—but did not permit significantly entering the global manufactured goods trade.

The oil hard-currency windfall of the 1970s was wasted as domestic subsidies supported inefficient producers. So the Brezhnev heritage was a foreign commercial policy restricted by reduced oil income and a heavy domestic debt that limited the prospects of the price reform necessary for improved efficiency and competitiveness in trade.

The Asian models of Japan, South Korea, and the other Newly Industrializing Economies stressed development of a domestic market economy guided toward export orientation to the world market. Soviets cannot and need not adopt the full Japanese model because they have a large domestic market and are rich in natural resources. The new Soviet commercial strategy for Asia may be headed toward a model conducive to large-scale foreign involvement in their economy based on improving the prospects of profitability to Western partners. Whereas the orientation toward the Federal Republic of Germany and other West European countries—the joint ventures and economic zones, such as the soon to be initiated Special Economic Zone (SEZ) near Vyborg (north of Leningrad)—places emphasis on industrial production, the expected SEZ in Nakhodka in the Far East would be more oriented toward developing the rich resource base of East Siberia and the Far East.

A key Soviet import strategy does reflect current priorities of food processing, medical supplies and equipment, and housing, with a long-term focus on imports that improve efficiency in material output (the materials chain) and provide entry into the world machinery market (automobiles).

The experience of Japan and South Korea suggests that imports be keyed to development needs—that they generate increasing domestic incentives and hard currency earnings in the short and long term. In consumer goods, imports of machinery and technology are especially important; what is needed in order for the USSR to enter the global manufactured goods market are capital and technology imports, to permit and improve the efficiency of extraction and marketing of Siberian natural resource riches, quality control, and a simulated Western environment. This approach may be likened to the role of the Ministry of International Trade and Industry of Japan (MITI) and its Korean counterparts in their takeoff stage of development.

A flexible balance-of-payments policy using all the techniques that Newly Industrializing Countries employ is also needed. Specifically, the Soviet Union may well need to run balance-of-payments deficits in the near term in order to shift its production possibilities curve to a higher plane. Investment in modernization of the economy will result in higher productivity and more competitive goods in the future, which may be exported to reduce the debts incurred in growth. They must not follow the Polish and Yugoslav examples of accumulating debt for meeting short-term balance-of-payments and consumption support needs.[17]

A flexible balance-of-payments policy would involve some of the following:

- Encouragement of direct investment, characteristically through joint ventures that would increase hard currency income from sale of energy, metal, and timber products in the world market. The Chevron oil field joint venture and Western joint ventures in petrochemicals may increase the efficiency of the energy chain and release more oil output for export. The Asian involvement would be more keyed to resource-rich land leasing and development of natural resources under a much more liberal policy than has been the case in the past.
- A prudent credit policy would be tied to joint ventures and prospects of domestic modernization and growth of hard currency earnings.
- A general assessment of all categories in the hard currency balance, with a view to obtaining more hard currency to pay for technology-related imports to facilitate improvement in the quality of domestic output and increase competitive exports to the world market.
- The establishment of foreign commerce zones, that is, sectoral or special regional zones, to foster the rapid development of a new export-import culture.

Possible special zones being discussed include ones near Nakhodka or Vladivostok, which might be developed by Seizo Ota, president of Tokyo

Mutual Life Insurance Company, who suggested that about $4 billion were available for investment.[18] The Republic of Korea has trade representative offices in the Far East. The Asian zones might parallel a special zone near Leningrad in the Vyborg area of Karelia (near the Finnish border). Each would be entrepôt developments to draw on the resources of the hinterland—in Nakhodka or Vladivostok, the rich natural resources of the Far East and East Siberia. Tourism could also be facilitated. The Leningrad SEZ could lead to development of underutilized Soviet research and development. Khabarovsk may be another economic zone, with potential involvement from Japan, South Korea, and the PRC. The Patrizansk, Pogranichny, and Khazan districts have also been discussed as special zones but are still restricted areas. The Soviet city of Blagoveshchensk has had workers from the Chinese city of Heihe in Heilongjiang province during 1988 and could be expanded to an economic zone. In the period before the Sino-Soviet Summit, large numbers of Soviet visitors to Shenzhen, the Chinese economic zone nearest to Hong Kong, suggests some parallel from that Chinese SEZ in the Soviet Far East.[19]

Soviet joint venture laws have answered many of the criticisms of Western partners in Chinese special zones: Labor and local supplies can be controlled and paid for by the Western partner, and the domestic market profits may be repatriated in hard currency not earned in third countries.

Transition toward eventual convertibility of the ruble would provide the basis for establishing a real exchange rate and a tariff system in line with international standards. This will become increasingly important for the Soviet Union's future export strategy—without convertible currency, even the expansion of joint ventures may well be curtailed due to the inability of Western firms to repatriate profits. The first step in joint venture and commercial relations is to allow profits from sale in the Soviet domestic market to be repatriated to Western partner countries at an agreed rate of exchange. As the value of the ruble is not predictable, some artificial rate could be negotiated that would provide a reasonable basis for estimating profits that could be repatriated.

There are a number of Soviet proposals toward convertibility—a dual currency system, for example, with sector-by-sector convertibility. A uniform convertible system is, in any event, a long way off. In the interim, some combination of goods convertibility (countertrade or supply of hard goods such as oil) and credit might facilitate development of a profitable environment.

Integration into the International Economic System

Adherence to international agreements covering trade protection and intellectual property rights would be helpful. Narrowing the function of espionage agencies to normal military espionage would likewise be a step

Table 1.1 USSR Estimated Hard Currency Balance of Payments (in millions of current U.S. dollars)

	1975	1980	1981	1982	1983	1984	1985	1986	1987	1988[a]
Current Account Balance	-4,565	1,470	-387	4,293	4,760	4,664	137	1,376	5,073	1,400
Merchandise Trade Balance	-4,804	1,814	365	4,468	4,712	4,727	519	2,013	6,164	2,700
Exports f.o.b.	9,453	27,874	28,254	31,975	32,429	32,173	26,400	25,111	29,092	30,000
Imports f.o.b.	14,257	26,060	27,889	27,507	27,717	27,446	25,881	23,098	22,928	27,300
Net Interest	-521	-1,234	-1,752	-1,275	-1,052	-1,163	-1,482	-1,737	-2,191	-2,400
Other Invisibles and Transfers	760	890	1,000	1,100	1,100	1,100	1,100	1,100	1,100	1,100
Capital Account-ing Balance	6,981	284	5,430	-2,965	-1,541	-124	1,869	1,966	-1,017	1,710
Change in Gross Debt[b]	6,786	-792	1,977	-640	116	224	6,804	6,983	4,768	860
Official Debt	1,492	-280	-1,370	967	340	-375	463	563	561	190
Commercial Debt	5,294	-512	3,347	-1,607	-224	599	6,340	6,420	4,207	670
Net Change in Assets Held in Western Banks	-163	-35	-166	2,122	277	-664	1,787	1,595	-527	20
Estimated Exchange Rate Effect[c]	-22	-411	-1,457	-817	-1,070	-688	3,248	3,322	5,012	-2,570
Net Credits to LDCs	715	950	870	2,120	3,200	2,700	1,700	4,100	4,800	5,500
Gold Sales	725	1,580	2,700	1,100	750	1,000	1,800	4,000	3,500	3,800
Net Errors and Omissions[d]	-2,416	-1,754	-5,043	-1,328	-3,219	-4,540	-2,006	-3,342	-4,057	-3,110

[a] Preliminary data.
[b] Including additions to short-term debt.
[c] A minus sign signifies a decline in the value of assets.
[d] Includes hard currency assistance to and trade with Communist countries, credits to developed Western countries to finance sales of oil, other nonspecified hard currency expenditures, as well as errors and omissions in other line items of the accounts.
Source: Testimony of CIA-DIA to Joint Economic Committee, April 1989.

forward. Domestic success in implementing market-oriented reforms should be the major criterion for the normalization of trade, finance, and investment and the basis for acceptance within the international economy. As socialist countries move toward meeting the rules and criteria for market-oriented trade, they should be encouraged to initiate relations of an institutional character with international organizations. Increased information exchange and technical assistance from such organizations as the International Monetary Fund and the World Bank could be utilized to further this process. Progress toward integration could be assessed and adjustments could be made on the basis of this progress. Professional assistance from such organizations as the World Bank could be utilized to further this process. An initial technical and informal consultative period could be a useful first step toward eventual membership.

In each case the partners would also want assurance of profitable commercial arrangements. New Soviet commercial strategy applying European policy parallels on joint ventures and direct investment to Asia would open the door.

1. Joint ventures: Political, economic, and social considerations limit the scope of joint ventures between the USSR, China, North Korea and other Western economies. Assuring control of quality, management, and supply require more than special zones; a special "commerce friendly" culture is needed. Special management schools and exchanges with Western countries might be arranged. Specific training in open-market procedures might also be a part of joint ventures. Selected steps in convertibility of currency would be useful, and probably critical, in arrangements for profit repatriation in hard currency for joint ventures; special contractual arrangements may permit conversion of profits on domestic Eastern markets to convertible currency on a case-by-case basis. Use of convertible currency auctions, such as instituted in Poland and undertaken on a limited basis for the USSR, may be helpful as a transitional mechanism.

2. Direct investment may be permitted and even encouraged by the Soviet government in some Special Economic Zones, as well as long-term lease of areas in natural resources development projects, providing for foreign rights to develop, manage, and market, e.g.:

- Products from East Siberian timber tracts for pulp production, or other marketable resources.
- In developing joint ventures and Special Economic Zones a single country and/or Western multinational corporations may be the developer of a harbor area and its hinterland.
- Broadened developments may include joint ventures involving the energy chain from exploration to marketing of refined products and by-products.

- Joint Western-Soviet exploration and assessment of profitability of developing various resource potential areas might be undertaken, modeled on the Urengoi gas assessment undertaken by the United States, Japan, and the USSR in the 1970s as a point of departure. Then bids for foreign development on long-term leases with priority on maintenance of environmental standards would be in order. The new lease law of the USSR is now being extended to foreign entities.
- Joint Soviet-Western scientific and technological assessments might be a basis of development plans for commitments to underdeveloped but competitive Soviet industrial capability through joint ventures. These could be considered, with the development planned by the Soviets, for the Special Economic Zones near Leningrad and Nakhodka.

Further assurances on issues that affect Asian security and stability would facilitate a process of economic normalization. The Soviets have a trade surplus with the PRC but could expand their trade if Soviet goods were more accessible, if Siberian natural resources were being developed, and if the expansion of Soviet imports required more industrial production to balance trade (e.g., investment in moderately modernized plants built by the USSR in the PRC during the 1950s). PRC-USSR trade (e.g., timber for consumer goods) may be facilitated by Japanese or Korean direct investment (harbors and transport) and joint ventures. Indeed, without access between the PRC and the USSR, achieved through improved facilities in each country's infrastructure brought about through Japanese and South Korean investment, commerce will be restricted.

With new foreign and security policies conducive to a less threatening and more stable environment, a commercially oriented Soviet Siberia and the PRC might be welcomed into the community of Asian Newly Industrializing Economies (NIEs). The substantial financial and technological resources of Japan and South Korea might profitably be invested by these open, developed commercial countries. Constraints on Japanese and South Korean trade with the PRC in the wake of Tiananmen Square are likely but difficult to measure at this time. Soviet constraints, for the same reason, are even more difficult to calibrate. It is even possible that the Soviet policy may be favorable to increased trade with the PRC if the Soviets deem that running counter to Western governmental policy may be in their self-interest.

Prospects and Options for the Developed Economies

1. Japan, the United States, and allied countries in Asia should follow a two-track policy to *ensure adequate* security forces and seek the reduction

of *tension*.[20] The United States and Japan should follow a policy of *facilitating* reduction of tensions and *sharing* responsibility.

2. If the Soviet Union translates to Asia its new military doctrine for Europe (defensive reasonable sufficiency), its New Thinking (using the Afghanistan withdrawal model), and the European pattern of major force reductions in Asia, including the China border and Trans Baikal military district, and moves toward resolution of outstanding issues barring the Peace Treaty with Japan, then a new modus vivendi in Asia may become negotiable. Negotiations on regional and defense issues should be pursued vigorously by Asian market economies to facilitate openness and a reduction of the Soviet threat.

3. Japan and the Asian NICs may foster globalism by opening markets, increasing global aid, pursuing direct investment, and participating in the Brady Plan (including not just ASEAN but also Latin America, Africa, and Eastern Europe).

4. Domestic reform, including market-oriented economic restructuring and democratization, may lead to the development of Eastern economies capable of competing in the global economy. Pressing domestic reform needs and democratization may incline Eastern countries to be less threatening in foreign policy and more inclined toward arms negotiations and reduction of defense burdens.

Notes

The personal views expressed are not necessarily those of the Congressional Research Service (CRS) or of the U.S. Congress.

1. See John P. Hardt and Sheila N. Heslin, "Perestroika: A Sustainable Process for Change," with commentary by Academician Oleg T. Bogomolov, Group of Thirty, Occasional Paper, 1989.

2. Minister of Finance Boris Gostev, *Izvestia*, March 31, 1989. Reform economist Nikolai Shmelev noted in an article for the April 1988 edition of *Novy Mir* that excess demand, defined as a greater supply of rubles than can be effectively absorbed by available supplies, stood at approximately 300 billion rubles, with 100 billion in mattresses, while large subsidies supporting unproductive but critical sectors (e.g., subsidies equal to about 90 billion rubles on meat prices and rent) represent about 25 percent of the state budget. Other official estimates place the overhang at about 100 billion rubles but acknowledge that it is probably larger, although the full magnitude is not officially known.

3. Interview with Minister of Finance Boris Gostev, *Izvestia*, March 31, 1989; Shmelev, "Interconnections Between World Markets and Planned Economies," paper presented at the International Economic Association meeting, Moscow, March 28–30, 1989.

4. John Hardt and Timothy Stanley, "Economic Indicators in Soviet Security Policy," Atlantic Council, April 1989.

5. See the discussion of P.A. Bunich, "Self-Financing of Principal Economic Elements: Prerequisitioning, Essence, Problems and Trends," *Sotsialisticheskiy Trud*, no. 7, July 1987, pp. 7-17, and no. 9, Sept. 1987, pp. 10-19. Also Nikolai Petrakov, "Prospects for Change in the Systems of Price Formation, Finance, and Credit in the USSR," in *Soviet Economy*, vol. 3, July-Sept. 1987, pp. 135-144; Shmelev, "Price Reform in the USSR," *Soviet Economy*, vol. 6, March 1989.

6. This seemed to be Gorbachev's point when he stated, "In-depth cooperation and integration must be implemented throughout the *entire cycle, from the field to the counter* (emphasis added). Second, it is necessary to restructure priority areas of state investments in the agro-industrial complex. At the present stage, no longer production itself, but production and social infrastructure, must increasingly become the leading target of expenditure." M.S. Gorbachev, Speech to Kolkhoz Congress, March 23, 1988, *Pravda*, March 24, 1988. See also O. Bogomolov, *Kommunist*, no. 16, 1987.

7. CRS Assessment of Gorbachev's UN Speech of December 7, 1988. Fyodor Burlatskii, *Novoye Misheleniye* [New Thinking], pamphlet, Moscow, Politizdat, 1988.

8. Discussions in Moscow, March 29, 1989.

9. Andrew Goodpaster, Atlantic Council, April 1989.

10. John P. Hardt, "Gorbachev's Policy May Be Pivotal to Significant Commercial Change in Northeastern Asia," prepared for the Senate Foreign Relations Committee, CRS Workshop on Sino-Soviet Summit, May 1989.

11. See chapter by Nicholas Lardy.

12. The views expressed herein were tested in discussions in Moscow, Seoul, Tokyo, and Geneva in 1988-1989 with involved officials.

13. Hiroshi Kimura, "The Soviet-Japanese Territorial Dispute," *Harriman Forum*, vol. 2, no. 6, June 1989.

14. Ibid.

15. V. K. Park, "Korea's Trade With PRC and other Communist Countries: Businessman's View," paper presented at the International Conference on the Soviet Union, China, and Northeast Asia, July 26-27, 1988, in Seoul, Korea.

16. Text of the Soviet-Federal Republic of Germany Treaty of June 1989.

17. Substantial imports of grain in 1989 and projected gold sales to import food and consumer goods is an ominous setback to this policy dictated by a short-term need to show results from perestroika to meet citizen unrest. Some of these short-term imports may be a response to coal miners' demands for more consumer goods.

18. From discussions in Tokyo. See also the *Wall Street Journal*, May 3, 1989, p. A14.

19. Cf. "Glasnost's Asian Frontier, Gorbachev's Benign Look-East Policy Aqueous Substance," *Far Eastern Economic Review*, August 4, 1988, pp. 24-29.

20. Policy Recommendations on "Long-Term Political Vision for Stabilization and Cooperation in North East Asia," The Japan Forum on International Relations, Inc., Tokyo, March 1989.

2

Japan's Role in Asia-Pacific Cooperation: Dimensions, Prospects, and Problems

Edward J. Lincoln

Japan's relationship with the world and especially with the Asia-Pacific region is changing rapidly. These shifts hold promise for closer and more productive interactions but also give rise to concerns over the possible exclusive nature of the evolving relationships. These changes stem from the macroeconomic developments considered in Dick Nanto's chapter—developments that have produced large net capital outflows and a strong appreciation of the yen. The purpose of this chapter is to explore Japan's role in the development of trade and investment ties in the Asia-Pacific region, review the changes now taking place in Japan's relationship with these countries, and speculate on future developments.

Economic ties among Asia-Pacific nations have increased over time, although most of the increase is due to larger flows between these countries and the United States and Japan. Even without these two, however, a gradual strengthening of trade ties has taken place. Japan and the United States have had trade and investment roles of roughly equal importance in the region, but the changes now taking place will strengthen Japan's role while diminishing the position of the United States. As this shift unfolds, there is some concern that Japan's stronger relationship with the region will take on an exclusive form, pulling other Asian nations closer to it while progressively excluding the United States and other non-Asian nations. Such moves would not be in the interest of the United States, and they could be economically and politically harmful throughout the region. This chapter concludes that cooperation in the region should not, therefore, take the form of any formal regional trade preference arrangement. Furthermore, while a new formal regional organization that would bring together government officials to discuss matters of mutual interest makes sense given the rising regional economic interdependence, most economic issues are properly discussed in a global setting rather than a regional one.

Background

The countries of the Asia-Pacific region have little in common other than geography. The United States is generally assumed to belong to the region, but it is not tied to Asia by any strong cultural features. Even within Asia, the cultural and religious differences among nations are quite large, although some common cultural traits characterize all or most of these countries. Furthermore, the economic differences are enormous, ranging from Japan and the United States, advanced industrial nations with very high per capita incomes, to China and the Indochina countries, which are close to the bottom of world incomes and development. This region, therefore, is very different from Europe, where common land borders and strong cultural and historical connections have driven a process of integration. In the Asia-Pacific area geography remains the main reason for close economic ties.

Economic relations among these countries can be considered in a number of ways. The discussion here concentrates on three of these: merchandise trade, direct investment flows, and foreign aid. Connections among these individual ties certainly exists, especially in the case of Japan, but it is convenient to begin by considering them separately.

Merchandise Trade. Data on intraregional trade are presented in Table 2.1, which is based on the detailed trade matrix presented in Table 2.2. For all the nations on the list, the share of exports destined to other nations in the region was almost one-half (48 percent) in 1986. This figure represents a very large gain of 27 percentage points since 1966. The only nations included in the table that clearly are not part of the region in terms of trade are Canada and the Soviet Union, and they are excluded from the discussion in the remainder of this chapter.

Much of the regional trade is accounted for by the United States and Japan, and the very rapid growth of the Japanese economy could account for a large portion of the results. Therefore, Table 2.1 also shows trade for a subset of the region—the list of countries in Table 2.1 minus Japan, the United States, Canada, and the Soviet Union. As might be expected, the share of exports going to others within the subset is much lower (24 percent in 1986) than the share for the whole region, and the growth over time is generally lower as well (up 9 percentage points from 15 percent in 1966). Nevertheless, it is significant that this share is increasing. The rise is especially noticeable for the three former British colonies—Australia, New Zealand, and Malaysia. Over the 20-year period covered by the table, these three lost much of their attachment to the British commonwealth

Table 2.1 Regional Exports

	Percent of Its Exports Destined to the Rest of the Region		Percent of Its Exports Destined to the Subregion	
Country	1986	Percentage Point Change 1966-1986	1986	Percentage Point Change 1966-1986
United States	26	11	14	6
Japan	68	7	27	-1
Canada	8	0	4	1
USSR	10	-1	4	4
China	66	14	42	10
South Korea	68	-8	11	1
Taiwan	78	10	15	-2
Hong Kong	72	13	33	10
Singapore	68	17	36	9
Philippines	76	-2	21	16
Thailand	62	6	28	1
Indonesia	85	23	20	2
Malaysia	73	15	34	24
Australia	68	16	29	24
New Zealand	61	27	29	21
Total Region	48	20	--	--
Subregion	--	--	24	9

Note: The subregion excludes the United States, Japan, Canada, and the Soviet Union.

Source: Calculated from the data in Table 2.2, which is taken from data in the International Monetary Fund, Direction of Trade, Annual 1966-70 (Washington, D.C.: IMF, 1971); and Direction of Trade Statistics, Yearbook 1987 (Washington, D.C.: IMF, 1987).

countries and became much more integrated with Asia, including both the entire group of countries represented in the table and the subregion.

As evident from Table 2.2, the nature of relationships between individual countries on this list and the major markets of Japan and the United States is diverse. In 1986, the countries in the subset sent 24 percent of their exports to the United States (a substantial gain from 14 percent in 1966) while only 14 percent went to Japan (*down* three percentage points over the same period). The downward shift for Japan is primarily due to the diversification of trade by Taiwan and South Korea, both of which were colonies before World War II and remained highly dependent on Japan as an export market for a time after the war.

In addition to the fact that a larger share of exports has gone to the United States than to Japan, there is a qualitative difference between the subset region's trade with the United States and its trade with Japan. Those few countries with a substantial share of their exports destined to Japan

Table 2.2 Regional Trade in Asia, 1966 (in millions of U.S. dollars)

Export by:	U.S.	Japan	Canada	USSR	China
U.S.	-	2,371	-	-	0
Japan	3,010	-	256	215	315
Canada	-	366	-	-	171
USSR	-	273	-	-	-
China	0	278	19	-	-
S. Korea	96	65	6	0	0
Taiwan	120	131	14	0	0
Hong Kong	375	77	34	0	12
Singapore	15	45	0	0	0
Philippines	333	278	2	-	1
Thailand	48	142	2	-	-
Indonesia	179	160	1	0	0
Malaysia	177	273	38	0	0
Australia	412	586	55	33	84
New Zealand	169	90	15	15	7

	S. Korea	Taiwan	HK	Sing.	Phil.
U.S.	339	237	229	51	348
Japan	335	255	369	138	278
Canada	15	8	15	0	17
USSR	0	0	3	0	0
China	0	0	441	0	1
S. Korea	-	2	9	2	1
Taiwan	11	-	34	9	7
Hong Kong	6	17	-	64	14
Singapore	2	3	32	-	5
Philippines	17	13	4	3	-
Thailand	0	9	45	50	8
Indonesia	1	1	21	0	26
Malaysia	13	12	10	0	12
Australia	7	22	69	58	35
New Zealand	0	0	2	0	7

Table 2.2 (Continued)

	Thai.	Indo.	Malay.	Aus.	N.Zea.
U.S.	128	60	46	661	127
Japan	301	119	95	298	59
Canada	6	1	15	110	39
USSR	3	0	0	2	0
China	0	0	0	26	0
S. Korea	5	1	1	2	0
Taiwan	18	6	5	4	2
Hong Kong	23	78	36	29	12
Singapore	13	0	0	8	0
Philippines	1	0	5	3	1
Thailand	-	22	56	2	0
Indonesia	19	-	0	65	3
Malaysia	10	0	-	29	8
Australia	24	6	54	-	199
New Zealand	0	0	6	49	-

	A World	B Total	C Sub.
U.S.	30,450	4,597	2,226
Japan	9,779	6,043	2,777
Canada	9,552	763	397
USSR	2,504	281	8
China	1,478	765	468
S. Korea	250	190	23
Taiwan	534	361	96
Hong Kong	1,323	777	291
Singapore	238	123	63
Philippines	843	661	48
Thailand	693	384	192
Indonesia	769	476	136
Malaysia	983	582	94
Australia	3,168	1,644	591
New Zealand	1,076	360	86

Table 2.2 (Continued)

	B/A	C/A	Japan/A	U.S./A
U.S.	15.1%	7.3%	7.8%	.0%
Japan	61.8%	28.4%	.0%	30.8%
Canada	8.0%	4.2%	3.8%	.0%
USSR	11.2%	.3%	10.9%	.0%
China	51.8%	31.7%	18.8%	.0%
S. Korea	76.0%	9.2%	26.0%	38.4%
Taiwan	67.6%	18.0%	24.5%	22.5%
Hong Kong	58.7%	22.0%	5.8%	28.3%
Singapore	51.7%	26.5%	18.9%	6.3%
Philippines	78.4%	5.7%	33.0%	39.5%
Thailand	55.4%	27.7%	20.5%	6.9%
Indonesia	61.9%	17.7%	20.8%	23.3%
Malaysia	59.2%	9.6%	27.8%	18.0%
Australia	51.9%	18.7%	18.5%	13.0%
New Zealand	33.5%	8.0%	8.4%	15.7%

Regional Trade in Asia, 1986

Export by:	Imported by:				
	U.S.	Japan	Canada	USSR	China
U.S.	-	26,882	-	-	3,106
Japan	81,926	-	5,571	3,178	9,936
Canada	-	4,238	-	-	765
USSR	-	1,807	-	-	1,338
China	2,633	4,742	307	1,230	-
S. Korea	13,730	5,417	1,227	-	-
Taiwan	18,995	4,545	1,271	-	-
Hong Kong	11,108	1,651	832	38	7,551
Singapore	5,254	1,931	168	130	571
Philippines	1,709	852	69	15	101
Thailand	1,575	1,235	121	72	256
Indonesia	2,902	6,644	60	52	139
Malaysia	2,297	3,113	111	130	163
Australia	2,389	6,065	372	698	1,065
New Zealand	951	863	100	111	214

Table 2.2 (Continued)

	S. Korea	Taiwan	HK	Sing.	Phil.
U.S.	4,355	4,604	3,030	3,380	1,363
Japan	10,557	7,430	7,215	4,611	1,098
Canada	680	437	234	110	36
USSR	-	-	55	33	15
China	-	-	9,776	1,217	157
S. Korea	-	296	1,801	498	184
Taiwan	350	-	2,915	931	329
Hong Kong	831	341	-	1,032	393
Singapore	324	306	1,462	-	248
Philippines	112	138	220	154	-
Thailand	239	146	354	783	29
Indonesia	356	321	345	1,239	108
Malaysia	722	-	311	2,366	247
Australia	928	795	511	441	119
New Zealand	89	-	92	85	40

	Thai.	Indo.	Malay.	Aus.	N. Zea.
U.S.	936	946	1,730	5,551	881
Japan	2,045	2,682	1,723	5,273	1,113
Canada	79	176	80	460	110
USSR	18	5	10	8	5
China	159	143	203	209	26
S. Korea	182	158	218	494	75
Taiwan	278	392	-	870	-
Hong Kong	279	377	231	667	90
Singapore	821	-	3,327	696	157
Philippines	67	28	97	69	10
Thailand	-	58	381	159	14
Indonesia	83	-	82	159	82
Malaysia	361	54	-	284	21
Australia	129	373	368	-	1,031
New Zealand	21	52	63	930	-

Table 2.2 (Continued)

	A World	B Total	C Sub.
U.S.	217,291	56,764	29,882
Japan	210,804	144,358	56,861
Canada	89,706	7,405	3,167
USSR	33,696	3,294	1,487
China	31,366	20,802	13,120
S. Korea	35,624	24,280	3,906
Taiwan	39,789	30,876	6,065
Hong Kong	35,420	25,421	11,830
Singapore	22,490	15,395	8,042
Philippines	4,787	3,641	1,011
Thailand	8,776	5,422	2,491
Indonesia	14,824	12,572	2,966
Malaysia	13,832	10,180	4,659
Australia	22,541	15,284	6,458
New Zealand	5,930	3,611	1,697

	B/A	C/A	Japan/A	U.S./A
U.S.	26.1%	13.8%	12.4%	.0%
Japan	68.5%	27.0%	.0%	38.9%
Canada	8.3%	3.5%	4.7%	.0%
USSR	9.8%	4.4%	5.4%	.0%
China	66.3%	41.8%	15.1%	8.4%
S. Korea	68.2%	11.0%	15.2%	38.5%
Taiwan	77.6%	15.2%	11.4%	47.7%
Hong Kong	71.8%	33.4%	4.7%	31.4%
Singapore	68.5%	35.8%	8.6%	23.4%
Philippines	76.1%	21.1%	17.8%	35.7%
Thailand	61.8%	28.4%	14.1%	17.9%
Indonesia	84.8%	20.0%	44.8%	19.6%
Malaysia	73.6%	33.7%	22.5%	16.6%
Australia	67.8%	28.6%	26.9%	10.6%
New Zealand	60.9%	28.6%	14.6%	16.0%

Note: The figures are based on the export data reported by each country. The columns, therefore, do not equal the imports reported by each recipient country because exports are reported on an f.o.b. (free-on-board, basically an ex-factory value) basis and imports on a c.i.f. (cost-including-freight--the cost at arrival in the recipient country) basis.

Source: International Monetary Fund, Direction of Trade, Annual 1966-70 (Washington, D.C.: IMF, 1971) and Direction of Trade Statistics, Yearbook 1987 (Washington, D.C.: IMF, 1987), various pages.

Table 2.3 Imports from the Asia-Pacific Region

	Share of Imports of Each Country Coming from:			
	U.S.	Japan	Region	Subregion
United States	.0%	20.8%	51.4%	13.7%
Japan	7.9	.0	43.3	29.8
Canada	64.8	6.3	75.7	4.5
USSR	3.6	6.3	17.0	5.5
China	11.2	23.3	68.6	27.8
South Korea	21.4	33.3	70.2	13.3
Taiwan	22.1	34.3	69.4	11.1
Hong Kong	8.5	19.0	72.5	44.1
Indonesia	9.4	33.4	65.6	20.4
Malaysia	18.7	21.7	75.0	33.5
Philippines	22.2	16.5	63.5	23.2
Singapore	14.7	20.5	68.7	32.9
Thailand	12.5	26.0	63.4	23.5
Australia	21.4	19.7	59.4	16.2
New Zealand	15.6	18.7	64.1	27.8
Total Region	11.4	16.1	55.1	18.5
Subregion	14.8	23.5	68.3	27.6

Source: Calculated from data in International Monetary Fund, Direction of Trade Statistics, Yearbook 1987 (Washington, D.C.: IMF, 1987).

are mostly raw material–exporting countries: Australia (coal and iron ore), Malaysia (tin), and Indonesia (oil and gas). Japan has had a reputation in the past for not welcoming manufactured imports from the world or from Asia. Indicative of Japan's reluctance to import manufactures is the fact that the ratio of manufactured imports to GDP remains considerably below that of other industrial nations.[1] Furthermore, the bulk of the increase in Asian exports in the first half of the 1980s was to the United States. Japan's imports from the rest of Asia stagnated (and in some cases dropped because of falling prices for raw materials).

On the import side (Table 2.3), similar relationships are visible, although the relative roles of Japan and the United States are reversed. For individual countries, the importance of the region or the subregion as a source of imports is largely the same as in the export picture. However, the share of imports in these countries sourced from Japan was 24 percent in 1986 (up substantially over 1966), while the share from the United States was a smaller 19 percent (virtually unchanged since 1966). The only Asian countries importing more from the United States than from Japan are the Philippines (with strong historical ties to the United States) and Australia. For a number of others, including China, Hong Kong, Indonesia, and

Table 2.4 Cumulative Foreign Direct Investment in Selected Asian Countries

Recipient Country	Share of Investment from: Japan	U.S.	ROW*	Total Inward FDI (in billions of U.S. dollars)	Date
Hong Kong	22%	54%	24%	$1.5	9/84
South Korea	48	30	22	2	6/84
Taiwan	30	42	29	3.3	12/84
Singapore	20	33	47	5	6/83
Thailand	23	9	68	7	12/83
Indonesia	35	8	58	14.4	12/83
Malaysia	18	7	75	3.4	12/83
Philippines	16	52	32	2.5	12/83

*Rest of World.

Source: Bank of Japan, Monthly Report of Research Department, January 1986, cited in Yasuhiko Torii, "Recent Trends and Role of Japan in Financing Growth of Asian Countries."

Thailand, Japan has a far greater share of imports than does the United States.

These data on exports and imports indicate that Japan and the United States are the major trading partners for these countries. But in no sense has Japan "replaced" the United States within the region. The United States has not lost share in the region, neither as a destination for exports nor as a source of imports. Japan's gain as a source of the region's imports has come at the expense of countries other than the United States. A better characterization would be to say that both Japan and the United States have come to dominate the trade of these nations to a greater degree than in the past. Nevertheless, Japan's large share in the imports of these countries, and the growth of that share, is a significant long-term development.

Direct Investment. Investment patterns appear roughly similar to trade. Table 2.4 presents basic data on direct investment. In the Asian Newly Industrializing Countries (NICs), the United States has generally had higher levels of cumulative investment (except in South Korea), while in the ASEAN countries, Japan has had the larger share (except for the Philippines). Only in Malaysia is neither Japan nor the United States the largest single foreign investor (with that position held by Singapore).

Traditionally, much of Japanese foreign direct investment has been destined toward Asia, but over time a declining share of investment has gone to Asia as the horizons of Japanese investors have expanded. A large share of Japan's direct investment in Asia in the past has also gone to resource development projects, mainly in Indonesia. Manufacturing investment in developing countries in Asia has not been a large part of Japanese investment activity in the past; and the manufacturing investment that did take place was motivated more by the desire to supply products to local markets or to third markets (especially the United States). An attempt to circumvent import protectionism in these countries or in the United States provided a stronger rationale for manufacturing investment than did the existence of low wages. In Japanese industry, there has generally been a strong belief that products of higher quality and competitive prices could be manufactured from a Japanese production base, even as the relative cost of labor rose steadily through the 1960s and 1970s. Japanese innovations in manufacturing processes, including methods of reducing inventory costs (such as just-in-time production) and reducing product defect rates, were assumed to be dependent on a geographic concentration of the manufacturing process and on the special nature of human relationships in the Japanese culture. Japanese firms generally sought to reduce labor costs through automation rather than by moving abroad.

With these perceptions of the advantages of Japanese manufacturing technology, investments abroad have tended to have an unusually high number of Japanese nationals in the management structure.[2] In addition, some countries, especially China, have been complaining for some time about the relative lack of technology transfer to these subsidiaries.

Foreign Aid. Unlike trade and direct investment, Japan is the dominant source of official development assistance (ODA) for Asian developing countries. The total amount of ODA from Japan now rivals that of the United States, and the dollar amount continues to grow at a fairly rapid pace. According to OECD data, total Japanese ODA grew at a 5.7 percent annual average rate from 1982 to 1987, while that of the United States grew at only a 2.2 percent rate.[3] Of Japanese ODA disbursed bilaterally, the largest amount continues to go to Asia, even though that portion has declined somewhat over time as Japan has added other, non-Asian countries to the list of recipients. As of 1988, the share of Japan's bilateral aid destined to Asia (broadly defined to include South Asia) was 63 percent.[4]

Figure 2.1 shows for the ASEAN countries the share of Japan, the United States, and the multilateral aid agencies in net total ODA receipts. Net receipts represent actual new disbursements minus repayment of concessional loans, and thereby represent a more accurate figure on actual foreign aid activity than do commitments. Two striking facts are evident from these data: Japan provides half or more of the ODA received by each of the ASEAN countries (far outdistancing funds from the multilateral agencies), and the United States provides virtually nothing except to the Philippines. For ASEAN as a whole, Japan provided 55 percent of net ODA in 1987, with the United States accounting for only 11 percent and the multilateral organizations only 10 percent.

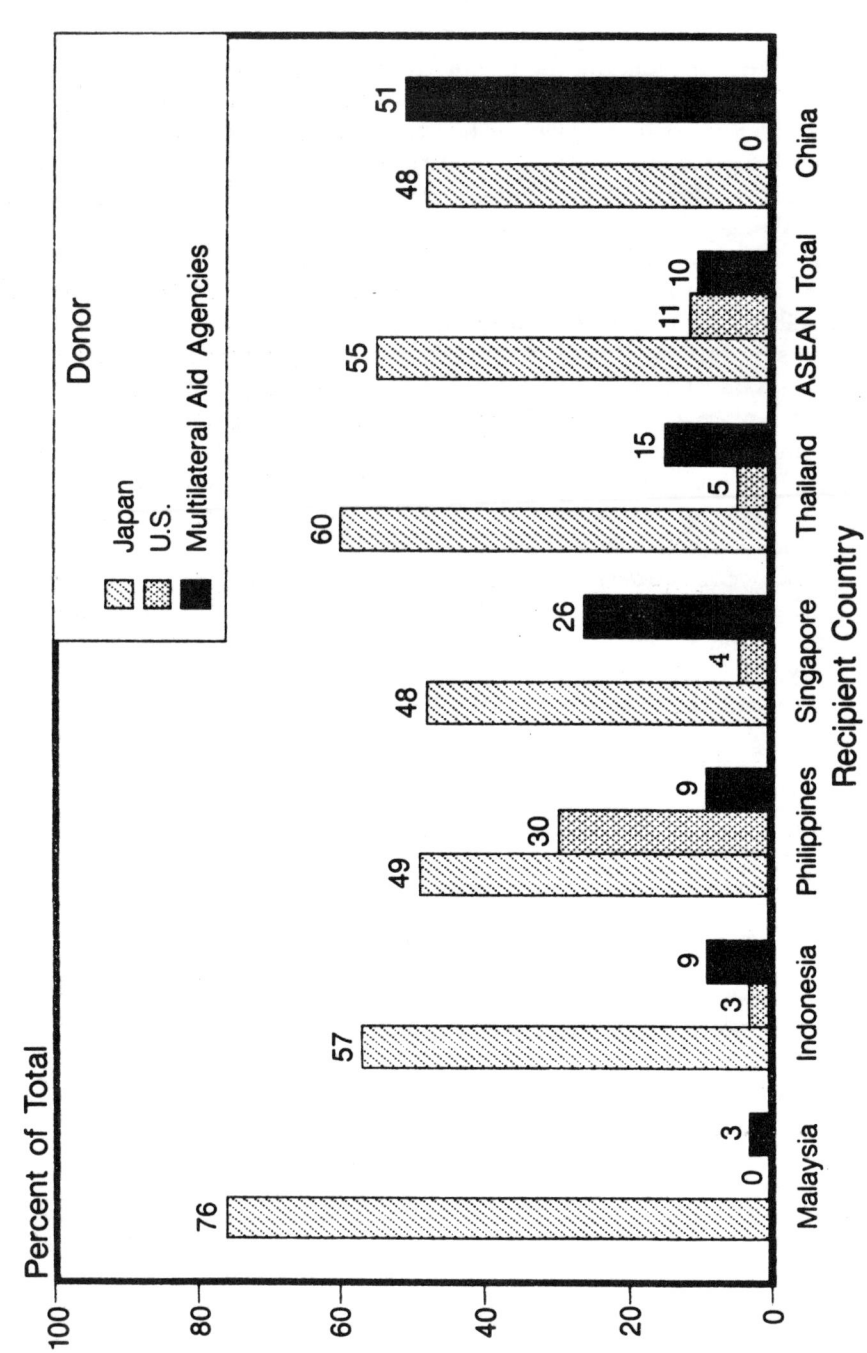

Figure 2.1 Shares of Net ODA Flow, 1987. *Source:* Calculated from data in Table 2.5.

Table 2.5 Net ODA Received by Southeast Asian Countries, 1987 (in millions of U.S. dollars)

Country	Total ODA New Receipts	Bilateral Net ODA from: Japan	Bilateral Net ODA from: U.S.	Net ODA from Multilateral Aid Agencies
Malaysia	$363	$276	$0	$11
Indonesia	1,245	707	36	112
Philippines	775	379	230	69
Singapore	23	11	1	6
Thailand	506	302	23	75
ASEAN Total	2,549	1,399	290	262
China	1,449	553	0	588
Burma	364	172	11	124
Kampuchea	14	0	2	5
Laos	59	14	0	28
Vietnam	116	1	1	51

Source: OECD, Geographical Distribution of Financial Flows to Developing Countries (Paris: OECD, 1989).

The dollar amounts of the ODA flows to Asian countries are displayed in Table 2.5. Except for the Philippines, U.S. ODA to ASEAN is pitifully small: none to Malaysia, $36 million to Indonesia, $23 million to Thailand, and $1 million to Singapore. Except for Singapore, Japan's ODA is measured in hundreds of millions of dollars, and it outspends the United States even in the Philippines. Furthermore, the top recipient of Japanese aid for the past several years has been China (with net receipts from Japan in 1987 of $553 million), a country to which the United States provides nothing.

The incident in Tiananmen Square in the spring of 1989 put a temporary hold on Japanese aid to China, but there was every indication that the hold would be very short-lived. The Japanese government has played a very low-key role in joining other industrial countries in criticizing the Chinese government, and the hold was officially implemented because of concern that the turmoil in China would disrupt the ability to handle incoming foreign aid monies. This approach left the Japanese government free to resume foreign aid quickly, with disbursements under existing commitments resumed in the fall, and negotiations for new loans begun as soon as the United States signaled some softening in its own position on China early in 1990. Although the Japanese government's position on the China problem was couched in terms of the delicate and special relationship between Japan and China stemming from the atrocities of the war, it also opened the way for Japan to play an even larger role in China's external financial ties by returning relations to normal in advance of other industrial nations.

The picture in Indochina is different. Burma, Cambodia, Vietnam, and Laos all receive some ODA from the world, but neither Japan nor the United States is heavily involved (except for Japan's provision of $172 million to Burma in 1987). The multilateral aid agencies and certain European nations play a much larger role here. Should the conflict in Indochina come to an end, though, the way would be opened for much larger aid flows. Devastated by decades of war and inefficient economic management, these nations are prime candidates for increased foreign aid efforts, and Japan, at least, would be in a position to provide much larger sums of money than in the past. Japan has remained cautious to date, apparently not desiring to move much beyond U.S. policy, especially in the case of Vietnam.

Japanese aid used to be criticized for having a high tied ratio and for being excessively motivated by Japanese commercial interests. Although the share of untied aid in Japan's aid mix has increased, it continues to have an unusually low grant ratio, and the complaints of commercial motivation continue unabated. The OECD puts Japan's grant element (the share of ODA disbursed as grants rather than as loans) at only 62 percent in 1986-1987, compared to an 87 percent average for the nations belonging to the Development Assistance Committee (DAC) and 97 percent for the United States. The grant element for Japan actually declined from 75 percent at the beginning of the 1980s.[5] Even untied aid from Japan is often structured in such a way (as through tied engineering studies) that Japanese manufacturers end up with the contracts. This bias is even true of multilateral loans from the Asian Development Bank (ADB), and U.S. officials involved with the bank have been complaining for at least the past decade that their Japanese counterparts do all they can to steer contracts for ADB-financed projects to Japanese corporations.[6]

Japan also continues to be plagued with a woefully inadequate bureaucratic infrastructure. The two principal Japanese aid agencies—the Japan International Cooperation Agency (JICA) and the Overseas Economic Cooperation Fund (OECF) are seriously understaffed and have very limited capabilities to monitor fieldwork. Partly because of the understaffing, the Japanese government continues its policy of providing aid only on a request basis; it responds only to project proposals submitted by recipient countries rather than using its own people to design an agenda of projects. This policy reinforces the tendency for a commercial bias in aid because Japanese trading companies operating in these countries often become the leaders in designing projects and helping the governments of these countries deal with the Japanese aid agencies. This tendency is not at all surprising since these companies have the planning expertise that is often lacking in developing countries and also have expertise in dealing with the Japanese bureaucracy, but their interests are obviously and inextricably tied to those of the Japanese manufacturing and commercial sectors.

Consider further that the principal institute in Japan designed to conduct research on developing economies is actually a subsidiary of the Ministry of International Trade and Industry (MITI). The Institute of Developing Economies is known in Japanese as Ajiken (Asian Research). The institute is a credible organization that engages in sophisticated economic research, but the fact that its research agenda is provided entirely by MITI is disquieting. MITI, one of several government ministries involved in overseeing Japanese foreign aid, promotes the interests of the Japanese manufacturing sector.

Changes and Implications

For many years Japan has been the "bad guy" in the Asia-Pacific region—accused of not importing enough, not transferring technology with investment, and driving hard bargains (tied financial assistance, sales of defective equipment, etc.), with remembrance of the militarism of the 1930s and 1940s always strong among other Asian countries. Whether these accusations were justified or not, current macroeconomic changes will bring major changes in Japan's reception throughout the region. The willingness of all these countries to attend the funeral of the Showa emperor in February 1989, who symbolized the wartime agony they suffered at the hands of the Japanese military, is one sign of the changes taking place.

Rapid shifts are now occurring in all three dimensions of the economic relationships explored above. First, Japan's imports of manufactured goods have been rising rapidly since 1986 and could continue to do so for some time. Second, Japan's foreign direct investment in the region is growing somewhat more rapidly, even though that growth is considerably lower than the high and rising growth in investment destined to other regions of the world. Third, ODA continues to expand at a substantial pace, and a large portion of the bilateral segment of this aid continues to be allocated to Asian countries.

As long as the yen remains very strong and the Japanese economy continues to expand through domestic demand, these trends should continue. The rise in the yen, up 100 percent against the dollar since 1985, has provided the motivation for the increase in imports. Even a country such as Japan, which can be described as protectionist (even though tariffs and quotas are no longer significant), must respond to movements in exchange rates. The landed cost of foreign products is now so much below that of domestic products in many cases that manufacturers and distributors cannot ignore them. Furthermore, attitudes among businesses and consumers toward the role of manufactured imports in the economy appear to be changing.

Table 2.6 Recent Trends in Foreign Direct Investment (in millions of U.S. dollars)

	12/31/80	12/31/85	3/31/89	Growth 85/81	Growth 89/86
Total	$12,179	$23,819	$49,843	14.4%	25.5%
North America	2,332	7,440	23,944	26.1	43.3
Asia	4,444	7,434	12,371	10.8	17.0

Source: Ministry of Finance of Japan, Kokusaikin'yukyoku Kin'yu Nenpo (Annual Finance Report of the International Finance Bureau), 1986, pp. 458-459, 1981 edition, pp. 352, 353; and 1982 editions; and Eileen Doherty, "Japan's Foreign Direct Investment in Developing Countries," JEI Report, no. 31A, August 11, 1989, p. 4.

Whereas government publications used to enumerate the reasons why Japan imported few manufactured goods, they are now extolling the virtues of imports (as a means of controlling inflation, increasing consumer choice, and providing competitive pressure on domestic industry).[7] The distribution sector, long considered part of the problem in getting manufactured goods into the country, is now undergoing some scrutiny from the government, and at least modest regulatory liberalization appears likely.

The strong appreciation of the yen has also provided a greater incentive to invest abroad. Despite the conviction that firms had concerning the virtues of keeping production centrally located at home, the disparity in costs between Japan and other countries is now causing them to change their attitudes. But even now the impact of these changes on Asia have been moderate. As shown in Table 2.6, Japan's cumulative direct investment in the manufacturing sector in Asia was growing at a 10.8 percent annual pace in the first half of the 1980s, rising to a 17 percent annual rate from 1985 through 1988. This acceleration was far more modest than the overall rate of direct investment growth after 1985 (25.5 percent) or the rather high growth of foreign direct investment (FDI) in North America (43.3 percent).

Even this moderate acceleration in Japanese foreign direct investment in the rest of Asia should make Japan more visible relative to other foreign investors and the local economies. Furthermore, new investment will likely be concentrated in a very small number of Asian countries (Korea, Taiwan, Thailand, and Malaysia principal among them) where the Japanese presence will be even more noticeable. Japanese investors also are more adept at tying local firms closely to themselves, even though their equity ownership position may be small, through retention of critical skills in Japanese staff dispatched to the local operation or through tight control over nonequity financing (bank loans and trade credit), which may make the perception of Japanese dominance far stronger than simple data on the dollar amount of investment would indicate.

Other indicators show a strong increase in Japanese attention directed toward Asia. The Japanese business media have been emphasizing Asia much more over the past several years, and one could term 1987 the year of the discovery of the Asian NICs and 1988 the year of the discovery of ASEAN by the Japanese press. With an upbeat assessment of the region, the media are promoting the idea that these countries are capable of producing goods of sufficient quality for the Japanese market, thereby endorsing the idea of increased direct investment.[8] Therefore, Japanese firms are seeing Asia as a base for production of goods destined for consumption in Japan (rather than for local or third markets as in the past). Data from a recent MITI survey indicate that the portion of output from Japanese-owned factories in Asia shipped to Japan has risen from 9.8 percent in 1980 to 16.7 percent in 1987. This portion is considerably higher than the 9.1 percent average for all Japanese overseas investment.[9]

Finally, the pressures that have caused Japan's foreign aid spending to increase continue to be present. As a major economic power, the Japanese government feels the pressure to provide a greater contribution to international peace and stability. Both the public and government continue to believe that Japan's primary contribution to the world should be economic rather than military, although defense spending also rose at an above average pace in the 1980s. Even though defense spending and foreign economic aid are by no means entirely substitutable commodities, there is some tendency to view them as such in Japan. Note, however, that in much of the discussion of these issues in Japan, the main motivation is one of obligation to the other industrial nations. By spending more on foreign aid, the Japanese government appears more intent upon impressing the United States and the European countries that it is doing more to carry the "burden" of international security than upon actually contributing to world development. Whatever the motive, though, Japanese aid is likely to continue to grow at an above average rate.

As it grows, Japanese foreign aid continues a close association with industry. Keidanren (known in English as the Japan Federation of Economic Organizations, and which acts as the organized voice of big business), for example, established a new organization, the Japan International Development Organization, Ltd. (JAIDO) in the spring of 1989 to promote direct investment in developing countries. This organization is one-third funded by the OECF—the government's soft loan agency mentioned above. Keidanren also has established an internal group, the Committee on International Cooperation Projects (CICP) to oversee and approve JAIDO investments.[10] In essence, JAIDO and CICP provide a vehicle to gain concessionary financing for Japanese commercial direct investment in Asian countries. U.S. officials also are concerned that this arrangement will provide a means for Japan to gain more influence over the Asian Development Bank as JAIDO begins to request cofinancing for its investments. JAIDO may be a useful tool in promoting beneficial investment and economic development in Asia, but it also provides an explicit combination of government and business to promote Japanese economic benefit, which runs counter to much of U.S. foreign aid philosophy and will raise serious concerns among U.S. officials that it is designed merely to further a mercantilist Japanese policy stance.

Over the next several years, the United States could easily follow the opposite trend. Recognition that the federal budget deficit is a major economic problem for the United States is now quite widespread, although progress in reducing the deficit remains limited. The progress in achieving this goal could be somewhat limited over the next several years, but the direction of change in the deficit will be downward and not upward. By taking some of the pressure off capital markets, and thereby reducing the net inflow of capital from the rest of the world, this scenario leads to a smaller U.S. merchandise trade and current-account deficit (brought about by a continued weak dollar and by slower growth of consumer demand).

A reduction of the U.S. global deficit must affect trade with Asia. These countries will find the United States a less vibrant market for their exports and will find themselves under more pressure from the United States to dismantle their own import barriers in order to facilitate absorption of swelling exports from the United States. These developments could also affect U.S. direct investment in Asia. To date, however, there is little evidence of a slowdown in the pace of U.S. direct investment in manufacturing in Asia. From 1985 to 1987, U.S. cumulative FDI in manufacturing in Asia and the Pacific in countries other than Japan grew at a 20 percent annual rate.[11] Nevertheless, the depreciation of the dollar ought to bring some reconsideration of new overseas investment when those investments are motivated by cost savings.[12]

With these economic developments in Japan and the United States comes a substantial role reversal in the region: Japan's image will improve while that of the United States will worsen. Japan will provide a growing market for Asian manufactured exports while the United States will not; Japan will become a source of a rising amount of direct investment (which may be quite welcome if it generates exports back to Japan) while U.S. firms may slow their investment; budget cutting in Washington may bring further reductions in the already small U.S. foreign aid budget, while Japan's continues to grow. Meanwhile, the antagonism that remains as a legacy of World War II will further diminish as generational transition continues (including the death of the Showa emperor, which eliminated a symbol of Asian distrust of Japan). The Japanese are, for example, touting the idea that the United States has eliminated the generalized system of preferences (GSP) for the Asian NICs while Japan has not. Prime Minister Noboru Takeshita also made a point of presenting issues of concern to Asian countries at the 1988 industrial-nation summit meeting, another symbolic gesture representing a unilateral assumption of a role as Asian spokesman. The intent appears to have been to impress Asian countries that Japan is different from other industrial nations and to demonstrate its interest and concern for the interests of regional nations at this meeting.

Implications for Japan's Role in Regional Cooperation

Japan has been a rather insular nation over the postwar period, willing to export to the world but unwilling to play much of an active role in any other way. Now Japan is inevitably drawn into a more active role by its ownership of overseas assets and provision of ODA. Furthermore, Japan is exhibiting a much greater interest in the Asia-Pacific region after years of largely ignoring its Asian neighbors. Given the general rise of economic ties within the region over time, some type of closer cooperative arrangement makes sense.

To the extent that Japan's outreach to the region promotes economic development, the recent changes are entirely welcome. However, there is room for concern about the nature of Japan's interaction with the region because the newfound interest may drift toward a regionalism that excludes the United States and other industrial countries. Despite the fact that little of the official rhetoric makes specific statements to this effect, the possibility of such a development must be recognized. What the Japanese see as so encouraging about the rest of Asia (and especially the four NICs plus Thailand) are the similarities to Japan's own past economic development. That is, the focus is on aspects of these economies and cultures that provide a link to Japan, and not to the West or the United States. Even the spread of offices of Japanese department and super stores through Asia has been described as part of this process (in an article envisioning a large Japanese-run regional distribution network throughout Asia in the not-too-distant future). Because they maintain both buying operations and sales outlets, Japanese firms are described as having a superior information-gathering ability and "greater trustworthiness" compared to U.S. or European distributors, who have operated purchasing offices in these countries for years.[13] Others have referred to Asia as a large high-quality market in which Japanese firms will plan their procurement from the "most appropriate production base."[14]

The key element in these and other commentaries on Asia is the sense of exclusivity. The United States or other industrial nations are rarely mentioned, or if they are, it is in a negative context. An aggressive tone has emerged in some articles, in which the Japanese portray the United States as being unfair to the rest of Asia, in explicit or implicit comparison to a more benevolent Japan. Consider, for example, the title of a recent cover story in a major Japanese business publication: "No More Japans! Japan and the U.S. Policy of Beating Up South Korea and Taiwan."[15]

Some Japanese have gone so far as to see evolving regionalism in the Western Pacific proceeding to the same extent as European regionalism, driven by both the high yen and the continuing economic development of other countries in Asia. In a recent roundtable discussion, one participant surmised that "Japan and other Asian countries will increasingly draw away from the United States," a trend viewed with favor because Asia has been "overly dependent" on the United States.[16] A long-term economic forecast to the year 2000 issued by the Research Institute on the National Economy (a respected private group) adopts a similar position, predicting that the continued rapid growth and development of the Asian NICs will make closer ties between them and Japan more likely. This report anticipates a greater horizontal division of industry and a rise of intra-industry trade, bringing about a de facto yen bloc as the portion of regional trade denominated in yen rises naturally.[17]

More conservative organizations avoid endorsing any exclusive regional grouping but point out the same trends in trade and investment, thus also implying that much closer ties between Japan and the rest of Asia are likely to develop. For example, a recent report from an advisory committee to MITI with a heavy representation of "internationalists" foresees a new posture for Japan toward Asia and makes a major point of Japan's continued GSP treatment for the Asian NICs. This same report speaks of Japan becoming a major market for the exports of these countries, although it generally casts its discussion in a multilateral framework that explicitly includes the United States. The report endorses initiatives such as JAIDO by stressing that Japan's Asia policy should be a coherent package that will draw Japan and Asian economies closer together. The elements of this coordinated package are to include importing more from Asia, using foreign direct investment to bring about industrial specialization, implementing an expanded medium-term foreign aid program, cooperating on energy policy, and increasing regional dialogue. The report stresses strongly the granting of foreign aid to specifically service Japan's private-sector investment activities in developing countries.[18]

As might be expected from such discussion, some debate has been occurring in Japan over new institutional arrangements for the Asia-Pacific region. Officially the Japanese government stands in favor of integrating the Asian NICs into the OECD, a position that should be applauded. At the same time, however, the Japanese government is also pursuing the creation of a new regional organization. A report on this topic by an advisory commission to MITI released in June 1989 supported the Australian call for ministerial-level meetings of Asia-Pacific nations to discuss economic development and cooperation issues. This report also specifically speaks of "outward-looking" regional cooperation and specifically includes the United States, Australia, and New Zealand. But it also indirectly promotes several MITI initiatives (such as JAIDO and a coordinated regional energy policy that would be dominated by Japanese firms). Other suggestions, including environmental protection, belong in a global framework (or at least one that transcends the boundaries of the Asia-Pacific region).[19]

A number of academics and government officials are also very interested in the concept of a free-trade zone, either bilaterally with the United States or regionally. In some sense this concept goes back as far as the late 1960s when the Japanese proposed a Pacific Free Trade Area.[20] At the present time, the Japanese claim their motivation is due to a perception that the United States is moving away from a multilateral approach to trade, as evidenced by the U.S.-Canada agreement. They also note the statements by former Ambassador Mike Mansfield and various members of Congress in favor of a bilateral free-trade arrangement with Japan. However, their interest appears to go beyond a simple reaction to an American position.

The concept of a bilateral free-trade zone with Japan or other Asian countries has very little support in Washington. Virtually no U.S. government official at all familiar with Japan is in favor of such an arrangement for a variety of reasons. Discussion of a regional arrangement is not likely to proceed very far either. The basic problem lies in the perception that trade barriers in Japan are not easily addressed in a free-trade agreement, so that such a move would not provide much increased access to Japanese markets. Furthermore, a bilateral deal with any single country or a limited group of Asian nations would be extremely poor diplomacy, raising immediate protests or demands for similar treatment from the rest.[21]

There is a scenario, however, in which a regional trade arrangement could emerge regardless of the U.S. government's position. If the European nations were to become somewhat more protectionist toward the rest of the world after 1992, and if the United States spurned the idea of a bilateral or regional trade arrangement with Japan or Asia, the rising trade and investment ties between Japan and Asia, as well as the increased interest of the Japanese in their Asian connection, could well lead to consideration of an Asian preferential trade zone exclusive of the United States. Other Asian nations would likely oppose such a move, but given rising exports to Japan (compared to stagnant sales to the United States), increasing pressure from the United States to open their markets, rising FDI from Japan, rising ODA from Japan, and other inducements, their acquiescence is possible in the 1990s.

Policy Implications

The scenario just sketched is a troubling one. An Asian economic zone centered on Japan would not be in the long-term interests of the United States and might be destabilizing to the region as well. Asian countries might go along with initiatives from Japan, but the exclusivity that would accompany such an arrangement would bring considerable tensions. In addition, U.S. commitment to a substantial military presence in the region would be severely damaged by any economic development that sought to exclude the United States. A diminished U.S. military presence would be a further destabilizing development, especially in the presence of an increasingly economically dominant Japan.

This scenario remains relatively unlikely. However, the following proposals would make it even less likely and would help to move the region in the direction of a more productive cooperation:

1. Japan should dramatically increase its training of specialists on the region. A stronger core of people in Japan who can speak to the needs and problems of Asian developing countries would improve the quality of Japanese foreign aid, counter the heavily commercial orientation of aid and other aspects of Japanese foreign policy toward the region, and provide a more human dimension to Japan's interaction with Asian countries. A major expansion of university area studies programs, including greater opportunities to study or travel abroad, should be the key element in this development. In addition, however, Japan could use a strong effort by the government to create something akin to the Peace Corps of the 1960s in the United States. Japan has an equivalent to the Peace Corps, but the missing element is any visibility or any evidence of substantial interest among the Japanese in working for such an organization. Service abroad, and especially in Asia, should be elevated to a more acceptable position. The point is not effectiveness (as many see the U.S. Peace Corps as ineffective in the 1960s) but generating international experience, understanding, and interest among the Japanese.

2. Japan should also continue its macroeconomic adjustment, expanding domestic demand as part of a program to both benefit the Japanese public and to reduce the trade surplus by absorbing more imports. This process must enable foreign firms to get a real chance to sell more to Japan; if increased imports come primarily from the overseas subsidiaries of Japanese firms, domestic demand expansion will have failed to bring about real change in Japan's position in the world. Conversely, the United States must also continue its macroeconomic adjustment. Admitting the dilemmas this poses for the image of the United States in Asia, the need for reduction or elimination of the trade and current-account deficit is overwhelming.

3. Japan should stick to a multilateral framework in dealing with the rest of the Asia-Pacific region. Moves such as promoting the NICs seminar

in the OECD in the spring of 1988 should be continued; discussion of bilateral or regional trade blocs should be discouraged. This is an area where the Japanese government could easily take a strong initiative, thus clarifying its commitment to GATT and the Uruguay round, disassociating itself from notions of bilateral or regional preferential trade schemes, and ending government-sponsored research on these ideas. There is no harm in the periodic ministerial conference proposed by Australia's Prime Minister Robert Hawke (and strongly supported by the Japanese), but many issues that the Japanese envision discussing—trade, environment, and promotion of foreign direct investment, for example—are more appropriate in nonregional settings.

4. The United States should also do all it can to encourage Japan to move in a more liberal, less mercantilist direction toward the rest of the Asia-Pacific region. Greater communication on issues of mutual interest where Japan can play a beneficial and useful role are important in order to ensure that Japanese policy toward the region evolves in a manner that is advantageous to all and not just to Japanese corporations. The United States must also maintain a presence in Asian matters. Foreign aid should be increased (despite the federal deficit problem) and Japanese efforts to gain greater control over the Asian Development Bank should be resisted. If the United States plays a more limited role in Asia in the future, Asian countries would have little choice but to accept Japanese policy initiatives.

These four points do not represent any innovation or major change in policy. The GATT, the United Nations, the IMF, the World Bank, and other institutions were created in the early postwar era out of a belief that regionalism was not desirable as a general principle. The reasons for opposing preferential regional arrangements are as strong today as they were forty years ago. The informal organizations that now provide an overlapping set of fora in which businesspeople, academics, and government officials of Asia-Pacific countries can interact are all positive steps; as we have moved toward greater economic integration, the need for enhanced communications and information exchange has become stronger. However, any stronger formal institutional framework is not advisable, especially if it includes any form of preferential trade. This would be true even if the United States were a participant in a regional scheme and is even more true if such an arrangement were centered on Japan without the United States.

Notes

1. Japan's relative lack of manufactured imports is discussed in detail in Edward J. Lincoln, *Japan's Unequal Trade* (Washington, D.C.: The Brookings Institution, 1990).

2. Yasumitsu Nihei, Makoto Ohtsu, and David Levin, "A Comparative Study of Management Practices and Workers in an American and Japanese Firm in Hong Kong," in Hong and Levin, eds., *Contemporary Issues in Hong Kong Labour Relations* (Hong Kong: University of Hong Kong, 1983).

3. Organization for Economic Cooperation and Development, *Development Cooperation*, 1988 Report (Paris: OECD, 1988), p. 172.

4. Gretchen Green, "Japan's Foreign Aid Policy: 1989 Update," *JEI Report*, no. 41A, October 27, 1989, p. 12.

5. OECD, *Development Cooperation*, 1988 Report, p. 174.

6. Officially, Japan and the United States have equal capital participation and equal numbers of personnel at the Asian Development Bank. By agreement, Japan has the directorship of the bank, which would seem to be a minor advantage. However, the sense among Americans is that the Japanese have an undue amount of influence over bank affairs.

7. See especially the Ministry of International Trade and Industry, *Tsusho Hakusho* (Trade White Paper), 1988 edition (Tokyo: Ministry of Finance Printing Office, 1988).

8. As an example of this trend, see "Ajia no Seiki: Nihon no Yakuwari" [The Asian Century: Japan's Role], *Toyo Keizai*, November 15, 1986; or Yukiko Fukagawa, "Ajia no Dainamizumu o Torikomu Nihon: Nihon-ASEAN-NICs no Shin Sangyo Chizu" [Japan Grasping Asian Dynamism: The New Industrial Map of Japan/ASEAN/NICs], *Ekonomisuto*, July 4, 1988.

9. Kenji Takeuchi, "Effects of Japanese Direct Foreign Investment on Japan's Imports of Manufacturers from Developing Economies," unpublished paper, World Bank, 1989.

10. *Japan Times Weekly Overseas Edition*, April 15, 1989, p. 10.

11. U.S. Department of Commerce, Bureau of Economic Analysis, *Survey of Current Business*, August 1988, pp. 47-52. U.S. data are not compatible with Japanese data cited earlier because the United States measures the current value of local investments (including reinvested earnings and local capital sources), whereas Japan measures only the cumulative flow of investment funds from Japan.

12. Some caution is in order here, since dollar appreciation in the first half of the 1980s did not bring any acceleration of outward foreign direct investment by U.S. firms. U.S. Department of Commerce, International Trade Administration, *International Direct Investment: Global Trends and the U.S. Role*, 1988 ed. (Washington, D.C.: U.S. Government Printing Office, 1988), p. 20.

13. "Yu'nyu Daikyosui II: Kaihatsu Yu'nyu ga Kasoku Suru Hyakkaten-Supa no Ajia Ryutsuken" [The Big Flood of Imports II: The Asian Sphere of the Department Stores and Super Stores' Accelerating Development Imports], *Toyo Keizai*, July 4, 1987, p. 14.

14. Yukiko Fukugawa, "Ajia no Dainamizumu o Torikomu Nihon," pp. 86-89.

15. " No Moa Japan! Beikoku no Kankoku-Taiwan Tataki to Nihon," *Toyo Keizai*, July 18, 1987, pp. 4-17. The article is actually somewhat more innocuous than the sensational title, dealing with the decision of the U.S. Trade Representative (USTR) to keep South Korea and Taiwan from becoming trade problems on the order of Japan by making them open up their markets earlier. But the tone of the title and

much of the writing emphasizes the U.S. fear of having more successful industrialized countries across the Pacific.

16. Roundtable discussion with Toshio Watanabe, Naoki Tanaka, and Masao Okonogi, "Kankoku ga Senshin Koku ni Naru Hi" [The Day South Korea Becomes an Advanced Country], *Ekonomisuto Rinji Zokan*, November 2, 1988. The remarks are from Professor Watanabe, a specialist on Asian economic development.

17. Kokumin Keizai Kenkyukai [Research Institute of the National Economy is the official English rendition of the Institute's name], *Choki Keizai Yosoku: 2000-Nen no NihonKeizai, Higashi Ajia Koiki Keizaiken no Kannosei* [Long-Term Economic Forecast: The Japanese Economy in the Year 2000—The Possibility of a Broad Economic Area in East Asia] (Tokyo: Kokumin Keizai Kenkyukai, August 1988), especially pp. 9-15.

18. Ministry of International Trade and Industry, *Nihon no Sentaku: Nyu Gurobarizumu e no Kokan to 'Shin Sangyo Bunka Kokka' no Sentaku* [Japan's Choices: Choices Concerning Contribution to the New Globalism and the New National Industrial Culture] (Tokyo: Tsusho Chosakai, 1988), pp. 46-47, 50-53.

19. *Report of the Council for the Promotion of Asian-Pacific Cooperation: Toward an Era of Development Through Outward-Looking Cooperation* (Summary), June 1989. See also *Japan Times Weekly Overseas Edition*, April 8, 1989. The genesis of the proposal was to provide Prime Minister Takeshita a "present" to take to ASEAN on a state visit in late April, but the report was not issued until after his demise as prime minister.

20. Harry Harding and Edward Lincoln, "The East Asian Laboratory," in John D. Steinbruner, ed., *Restructuring American Foreign Policy* (Washington, D.C.: The Brookings Institution, 1989), p. 193.

21. For a review of these and other arguments both for and against a free-trade area with Japan or other Asian countries, see the International Trade Commission's survey of pros and cons on a free-trade area with Japan and with other Asian nations.

3

Asia-Pacific Economic Cooperation and U.S.-Japan Relations

Dick K. Nanto

As the Mediterranean Sea defined the world of the Middle Ages, so the Atlantic Ocean has been the center of power and wealth in the modern era. Now the Pacific perimeter burgeons with vitality and promise for the future. The locus of world economic activity has been shifting from the Atlantic to the Pacific. Although the European Community with its plan for economic integration by 1992 has attracted considerable attention, the fastest economic changes are occurring among the nations bordering the Pacific Ocean. World growth and international trade flows have been altered substantially by the strong economic performance of countries and areas such as Japan, South Korea, Taiwan, Hong Kong, and Singapore. Yet no official international organization links these Pacific Rim economies and provides a forum for them to discuss and coordinate important economic policies.

Other changes in world conditions also have raised the importance of the Asia-Pacific region. The easing of East-West military tensions has elevated the significance of economic issues in discussions of national security. As the prospect of global war recedes for the United States, the likelihood rises that economic, not military, forces will disrupt domestic tranquility. In the minds of many Americans, the economic threat to U.S. well-being presented by Japan and its Asian neighbors is beginning to displace the military threat of the Soviet Union.

Such perceptions have combined with a chronic bilateral trade deficit with Japan of about $50 billion to further focus attention on Asia. Despite the drop in the value of the dollar from 240 yen in 1985 to 140 yen in 1989, this trade deficit has scarcely declined at all. Like a burr under a saddle, it has generated friction over perceived unfair trade practices and economic threats posed by Japanese competitors. Policymakers are searching for alternative mechanisms to resolve these issues without such intense political and economic confrontations and are virtually going to the top to settle them. Should presidents and prime ministers have to discuss trade in semiconductors?

On the Japanese side, concessions made by the Japanese government on imports of beef and citrus products, along with the prospect of liberalizing rice imports, contributed to a defeat of the ruling Liberal Democratic Party in an Upper House election on July 23, 1989. Trade squabbles are beginning to take their toll by eroding political support for the faction in Japan that remains the most supportive of U.S. objectives.[1]

The Japanese also see the world dividing into trading blocs. Economic integration in the European Community by 1992 and the Canada-U.S. Free-Trade Agreement have raised the prospect that Japan and its neighbors could be excluded from these preferential trading arrangements. A unified EC can exert considerable leverage in multilateral trade negotiations that either Japan or the United States could find difficult to counter without joining forces.

Meanwhile, the rising debtor status of the United States, along with Japan's emergence as the world's largest creditor nation, has fundamentally altered the ability of the United States to resolve world financial problems. Issues such as Third World debt or currency misalignment, for example, are unlikely to be resolved without financial support from the government and banking community of Japan.

In essence, the diminished relative economic power of the United States and the increased power of Japan are changing the structure under which international economic policy is conducted. One response to this trend is to examine a more formal institutional framework to deal with economic relations among nations/areas in the Pacific Basin.

U.S. Economic Outlook

The United States is currently passing through a precarious stage in its business cycle. Recovery from the recession of 1981-1982 and subsequent expansion has continued longer than most economists anticipated, and the Federal Reserve has been attempting to ease a somewhat overheated economy into a "soft landing." The danger is that rising interest rates could push the U.S. economy into a recession, although indicators of economic activity in the first half of 1990 continued to be fairly strong.

Economic forecasts call for real economic growth in the United States to average about 2 to 3 percent per year during the 1990s.[2] The major macroeconomic problems are the twin deficits in the U.S. international and fiscal accounts.

The current account deficit, which dropped from $144 billion in 1987 to $111 billion in 1989, is expected to remain stubbornly high, at $112–$120 billion, through 1992.[3] Likewise, the U.S. federal budget deficit is expected to decline slowly, from $152 billion in 1989 to $100–$110 billion by 1992. As a result of these twin deficits, total U.S. net foreign debt is likely to exceed $1 trillion in the early 1990s. This rising debt has already educed U.S. net worth below that of Japan.

The gap between the escalating debtor status of the United States and the rising creditor status of Japan implies that Japanese citizens will continue to accrue net income through their overseas investments, while Americans will have to shoulder increasingly burdensome interest payments on their debts. In the future, this net outflow of capital from the United States will have to be offset by rising U.S. net exports of goods and services and a surplus in the U.S. current account. Much of this shift is likely to come out of the trade surpluses that East Asian economies are currently enjoying with the United States. Japan, in particular, will probably have to cut its exports or increase imports from both the United States and its Asian neighbors.

A significant improvement in the U.S. trade deficit depends primarily on U.S. macroeconomic policy, particularly in reducing the U.S. budget deficit. Econometric estimates, however, indicate that a total elimination of the U.S. budget deficit would likely reduce the trade deficit by only 50 percent or so.[4] About half of the trade deficit, therefore, depends on other factors, such as enhancing the competitiveness of U.S. firms, reducing trade barriers abroad, and promoting U.S. exports.

The 1988 Omnibus Trade and Competitiveness Act (P.L. 100-418) requires the United States to undertake aggressive action under the "Super 301" provisions to counter what it considers to be unfair trade practices abroad. It also eases the process by which U.S. firms can secure protection from import competition. As the provisions of this act are implemented, acrimony between the United States and its trading partners in Asia is likely to heighten.

The prospect for the United States, therefore, is that even if its budget deficit is reduced significantly, the trade deficit will remain at such a high level that pressures to lower it will continue. It is unlikely that Japan and other East Asian economies can go on running large bilateral trade surpluses with the United States without a major flare-up in trade friction or having to face numerous trade complaints from the United States. This is an important reason to examine an institution for Pacific Rim economic cooperation.

Japan's Economic Outlook

Japan's economic system seems to have a resilience that surprises even the Japanese themselves. After each external shock, their economy seems to recover and emerge even stronger than before. The two oil shocks during the 1970s and the post-1985 yen appreciation crisis seem to have come and gone without major disruption.

Currently, the Japanese economy is booming despite rising interest rates and a sagging stock market. Domestic demand has been strong, and a resurgence in Japanese exports, especially of partially assembled components to overseas manufacturing subsidiaries, has pushed growth rates up to the point where authorities are beginning to worry about overheating and a resurgence of inflation. Growth in real gross national product, which ranged from 2.5 percent in 1986 to 5.9 percent in 1988, dropped to 4.9 percent in 1989 and is forecast to remain at about 4 percent through the 1990s.[5]

Japan's surplus on current account, which rose from $7 billion in 1982 to $87 billion in 1987, is expected to continue to decline gradually, from $80 billion in 1988 to $60 billion in 1993. Whether this drop will be sufficient to quell protectionist forces in the United States and other nations cannot be determined. But the prospect is for more trade friction, particularly given the 1988 Omnibus Trade and Competitiveness Act in the United States and unification in the European Community.

Japan is currently enjoying an "embarrassment" of riches, both in terms of tax collections and in corporate profits. The fiscal year 1989 budget included the largest increase in spending since 1981 but still allowed for significant deficit reductions. Deficit financing was projected to drop by nearly half that in 1988. Outlays for foreign aid and defense are likely to rise as a response to strong foreign pressures on Japan to assume a larger international role.

Given the strength of the Japanese economy, its surplus of riches, and the friction in trade that it has had with nations around the Asia-Pacific region, the time seems ripe for it to consider broadening the framework under which it conducts relations with its neighbors.

Growing Asia-Pacific Trade and Investment

Patterns of international trade around the Pacific Basin are shifting. The economies of Asia are becoming more horizontally integrated, and a de facto trading bloc is arising. As indicated in Figure 3.1, however, the United States still remains the region's largest export market. The figure shows imports and exports with the arrows drawn in proportion to the size of those flows. The thickest arrows still point toward the United States. Any trading bloc that excludes the United States, therefore, would threaten a market upon which Asian exporters are highly dependent.

Trade within East Asia is taking a larger and larger share of total Pacific Basin trade, and Japan is becoming a hub for that trade. Between 1980 and 1988, for example, imports into Japan from the three East Asian Newly Industrializing Economies (South Korea, Taiwan, and Hong Kong) grew by

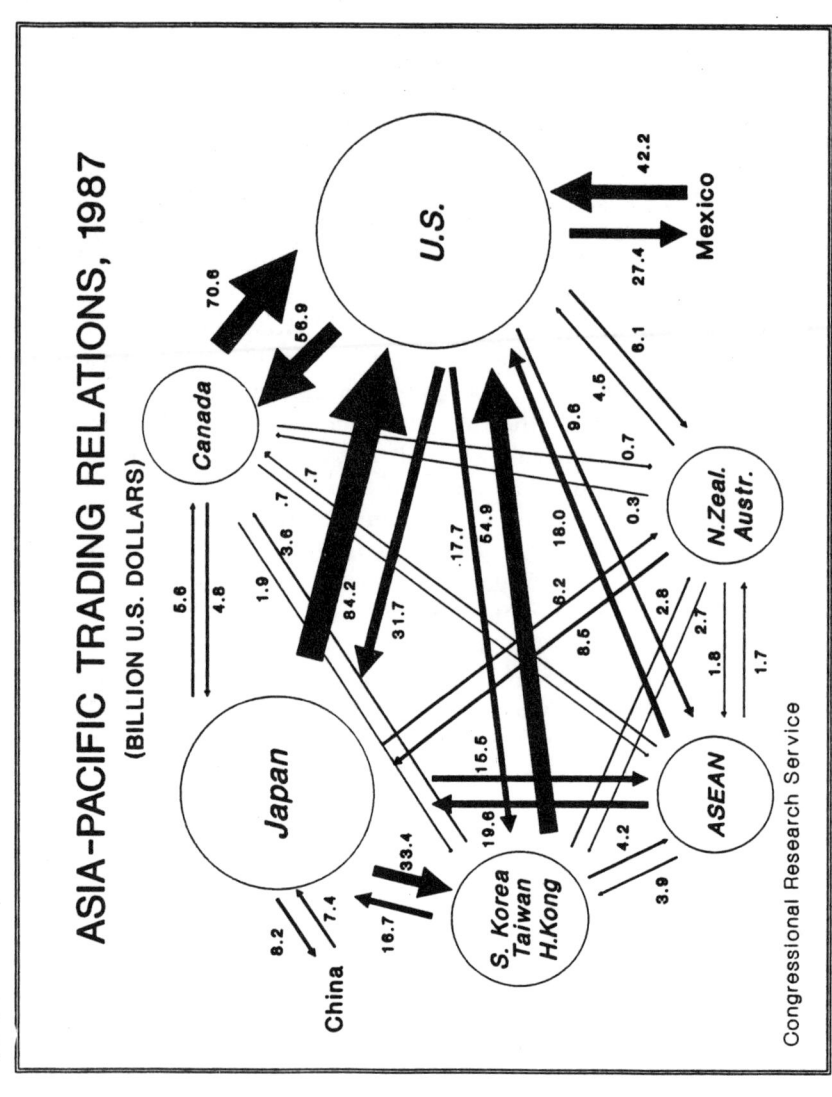

Figure 3.1

ASIA-PACIFIC TRADING RELATIONS, 1987
(BILLION U.S. DOLLARS)

Congressional Research Service

an average of 18.4 percent per year. This was almost five times the rate of growth in Japan's overall imports, which was 3.7 percent per year. Japan's exports to those economies grew by 13.3 percent over the same period, which was also higher than its 9.4 percent annual growth in overall exports.

Despite this surge in imports, however, Japan's trade surplus with these three East Asian Newly Industrializing Economies (NIEs) has remained quite high. It jumped from $16.6 billion in 1987 to $18.8 billion in 1988 (up considerably from $9.4 billion in 1980). Since Japan exports to these NIEs almost twice what it imports from them, imports need to grow almost twice as fast as exports in order for the bilateral trade surplus to fall.

Trade within industrial sectors is also growing. In transport equipment, for example, Japan's imports from the three East Asian NIEs increased an average of 45 percent per year from 1980-1987 and jumped 158 percent in 1987 alone. Japan's exports of transport equipment to these economies have been growing at 13 percent per year and rose by 58 percent in 1987. Such trends point toward increasing cross trade within sectors.

Japan's direct investment in manufacturing or distribution systems in Asia likewise has been moving forward rapidly. Much of the surge in imports of manufactured goods into Japan, in fact, originates from subsidiaries of Japanese corporations. As of March 1989, of the total Japanese overseas direct investment of $186.4 billion, $32.2 billion was in Asia. This amount included $9.8 billion in Indonesia, $6.2 billion in Hong Kong, $3.8 billion in Singapore, and $3.2 billion in South Korea.[6] By way of comparison, investments in the United States amounted to $53.3 billion at the end of 1988.

Japan is by far the largest donor of foreign aid to the Asian nations. In the fiscal year ending in March 1988, it provided $3.4 billion, about twice the amount provided by the United States. Although much of this aid has been tied to purchases of Japanese capital equipment, recently the government has been striking its buy-Japanese provisions.[7]

The yen, moreover, is assuming a larger role in Asian trade, capital markets, and in foreign exchange reserves. In 1987, 33.4 percent of Japan's exports (up from 29.4 percent in 1980) and 11 percent of its imports (up from 2.4 percent in 1980) were denominated in yen. Likewise, yen-denominated bonds and foreign exchange holdings of yen have grown. South Korea and Thailand give the yen a large weight in determining the value of their currencies.[8]

Hence, whether or not a formal Asia-Pacific trading bloc is created is somewhat immaterial because a de facto trading bloc is already emerging. It is arising out of economic necessity and, barring draconian barriers, will continue to grow regardless of whether free trade develops among the various economies.[9]

If Japan and other Asian or Pacific exporting nations perceive that Europe and North America are moving to lock them out of their economies, however, they could proceed toward formalizing an Asia-Pacific trading bloc, probably yen-based. Currently, the probability of such a formal relationship, particularly one that excludes the United States, is small. Most of the Asian and Pacific nations are committed to the multilateral GATT liberalization process rather than a plurilateral trading bloc arrangement.

As for the Asian NIEs, they seem much more interested in establishing a trading bloc arrangement with the United States than with Japan. They already rely heavily on the U.S. market for export sales and also share important security and other ties. Although trade within the Asia-Pacific region is growing, the United States is still the major export destination for these countries. Any trading bloc that excluded the United States would threaten a substantial market upon which Asian exporters depend highly.

U.S. Trade Policy Toward Japan

One reason for considering a new institution or trading arrangement to deal with Pacific Basin economic affairs is that a significant body of opinion is emerging in both the United States and Japan that something more needs to be done to resolve trade issues.[10] In the United States, current thinking takes four paths.

The first line of thought opposes more change and holds that the modifications made by the 1988 Omnibus Trade and Competitiveness Act were substantial and should now be allowed to operate. The mechanisms are already in place to resolve virtually any trade issue. Specific requirements in the Omnibus Trade and Competitiveness Act, particularly the Super 301 provisions, along with existing trade statutes, are forcing the U.S. government to deal with trade issues on a bilateral, sector-specific basis.[11] This activity will proceed regardless of any increased regional economic cooperation. Combined with the ongoing Uruguay Round of Multilateral Trade Negotiations under GATT, this process will continue to monopolize most of the resources of U.S. agencies with international trade responsibilities.

The second line of thought calls for a completely new approach, particularly for trade with Japan. This would be a type of "affirmative action" or legalistic method of reducing the bilateral trade deficit. It has been referred to as "managed trade." Managed trade is based on results rather than rules of operation. One model for managed trade has been the Multifibre Arrangement, which allows industrialized member nations to allocate quotas for imports of textiles and apparel from developing nations. Other models include Japan's voluntary export restraints on automobiles and the U.S.-Japan semiconductor arrangement, in which Japan purportedly agreed to establish a certain market share for U.S. semiconductor exports in the Japanese market.

Current versions of managed trade are not yet well defined, but it likely would include specific targets for import market shares in Japan's home market, quotas on exports from Japan, or even a target for the overall bilateral trade deficit.

Proposals for managed trade originate from the suspicion that Japan is implicitly managing its trade anyway, so the United States might as well make that management explicit and more consistent with U.S. wishes. Managed trade calls for Japan to do the management with a threat of retaliation from the United States if targets are not met.

One problem with managed trade is that the United States would be asking Japan to follow policies that would strengthen the hand of government over business. This idea counters U.S. negotiating objectives over the past two decades, which have called for Japan to stop intervening in its economy, particularly in regard to controlling imports. Japanese businesses likewise have been pushing for deregulation. Another problem is that retaliation under managed trade could amount to veiled protectionism. Would such sanctions be consistent with U.S. obligations under GATT and other treaty obligations?

As an alternative to managed trade or allowing the new trade law to operate, a third approach would be to negotiate a free-trade area (FTA) or other such cooperative arrangement with Asian trading partners, particularly Japan. The rationale for this approach is that the level of interdependence between the United States and Japan is so great that the relationship should not be threatened by constant bickering over market access and unfair trade practices. Trade friction has often threatened to damage other economic ties as well as political, security, and diplomatic cooperation.[12]

The idea would be to first eliminate official trade barriers in both countries, set up a dispute settlement mechanism that would be less taxing on the relationship, and then begin work on the more difficult cultural and institutional barriers to trade. FTAs are discussed in more detail below.

A fourth approach would be to allow current U.S. laws and processes to operate to resolve specific issues but to also step up the cooperative and consultative process with Japan and other nations of the Asia-Pacific region by creating a separate institution or forum. This approach would shift the focus of public debate from specific issues to broader questions, such as how the new wealth of Japan and other Pacific nations could be used to support the world economy and how the Pacific Rim countries could cooperate to solve major world problems, such as the Third World debt crisis.

This Pacific Rim institution would not focus primarily on issues such as trade barriers, which are being handled mainly in the GATT and on a bilateral basis. It instead would provide a forum for discussing and coordinating economic policies on issues such as exchange rates, capital flows, negotiating strategy, and product standards.

Pacific Rim Proposals

The proposals being considered for an FTA or Pacific organization are as numerous as they have been varied.[13] In the United States, versions of such proposals have been advanced by former U.S. Ambassador to Japan Mike Mansfield, former Senate Majority Leader Robert Byrd, former Secretary of State George Shultz, and Secretary of State James Baker as well as current members of Congress. Japan similarly has advanced such concepts.

The proposals fall into two groups. The first calls for new bilateral trading arrangements, particularly a free-trade area between the United States and Japan. The second aims at broader Pacific Basin cooperation and the establishment of a plurilateral system.

U.S.-Japan Free-Trade Agreement

In the 101st Congress (1989-1990), Senator Max Baucus introduced a bill (S. 292) that would require the initiation of trade negotiations with Japan for the purpose of entering into one or more agreements. Senator Baucus pointed out that the United States has chosen to address each bilateral problem that arises through a separate negotiation. This approach has shortcomings because U.S. objectives have been poorly chosen, the seemingly endless series of disputes has alienated many Japanese, and separate agencies in the United States have conducted independent negotiations without establishing a central agenda.[14]

The Baucus proposal would possibly include an FTA with Japan. The pros and cons of initiating negotiations to establish such an FTA have been surveyed in a report by the International Trade Commission done at the request of Senator Lloyd Bentsen.[15]

In addition to an FTA, the Baucus proposal includes an agreement to coordinate macroeconomic policies more closely. A type of G-2 (between the United States and Japan) could be formed (named after G-7, the group of seven Western nations who coordinate exchange market intervention) to establish target zones for exchange rates and coordinate economic policy. It also includes a version of managed trade. The two countries would set trade-flow targets aimed at increasing trade while restoring some trade balance. The tools used to reach the goals would primarily involve macroeconomic mechanisms or market opening—not protection of U.S. markets.

Representative Philip Crane has introduced bills (H.R. 1051, 1748, 1751, and 1752) that would authorize the establishment of FTAs between the

United States and Japan as well as with Taiwan, South Korea, and ASEAN. For the U.S.-Japan FTA, the advantages envisaged include mutual economic benefits in the form of trade creation, greater economic efficiency, enhanced competition, and lower consumer prices; removal of the remaining formal and informal barriers to trade in both countries, identifying and addressing remaining systemic barriers in Japan, such as the distribution system; provision of an effective vehicle for developing rules in nontraditional areas, such as services, trade-related investment, and intellectual property rights; and the creation of a less controversial and formalized dispute settlement mechanism to resolve bilateral problems.

Representative Donald Pease has introduced a concurrent resolution (H. Con. Res. 166) expressing the sense of the Congress that the United States should pursue the establishment of a United States–Japan bilateral framework agreement.

The earliest that Congress could give serious consideration to the FTA bills would probably be in the 102nd Congress (1991-1992). Most of these bills contain language that give other trade issues immediate priority. The focus of U.S. trade policy in 1990 was to proceed multilaterally to complete the Uruguay Round of GATT Negotiations and to continue bilateral efforts under existing trade law to resolve trading problems.

Although an FTA with Japan or other Asian economies could reduce trade tensions, it could also worsen bilateral trade deficits. The United States could lose some of the leverage with which it has gained some successes in opening the markets of its Asian trading partners. The United States would have fewer concessions to give and would probably find the threat of cutting off access to the U.S. market less convincing to its trading partners. (Even under an FTA, U.S. trade remedies would be available to U.S. industries unless specifically excluded by the agreement. For example, antidumping or countervailing duties could be assessed, or escape clauses could be invoked.)

A recent study by Jeffrey Schott of the Institute for International Economics recommends that the United States consider FTAs only as a third-best option after the GATT Multilateral Trade Negotiations and some sort of GATT-plus concept in which the United States would join with those nations willing to reduce trade barriers beyond those agreed to under GATT on a conditional, most-favored-nation basis.[16]

The Japanese themselves have expressed considerable interest in the concept of a free-trade area with the United States in order to keep from being shut out of what they perceive to be a growing North American trading bloc. While Japan opposes trading blocs in principle, they definitely do not want to be locked out of any that do develop. In a report examining an FTA with the United States, a quasi-governmental Japanese study group concluded that such an FTA could have great value but that a traditional

FTA that benefits the two countries exclusively could have a negative impact on third countries and a devastating effect on the GATT multilateral trading system as well. The group instead proposed to establish a Japan-U.S. economic charter, a framework for wide-ranging cooperation that would include a provision for dismantling border barriers, rules for activities not covered by GATT (intellectual property rights, services, and investments, for example), a method of harmonizing systems (such as tax, financial, distribution, anti-monopoly, and industrial policies), macroeconomic policy coordination, joint responsibility, and dispute settlement mechanisms.[17]

A separate innovative proposal calls for Japan to negotiate FTAs with Asian neighbors in exchange for an FTA with the United States. Japan would then be guaranteed access to the U.S. market in exchange for guaranteeing the United States and certain Asian economies access to its own market. Japan already provides special tariff preferences (GSP) for imports from Asian and other developing countries. It provides duty-free imports for 800 items and half the duty rates on 400 other items for countries with most-favored-nation status. It does plan, however, to raise duties on competitive imports from the NIEs. These include steel, textiles, and some other products that are becoming highly competitive on international markets.[18]

Japan also has intervened to protect its industries against too rapid incursions by imports from its Asian neighbors. It has already pressured South Korea to control its exports of cement and certain textiles. It recently asked Indonesia to restrain its exports of plywood, although Indonesia refused to do so. The idea of an FTA that allows free imports from Asian neighbors, therefore, seems contrary to current Japanese government behavior.

A further barrier to a formal Asian trading bloc, particularly one that is yen-based, is that next to trade friction with the United States, the second largest problem for the Asian NIEs is their deficit in trade with Japan. South Korea has become so distressed over its chronic trade deficit with Japan that it has begun a program to diversify imports away from Japan and toward the United States. It has gone so far as to compile a list of imports from Japan and designate alternative Korean or U.S. suppliers.[19] Taiwan has been following a buy-U.S. policy in its public procurement, although it recently scaled the program back for public construction projects. Each of these economies has been frustrated in its trading relations with Japan.

The irony, however, is that as much as these countries say they do not want to buy from Japan, their businesses continue to do so. Japanese exporters seem to have the products they need at a competitive price and provide the desired after-market service. Dependence on Japan continues to grow.

Japan's strategy seems less aimed at dominating the region than ensuring that it has stable sources of supplies of raw materials, locations for overseas plants, and markets for its products. Japan's businesses and government appear to be expanding the Japanese economy beyond the country's geographical borders.

The likely strategy for Japan will be to pursue greater economic cooperation among the nations of the Asia-Pacific region but not to pursue a formal trading bloc based on free trade. The most likely type of trading bloc for Japan to pursue would be one that included the United States. The Japanese government and many Japanese think tanks are now studying this issue.

A series of bilateral FTAs in the Pacific Rim could provide a type of Pacific Rim economic cooperation focused primarily on reducing barriers to trade and not wider economic issues. As in the case of the European Community, however, FTAs can be a first step toward further cooperation on a range of other economic and political issues.

For Americans now, an FTA with Mexico or with the EC seems more likely than one with Japan or other Asian countries. The high level of trade friction with Asian exporters, the differences in level of development, plus the likely protectionist backlash from unrestricted imports from Japan make generating the national support for approval of such an FTA quite difficult at this time.

In terms of the effects of FTAs or trading blocs, a significant contradiction is apparent. Currently, the world has more trade with fewer trade barriers (either natural or artificial) than at any time in history. Despite the warnings of increased protectionism, trade barriers actually are going down in most countries. Average tariff rates among the industrialized countries are only a fraction of the level prevalent during the Great Depression or even the 1950s, and shipping costs are relatively low. Cooperative arrangements such as free-trade areas, therefore, seem less necessary now than in times past.

On the other hand, the interdependence of countries is greater now than ever before because of their trading and investment relations. Vulnerability to foreign events and actions is more severe and apparent. For example, movements in exchange rates are large and can have major effects on countries. The 50 percent appreciation of the yen versus the dollar beginning in 1985 amounted to the equivalent of a 50 percent tariff being raised against imports from Japan into the United States. International capital flows also have major effects on domestic interest rates and economic growth. Given such interdependence and instability, economic cooperation and coordination seems more necessary now than in times past. Any FTA agreement should, following this line of reasoning, extend beyond merely lowering import barriers.

Proposals for Multilateral Pacific Cooperation

In November 1989, twelve Pacific Rim nations met in Canberra, Australia, to form the Asia Pacific Economic Cooperation conference (APEC). Twenty-seven representatives from the United States, Japan, Australia, New Zealand, South Korea, Canada, and the six ASEAN nations met at the initiative of Prime Minister Robert Hawke of Australia to exchange views and explore ways of creating a formal regional organization.[20] Mr. Hawke had envisaged an economic organization modeled after the OECD that would include a permanent secretariat for "core" nations. This organization would not constitute a trading bloc but would be intended to provide a boost to the GATT liberalization process.

At the conference, the ministers decided to meet again in 1990 in Singapore and 1991 in South Korea. They reiterated that APEC was not intended to form a regional trading bloc and agreed on the need to improve data collection and explore ways to improve investment and technology transfer between countries of the region. APEC follows on a number of proposals from the United States, Japan, and other Asia-Pacific nations.

On June 26, 1989, U.S. Secretary of State James Baker announced that the Bush administration would explore the possibilities for a new mechanism for multilateral cooperation among the nations of the Pacific Rim. The key principles of such a mechanism would be as follows:

1. It would encompass a wide variety of issues, extending from trade and economic affairs to cultural exchange and protection of resources.
2. A Pacific-wide institution would be inclusive; it would expand trade and investment and not hinder existing efforts or institutions.
3. A Pacific entity should recognize the diversity of social and economic systems and differing levels of development in the region.

Secretary Baker indicated that he did not intend to offer a definitive blueprint but would be looking for a consensus from Asia-Pacific leaders. This Pacific Rim initiative follows along the same lines as the ideas suggested by former Secretary of State George Shultz in a speech in July 1988. He called for a Pacific Basin forum to be created in which like-minded countries could compare experiences, discuss ideas, and prepare analyses on subjects that are of interest to most countries in the region. Shultz proposed focusing initially on regional infrastructure projects, particularly in transportation, telecommunications, education, natural resources, and the environment.[21]

In the 101st Congress, Senator Bill Bradley proposed forming a coalition of eight Pacific nations that would organize to coordinate exchange rates, seek solutions to the Third World debt crisis, and negotiate common positions for GATT negotiations. The so-called Pac-8 would include the industrialized countries of the United States, Canada, Japan, Australia, and the Newly Industrializing Countries (NICs) of Mexico, South Korea, Indonesia, and Thailand.[22]

The idea behind the Pac-8 proposal is to form a group of countries that cooperate on international economic policy but do not give each other trade preferences. In terms of macroeconomic cooperation, the group would work toward forming a monetary system similar to that of the European Community in which exchange rates could be stabilized and adjusted. For Third World debt, the group could establish a framework to resolve debt problems and make proposals to other creditors of the world.

For negotiating in fora such as the Uruguay Round of GATT negotiations, the Pac-8 could present a united front representing both industrial and industrializing countries of the Pacific. Unlike the Cairns Group[23] of agricultural exporting countries, the group would include industrial powers as well as agricultural exporting nations. Together, they probably could offset the power of the EC with its expanded membership.

Senator Alan Cranston and Representative Mel Levine have introduced bills (S. Con. Res. 27, H. Con. Res. 93) calling for a Pacific Basin forum to discuss economic, diplomatic, and other issues unique to the region. The forum would include annual meetings with a permanent secretariat to perform research and pursue dialogue on the long-range concerns of mutual interest in the Pacific. The purpose of the forum would be for the United States to work cooperatively with other nations in Asia to shape a mutually beneficial future. This proposal is a response to what is perceived to be a pressing need to reinvigorate U.S. diplomatic efforts in the Asia-Pacific region in the face of aggressive Soviet diplomacy and new initiatives by South Korea, China, Indonesia, and Japan. The forum would pursue issues such as free trade, economic development, and security confidence building.[24]

Japan also has favored more multilateral cooperation and is beginning to bolster formal ties and cooperative relationships among the economies in East Asia. In 1988, former Prime Minister Yasuhiro Nakasone proposed that the Pacific Forum for Economic and Cultural Cooperation be established with membership open to any country or area in the region. He also called for study of the idea of a Pacific free-trade zone, with the intent of a loose association at first as a means of bringing out more of the dynamism of the countries of the region.[25]

Japan's Ministry of International Trade and Industry (MITI) joined with Australia in pushing for the APEC conference of trade and industry ministers from "core" Asian Pacific nations (including the United States) that would concentrate on trade and investment issues. In March 1989, Prime Minister Noboru Takeshita asked MITI to quickly work out the details of a possible Asia-Pacific economic cooperation pact. The organization would include regularly scheduled meetings of trade and industry ministers with an eye toward promoting an outward-looking, nonexclusive, Asia-Pacific region.[26]

A MITI study group that examined Asia-Pacific cooperation has concluded that such Pacific cooperation is an inevitable development. It emphasized that regional cooperation should be outward looking and should not be aimed at forming a block economy. Any trade barriers eliminated should be applied on a most-favored-nation basis. New business opportunities generated by improving the infrastructure for economic development should be offered internationally to all enterprises.[27]

The group established the following principles of cooperation:

- Promotion of multifaceted cooperation. The approach to problems would be gradual and phased.
- Mutual respect and equal footing in participation by all participants.
- Promotion of multilayered cooperation. Asia-Pacific cooperation should complement existing regional cooperative arrangements, such as ASEAN, the Australia–New Zealand Closer Economic Relations agreement (CER), and the Canada-U.S. Free-Trade Agreement.
- Cooperation based on private-sector vitality and the free-market mechanism.

The group also established the following five targets to be focused upon in order to achieve sustained economic growth for the region:

- Further expansion of trade.
- Improving the industrial infrastructure of the region's developing nations.
- Reenforcement of measures for maintaining high growth.
- Attainment of balanced economic development. This includes lessening the heavy dependence on the U.S. economy, improving trade balances, and coordinating macroeconomic policies.
- Consolidation of conditions for cooperation. This includes providing adequate funds for cooperative projects, compiling economic statistics, harmonizing standards, protecting intellectual property rights, and promoting industrial cooperation.

Japan's Ministry of Foreign Affairs joined in the APEC meetings but also is supporting the Pacific Economic Cooperation Conference (PECC), which was established in September 1980. PECC is an unofficial body composed of representatives of business, academia, and governments who attend in their private capacities. It sponsors task forces that study possible areas of economic cooperation on topics such as trade policy, investment, capital flows, minerals and energy, and renewable resources. Since the conference is nongovernmental, it tends to provide a forum for discussion of important economic issues rather than to issue specific policies.[28]

The PECC is increasingly being viewed as the nucleus of a Pacific economic organization. It is expanding its role in the region, and in 1989 it began publishing an economic outlook for the Asia-Pacific region similar to that issued by the OECD.[29] For Japan, PECC seems to be emerging as a favored vehicle, a mechanism that "looks multilateral but which can be kept under Japanese sway." It has the potential to become a primary regional forum and could evolve into the same type of consultative policy-promotion club that the OECD is for rich countries.[30]

In 1986, the PECC expanded its membership to include representatives from Beijing and Taipei. It now has fifteen national committees representing the United States, Canada, Japan, South Korea, China, Taiwan, Australia, New Zealand, the Pacific Islands, and the six ASEAN members. The Soviet Union, Mexico, Chile, and Peru have expressed interest in joining PECC.

A major problem for Japan is that the nations that were victims of its aggression in World War II simply do not relish the thought of being a member of a regional trading bloc dominated by the Japanese. Japan has been trying to erase lingering memories of World War II and its attempt to establish the Greater East Asia Co-Prosperity Sphere, but considerable latent hostility still remains. This hostility occasionally surfaces, as when, for example, Japan rewrites its history books to downplay its aggression in China. The strength of the hostility continues to dog Japan's efforts to suppress it, despite the fact that those directly affected by the war are becoming a smaller and smaller proportion of the population throughout Asia.

Despite the legacy of past Japanese militarism in Asia, the ascendancy of that country as a dominant economic and political power in East Asia should not be discounted. The reality of Japanese economic power can take precedence over negative perceptions.

In order to gauge attitudes toward Japan among the dynamic economies of Asia, in the summer and fall of 1988 the Congressional Research Service conducted in-depth interviews with elite economic decision makers in South Korea, Taiwan, Hong Kong, Singapore, and Thailand. The first question asked was which countries will play a dominant politico-economic role in East Asia in the next five to ten years.

In South Korea, Japan stood out as the leading choice of the vast majority. The reasons were that Japan had the economic power, was the largest creditor nation, was exporting capital in the form of direct and portfolio investment, and was providing aid throughout East Asia. Japan, however, had to be cautious because of anti-Japanese feelings.[31]

In Taiwan, slightly more than half of the interviewees thought that Japan would be the number one country in the region over the next five to ten years.[32]

In Singapore, all the respondents rated the United States as being highly important to Singapore and the East Asia region, both in economic and security terms, but the vast majority saw U.S. power and influence as slipping. All saw Japan as the main beneficiary of the U.S. decline and as the power to watch in the future.[33]

In Hong Kong, most of the interviewees confined their answers to countries within the Asian region and named Japan as the country that would play the dominant role in East Asia over the next five to ten years, largely for economic reasons. They saw Japan as having economic power, which is the main determinant of influence today.[34]

In Thailand also Japan was seen as becoming the dominant economic power in East Asia and as already moving toward an expanded relationship with Thailand. Booming trade, investment, and economic assistance, along with the power vacuum created in the aftermath of the Vietnam War, were seen to be moving Japan toward a larger political role as well.[35]

Policy Discussion

U.S. policy has long favored close cooperation among Pacific Basin states. In 1985, President Ronald Reagan issued National Security decision Directive No. 185 (September 4, 1985), which directed executive branch officials to promote closer cooperation with countries in the Pacific Basin through expanded involvement in such regional fora as the ASEAN 6+5 dialogue framework and PECC.[36]

The APEC conference in November 1989, however, produced no agreement on a detailed plan for creating a governmental Pacific Basin institution.[37] Proposals are still sketchy. Some of the objectives for a Pacific Rim institution could be:

- To provide a forum in which to discuss common economic issues and resolve conflicts.
- To coordinate solutions and outside assistance to resolve economic problems in the region, including development aid, burden sharing, exchange rates, technology transfer, foreign investment, and environmental pollution.
- To promote international trade in the region in a manner also beneficial to other member states, particularly with respect to market access and

trade imbalances (to shift Asian export dependency away from the U.S. market and toward Japan and other economies of the region).
- To promote market-oriented growth to facilitate private-sector vitality and to provide both a model and a system into which the Chinese and other centrally planned economies could be integrated.
- To develop a unified negotiating strategy and counterweight to the economic and political influence of the European Community.
- To lift the level of performance of Asia-Pacific industrializing nations with respect to rules of bodies such as the GATT, IMF, and OECD in order to induce greater participation in the international economic system and ensure that Asian and Pacific nations develop outward-looking economic policies.
- To promote infrastructure development in developing nations, including information, communications, and transportation, in order to facilitate economic development and trade.

Given objectives such as these, several questions still exist about a Pacific Basin institution and how it would function. First, what problem areas should the institution address? Trade and economic issues are assumed to be central, but what associated issues would be in its purview? Should it include information flows, technology transfer, intellectual property rights, aid and investment flows, product standards, or natural resource issues? What about noneconomic issues, such as global warming, drug trade, human rights, educational exchange, and immigration? Presumably, certain economic issues are often best addressed in a bilateral context. These include particular nontariff barriers to trade. Other issues are broader and more regional. These include trade imbalances, currency adjustment, structural reform, capital flows, and general trade policies. Most regional issues also are global.

A useful role for regional institutions is to provide accurate economic and sociological data on the countries and economies of the region. One of the first tasks of such an institution could be to publish statistics similar to those compiled by the OECD.

Another central question deals with institutional membership. Which countries should be members? Presumably, the major market economies of the Pacific (the United States, Canada, Japan, South Korea, ASEAN, Australia, and New Zealand) that attended the APEC conference would comprise the core nations. China, Taiwan, Hong Kong, and the Soviet Union could be offered either membership or observer status. Both Taiwan and China belong to the PECC. Vietnam, Cambodia, Laos, North Korea, the Pacific Island nations, and Latin America also could be considered, but as membership grows, so do logistical problems. The initial membership could be restricted to a core group representative of other members.

China, Taiwan, and Hong Kong would pose thorny membership problems. A membership formula similar to that of the Asian Development Bank is a possibility (both China-Taipei and the People's Republic of China are members), but any membership decision would make a political statement.

A third question is how the institution would be funded. Each member would likely be expected to contribute according to its ability to pay. In the case of PECC, Japan was instrumental in setting up a central fund. Japan's growing foreign aid budget might be tapped, but it would likely expect a proportionately large voice in the operation of the institution. What seems almost certain is that U.S. budget constraints are unlikely to allow the United States to devote large sums of money to such an institution.

Fourth, where would the secretariat be located and how extensively would it be staffed? Australia has stated that for APEC it does not envisage a large body, particularly a massive new regional bureaucracy. It notes that initially a small number of officials, possibly seconded from regional governments, would be sufficient to act as a focal point and to draw together analysis needed to develop regional cooperation. This group of analysts would not do all the required analytical work but would draw on the resource network of existing regional bodies, such as PECC.

Fifth, how would the activities of the institution relate to existing institutions or processes? Would the institution help or hinder multilateral trade negotiations under GATT? Would it divert attention away from pressing bilateral trade issues, such as market opening? By providing a forum to discuss trade issues on a regional basis, could it postpone resolution of bilateral trade complaints? Could ministerial conferences, for example, be used as an excuse to postpone market opening? Or would the threat of criticism in such conferences be sufficient to induce nations to make concessions on trade?

How would the activities of this institution relate to the activities of the OECD, IMF, Asian Development Bank, World Bank, PECC, or the Pacific Basin Economic Council? Could the OECD be expanded rather than creating a new Pacific Rim institution?

If the institution were to lead to trade concessions, would such concessions be provided only to members of the group or to all nations? A free-trade area obviously would provide for free trade only among the direct participants, but some in Japan and ASEAN are recommending that any trade concessions be made on a most-favored-nation (MFN) basis. This would open them to all with MFN status. Both Australia and Japan have emphasized repeatedly that they do not wish to create an Asia-Pacific trading bloc.

Sixth, how could the institution be structured to account for the great diversity in economic development, culture, and political systems of the economies of the region? Would it lead to more demands to redistribute resources from the developed to developing nations?

Many questions remain to be asked and to be answered. The ultimate question, of course, is whether such an institution is necessary at all. In 1989 as APEC was developing, the Bush administration pursued the topic, remained engaged, but allowed Australia and Japan to take the lead. U.S. participation seems prudent, however, if only to avoid formation of an organization essentially devoted to the pursuit of Western Pacific interests at the expense of the Eastern Pacific Rim.

The focus on creating an institution, moreover, should not divert attention from the underlying need for greater economic cooperation and coordination among the nations of the Pacific Rim. Much can be done while a new institution is evolving. The ultimate question remains—whether the objectives of such an institution could better be achieved through existing mechanisms.

Japan's approach appears to be to proceed with measures that will lead to greater access to economic resources of the region and greater economic security regardless of whether a new Pacific Rim institution is created. It is beginning to view East and Southeast Asia as a single vast economy that needs basic infrastructure, information, and telecommunications systems in order to become an integrated region. Most of the specific recommendations for Asia-Pacific cooperation coming out of Japan are focused less on creating a plurilateral institution and more on adopting measures that strengthen the economic base of the Asia-Pacific economies.

The United States is supporting the APEC initiative, but even without U.S. support, Japan and Australia seem determined to formalize APEC into the primary governmental institution for the Pacific Basin. Japan is proceeding because it needs to avoid painting itself into a corner by not dealing effectively with a growing coalition of nations that view it as protectionist and an unfair trader. It also seeks a forum in which its vast wealth and business successes can be recognized and used to further international goals. Likewise, Australia sensed a growing isolation from other members of the former British empire as the United Kingdom sealed its ties with the EC and Canada joined in a free-trade agreement with the United States.

Hence, for Japan, the United States, and other Asian and Pacific countries, the time seems ripe to consider some form of greater economic cooperation.

Notes

Opinions expressed in this chapter are the author's and do not necessarily represent those of the Congressional Research Service or the Library of Congress.

1. Other factors leading to the defeat were an unpopular consumption tax, a sex scandal, and the Recruit (bribery) scandal.

2. *Blue Chip Economic Indicators,* vol. 14, March 10, 1989, p. 1.

3. DRI/McGraw-Hill, "U.S. Forecast Summary," *Review of the U.S. Economy,* March 1990, p. 12.

4. John F. Helliwell, *The Effects of Fiscal Policy in International Imbalances: Japan and the United States,* National Bureau of Economic Research, 1988, Working Paper No. 2650, p. 23.

5. Data Resources Inc., *Japanese Review,* first quarter 1989, p. 18.

6. Keizai Koho Center, *Japan, 1990, An International Comparison* (Tokyo: Keizai Koho Center, 1990), p. 56.

7. Urban C. Lehner, "First in Foreign Aid, Japan Still Isn't Sure What Purpose It Serves," *Wall Street Journal,* July 3, 1989, pp. 1, 4.

8. "The Yen Block: A New Balance in Asia? Japan Survey," *The Economist,* July 15, 1989, p. 9.

9. Several studies of Asia-Pacific economic ties have been done in Japanese. These include: Bank of Japan, "Ajia Shokoku no Hatten to Nichi-Bei-Ajia Keizai no Kinmitsuka" [Development of the Countries of Asia and the Growing Closeness of the Economies of Japan, the United States, and Asia], *Chosa Geppo,* August 1988, pp. 1–38.

10. For further discussion see: U.S. Library of Congress, Congressional Research Service, *U.S. Trade Policy Towards Japan: Where Do We Go From Here?* Report No. 89-307E, by William H. Cooper, Washington, D.C., 1989, 23 p.

11. See: U.S. Library of Congress, Congressional Research Service, *The Omnibus Trade and Competitiveness Act of 1988 (Public Law 100-418): An Analysis of Major Trade Provisions,* Report No. 88-390E, by William H. Cooper et al., Washington, D.C., 1988, 34 p.

12. Mike Mansfield, "The U.S. and Japan: Sharing Our Destinies," *Foreign Affairs,* vol. 68, Spring 1989, pp. 3–4.

13. For a historical overview of proposals for Pacific Basin economic cooperation see: Michael W. Oborne and Nicolas Fourt, *Pacific Basin Economic Cooperation* (Paris: Organisation for Economic Co-operation and Development, 1983), pp. 4–21; U.S. Library of Congress, Congressional Research Service, *Pacific Rim Initiatives,* Report No. 89-405D, coordinated by John P. Hardt, Washington, D.C., 1989, 14 p.; Richard L. Sneider and Mark Borthwick, "Institutions for Pacific Regional Cooperation," *Asian Survey,* vol. 23, December 1983, pp. 1245–1254.

14. Max Baucus, "Initiation of Trade Negotiations with Japan," *Congressional Record* (daily edition), January 31, 1989, pp. S858-S859.

15. U.S. International Trade Commission, *Pros and Cons of Initiating Negotiations with Japan to Explore the Possibility of a U.S.-Japan Free Trade Area Agreement,* USITC Pub. 2120, Washington, D.C., 1988, 61 p.

16. Jeffrey J. Schott, *More Free Trade Areas?* (Washington, D.C.: Institute for International Economics, 1989), p. 60.

17. Nichibei Jiyu Boeki Koso Kenkyukai, *Nichibei Jiyu Boeki Koso Kenkyukai, Chukan Torimatome* [Interim Report of the Study Group on Japan-U.S. Free-Trade Arrangement] (Tokyo: Nichibei Jiyu Boeki Koso Kenkyukai, June 1989), pp. 18–20.

18. "Japan to Lift All Duties for LDCs," *Japan Economic Journal,* April 15, 1989, p. 14.

19. See: U.S. Library of Congress, Congressional Research Service, *Japan–South Korea Economic Relations: South Korea's Approach to the 'Japan Problem,'* Report No. 87-953E, by Dick K. Nanto, Washington, D.C., 1987, p. 18–21.

20. Keith Richburg, "Pacific Rim Meeting Called Step Forward," *Washington Post*, November 8, 1989, p. B2.

21. U.S. Department of State, Summaries of Subject Proposals, Attachment to press release on address by James A. Baker III on "A New Pacific Partnership: Framework for the Future," June 26, 1989.

22. "Sen. Bradley Calls for Establishment of Eight-Nation Trade, Economic Coalition," *International Trade Reporter*, vol. 5, December 14, 1988, p. 1628.

23. The Cairns Group consists of a number of agricultural exporting nations, including Australia and New Zealand, that coordinate negotiating positions in multilateral fora.

24. Alan Cranston, "Senate Concurrent Resolution 27—Relating to the Establishment of a Pacific Basin Forum," *Congressional Record* (daily edition), April 13, 1989, pp. S3944–S3945.

25. Yasuhiro Nakasone, "The Pacific Future: A Prescription for Solidarity and Interdependence," *Speaking of Japan*, June 1988, pp. 27–32.

26. Bureau of National Affairs, "Japanese Prime Minister Requests Study of Possible Asia-Pacific Cooperation Pact," *International Trade Reporter*, vol. 6, March 19, 1988, p. 400.

27. Ajia Taiheiyo Kyoryoku Suishin Kondankai [Council for the Promotion of Asia-Pacific Cooperation], *Ajia Taiheiyo Kyoryoku Suishin Kondankai Hokoku* [Report of the Council for the Promotion of Asia-Pacific Cooperation: Toward an Era of Development Through Outward-looking Cooperation] (Tokyo: June 15, 1989).

28. Eric A. Trigg, "The Pacific Economic Cooperation Conference," *Pacific Economic Cooperation*, vol. 2, Fall 1986, pp. 2–5.

29. See: Kumao Kaneko, "A New Pacific Initiative: Strengthening the PECC Process," *Japan Review of International Affairs*, vol. 2, Spring/Summer 1988, pp. 67–90.

30. "The Yen Block," p. 12.

31. U.S. Library of Congress, Congressional Research Service, *U.S.–South Korean Economic Relations: Views of Some Members of the Korean Economic Elite*, Report No. 88-656E, by William H. Cooper, Washington, D.C., 1988, pp. 7–8.

32. U.S. Library of Congress, Congressional Research Service, *U.S.-Taiwan Economic Relations: Views of Some Members of the Taiwan Economic Elite*, Report No. 89-21E, by Arlene Wilson, Washington, D.C., 1989, pp. 10–11.

33. U.S. Library of Congress, Congressional Research Service, *Singapore-U.S. Economic Relations, Some Views from Singapore's Economic Elite*, Report No. 89-49F, by Richard P. Cronin, Washington, D.C., 1989, pp. 16–17.

34. U.S. Library of Congress, Congressional Research Service, *Hong Kong–U.S. Economic Relations: Some Views from Hong Kong's Economic Elite*, Report No. 89-23F, by Kerry Dumbaugh, Washington, D.C., 1989, p. 13.

35. U.S. Library of Congress, Congressional Research Service, *Thai-U.S. Economic Relations: Some Views of Thailand's Economic Elite*, Report No. 89-60F, by Raymond J. Ahearn, Washington, D.C., 1989, pp. 15–16.

36. U.S. Department of State, Memorandum from EAP/EP (East Asian and Pacific Affairs/Office for Economic Policy), Fred McEldowney, acting director to counselor of the department, J. Sour et al. Subject: Pacific Basin Economic Cooperation, May 2, 1989. Note: The ASEAN 6+5 refers to the six ASEAN members plus the five members of the OECD from the Pacific region.

37. For a useful early analysis, see: U.S. Congress, Senate Committee on Foreign Relations, *An Asian-Pacific Regional Economic Organization: An Exploratory Concept Paper*, Committee Print, prepared by the Congressional Research Service (Washington, D.C.: U.S. Government Printing Office, 1979), 74 p.

4

Trade, Policy, and Korea-U.S. Relations

Paul W. Kuznets

Economic development in South Korea, the largest of four East Asian "miracle economies" (the others are Taiwan, Singapore, and Hong Kong), has been distinguished from development in most other developing countries since the mid-1960s by the unusual speed and quality of growth. Korea's average annual GNP growth rate, a mediocre 4.3 percent from 1953 to 1963, soared to almost 10 percent from 1963 to 1973 and—at 8 percent— was still one of the world's highest from 1973 to 1987. During the past quarter of a century, Korea has been transformed from a predominantly rural, agricultural country to an urban, industrial one, real per capita income has more than quadrupled, and income inequality has remained low so that most Koreans have enjoyed the benefits of rapid development. Growth has been export led: The industrial sector has expanded most rapidly; within the industrial sector manufacturing has grown fastest; and within manufacturing, manufactures for export have expanded the most. Exports that, at $175 million, accounted for less than 10 percent of GNP in 1965 had increased to $46 billion and 46 percent of GNP by 1987.

Imports also rose during these years, particularly with the oil shocks of 1973-1974 and 1979-1980, and so Korea's external debt reached a peak of $47 billion at the end of 1985. However, current-account surpluses in subsequent years have permitted rapid repayment in contrast with most other major debtors; there has, consequently, been no rescheduling or default. Export-led growth has been implemented by a set of export-promotion measures that restructured producer incentives to favor output for export rather than the import replacements that were favored earlier. An activist government has also employed industrial policy to target new industries with particularly promising export prospects.

One might expect Korean policymakers to continue an outward-oriented or export-expansion strategy, given the country's unusual success with export-led growth, but a new pessimism is evident in the current five-year plan (the Sixth Plan of 1987-1991), which reveals "the government's desire to reduce the country's heavy dependence of economic growth on international trade."[1] There is as yet no evidence of a shift from outward- to inward-oriented strategy, and no indication of what is to replace exports as Korea's engine of growth in the 1990s, but recent developments provide good reasons for wanting to reduce dependence on trade. Chief among these, perhaps, is that Korean exports have proven unusually protection prone. This follows from the commodity and country composition of Korea's trade, particularly the heavy concentration of new exports to U.S. markets. These exports have triggered protectionist responses, partly because they tend to disrupt domestic markets, partly because the worldwide recession of the early 1980s and very large balance-of-payments deficits of more recent years have strengthened protectionist interests in the United States. Trade friction between the two countries has also mounted since 1986, when Korea's balance of payments shifted from deficits to surpluses, and growing pressure from the United States to liberalize Korean imports has collided with industrial policies and domestic interests in Korea. In addition, friction was increased—and acrimony heightened—by the election in early 1988 of an opposition-dominated National Assembly in Korea. Domestic political rivalry now requires that both governments cater to economic interest groups, thus strengthening protectionism in the United States and opposition to U.S. demands for liberalization in Korea.

Trade friction between the two countries is significant for several reasons. One is that it undermines a tradition of friendship between Koreans and Americans that dates back to the late nineteenth century. It also threatens the political, social, and strategic ties between the two countries that were established with Korean independence in 1948 and strengthened after 1965 by large-scale Korean emigration to the United States. Some disruption of Korean-U.S. relations was inevitable with the recent elections in Korea because many Koreans believe that the United States sacrificed Korean democracy for strategic considerations in supporting the authoritarian Park Chung-hee and Chun Doo-hwan regimes, but trade friction has clearly added to the disharmony. Trade friction is also significant because it is a sign of policy failure. In this instance U.S. protection threatens Korea's export expansion while Korean import restrictions foil U.S. demands for reciprocity, and so the two countries' trade policies appear to be mutually inconsistent. Either new policies, new adjustment mechanisms, or both are needed if economic harmony is to be reachieved. Finally, trade friction between the two countries is significant because the issues involved follow mainly from shifts in comparative advantage and therefore apply—though in less acute form—to economic relations between other industrial countries, like the United States and the other Newly Industrializing Economies (NIEs) of Asia.

Focus here is on the sources of trade friction and the policy options that might be employed to reduce friction and restore harmony. Because trade between the two countries is much more important for Korea than for the United States, and the U.S. trade and payments position and policy regime are better known than Korea's, the Korean situation is emphasized in this chapter. In the first section I will examine Korean trade and payments. In the next two sections I will discuss U.S. trade policies and Korean trade policies. Finally, in the fourth and fifth parts of the chapter I will discuss bilateral and global (GATT) options and other policy options.

Korea's Trade and Payments

Trade structure can be analyzed according to the distribution of exports and imports by commodity and country. Data from the United Nations for the year 1986 are used in Table 4.1 to show Korea's major exports to the world, to the United States, and to Japan as well as Korea's major imports from all sources. The table shows that traditional, relatively labor-intensive manufactures like clothing, footwear, and textiles still accounted for 30 percent of Korea's exports in 1986 while machinery, transport equipment, iron and steel, and electronic goods (mainly telecommunications and sound equipment), which are capital intensive and/or technologically sophisticated products, comprised almost 40 percent. Imports, in turn, were concentrated in food, fuels, and other raw materials (34 percent of the total) and machinery and equipment (23 percent). Imports were more diversified than exports, as is usual, and were consistent with the needs of a rapidly industrializing, natural resource–poor country like Korea.

Two things the table does not show are the composition of imports by expenditure category and the proportion of freely importable imports by category. When imports are classified by expenditure category, as has been done for the 1968–1982 period, one finds that consumer goods accounted for 3.4 percent or less of total imports and represented an even smaller proportion of freely importables.[2] These findings indicate that Korea's import regime was highly restrictive, at least through 1982, which is puzzling because import-liberalization ratios (the proportion of import categories entitled to automatic approval) widely quoted by the Korean government and press reached 75 percent by 1982 and almost 95 percent by 1988—so that there was evidently little left to liberalize. However, when the liberalization ratio for 1982 was adjusted to reflect measures that undo automatic approval—such as special laws on safety, health, and packaging; restrictions by source; licensing of certain imports; surveillance measures for "sensitive" items requiring prior approval; and government and end-user managed

Table 4.1 Korea's Major Exports and Imports in 1986 (in millions of U.S. dollars)

Sector (SITC)	Total	To U.S. (%)	To Japan (%)
Exports			
Textiles (65)	3,218.5	12.4	9.8
Iron, Steel (67)	1,970.6	29.7	21.2
Metal Mftrs. (69)	1,423.4	39.5	2.6
Telecomm., Sound Equip. (76)	3,108.9	51.7	5.9
Elect. Machinery (77)	2,856.5	48.6	5.7
Road Vehicles (78)	1,835.0	4.7	neg.
Other Transport Equip. (79)	2,158.7	1.1	neg.
Clothing (84)	5,482.8	49.9	18.0
Footwear (85)	2,059.1	75.9	7.0
Misc. Mftrs. (89)	2,252.4	58.6	8.6
Subtotal	26,365.9		
Total	34,714.5	40.0	15.6
Imports			
Food, Live Animals (0)	1,424.1		
Crude Materials Excl. Fuels (2)	4,291.4		
Coal, Coke (32)	1,027.8		
Petrol. and Prods. (33)	3,917.6		
Chemicals (5)	3,493.5		
Iron and Steel (67)	1,343.9		
Special Indust. Machinery (72)	1,294.2		
General Indust. Machinery (73)	1,691.9		
Electrical Indust. Machinery (77)	3,087.3		
Other Transport Equipment (79)	1,106.8		
Subtotal	22,678.5		
Total	31,583.9		

Source: UN, International Trade Statistics Yearbook, 1986.

imports—the ratio dropped from 74.7 to 7.3 percent![3] The task of import liberalization is evidently much greater than is suggested by Korea's published liberalization ratios.

Korea's export structure has become more capital and technology intensive in accordance with shifts in comparative advantage as investment in physical and human capital has outpaced labor-force growth. Exports, as imports, have been influenced by government policies, in this case by policies that targeted for development industries with particularly significant technologies, large employment effects, strategic benefits, and export potential. These included heavy industries and chemical plants during the 1970s and, more recently, industries that produce skill-intensive products, such as machinery and electronics (Fifth Plan, 1982-1986) and automobiles (Sixth Plan, 1987-1991). Not all targeted industries have become sufficiently competitive to export, nor have all export industries been targeted by policymakers, but Korea's exports—especially more recent ones—clearly bear the imprint of industrial policy. Also, according to a recent study by Petri, Korean industrial policy follows Japan's: "[The] Korean-Japanese relationship provide[s] a remarkable study in the 'economics of following'"; this similarity is seen in Korea's export structure (as measured by revealed comparative advantage), which is highly correlated with Japan's export structure of fifteen years ago.[4] Korea is no "second Japan," because the two countries differ significantly in market size, per capita income, and the economic role of government, but Petri's findings suggest that Korea is in fact a second Japan when it comes to exports.

The commodity composition of Korea's exports, mainly manufactures, is well diversified. In 1985, for example, the ten largest three-digit categories of manufactured exports accounted for 66 percent of total manufactured exports. The same figure for the United States was 65 percent. Country composition, however, is not well diversified. Since 1980 approximately 30-40 percent of exports have been shipped to the United States, 14-16 percent to Japan. The United States takes a large portion of most of Korea's leading exports (see Table 4.1) because it has been relatively open compared to Japan and Europe, the other large markets. It has been particularly important for Korea's new exports because U.S. sales permit the scale economies without which they would not be competitive.

Rapid export expansion has contributed to a shift from long-standing deficits to surpluses in Korea's current balance of payments (see Table 4.2). Surpluses starting in 1986 are also credited to "three blessings": (1) the drop in world oil prices, (2) the decline in international interest rates, and (3) yen appreciation. As oil prices and interest rates could rise again and the yen could fall, the sustainability of the surplus has been questioned, but a long-term and fundamental shift in Korea's saving-investment relation, such that saving now exceeds investment, indicates that surpluses are likely to prevail in the future. The current-account surpluses also have been associated with large commodity imbalances, particularly surpluses with the United States that have not been fully offset by deficits with Japan.

Some features of Korea's trade and payments have contributed recently to growing trade friction with the United States. Shifts in comparative advantage, for example, have caused Korea's new exports to compete with previously unaffected domestic products in the U.S. market. Another problem is that concentration of Korean exports in the U.S. market increases any disruption that might result from new competition. Also, insofar as Korea's exports follow Japan's, earlier Japanese market penetration would have

Table 4.2 Korea's Current Account Balance of Payments, 1984-1987 (in millions of U.S. dollars)

	1984	1985	1986	1987
A. Current Account	-1,372	-887	4,617	9,854
Trade	-1,036	-19	4,206	7,659
Exports	26,335	26,442	33,913	46,244
Imports	27,371	26,461	29,707	38,585
Invisibles, Net Transfers	-336	-868	411	2,195
B. Trade with U.S.				
Exports	10,528	10,789	13,920	18,382
Imports	6,877	6,554	6,548	8,761
Balance	3,657	4,235	7,372	9,621
C. Trade with Japan				
Exports	4,602	4,543	5,426	8,437
Imports	7,640	7,560	10,869	13,657
Balance	-3,038	-3,017	-5,443	-5,220

Sources: International Monetary Fund, Direction of Trade Statistics, International Financial Statistics, various issues.

initiated protection that should eventually affect Korea's exports as well. In addition, Korea's restrictive commercial policies and growing bilateral surpluses have provoked demands for reciprocity and encouraged U.S. industries affected by Korean exports to seek protection. Beyond this, recession during the early 1980s increased protectionism worldwide because unemployment soared and imports were seen to threaten employment. Trade friction has also grown as U.S. policy has become increasingly restrictive in response to the inept macroeconomic policies of the Reagan presidency. Whatever the reason, Korea's exports have been particularly protection prone, and this too increased trade friction between the two countries.[5]

U.S. Trade Policy

Central themes of U.S. trade policy have included advocacy of greater liberalization, support for multilateralism and multilateral institutions such as the GATT, and insistence on reciprocity in trade relations. Any policy is inevitably influenced by economic circumstance, and U.S. trade policy has clearly been affected by the unprecedented trade deficits of the late 1980s. These deficits and self-imposed fiscal restraints have focused attention on trade issues, inspired new trade legislation, and encouraged protectionist interests in the United States. While recent policy has promoted free-trade-area agreements (with Canada, for example), it also has fastened on administrative criteria and procedures for import relief from discriminatory foreign practices. This "process protection" can be seen in the Trade Act of 1974 and, more recently, in technical changes in administrative procedures under the Omnibus Trade and Competitiveness Act of 1988. In particular, whenever the courts, the Department of Commerce, or the U.S. International Trade Commission (USITC) has decided trade cases against a particular U.S. firm or industry, legislation covering import-relief requirements for all firms or industries has been altered to meet the needs of the particular interest. Such blanket procedural changes conceal the objects of protection, make the import-relief process increasingly protectionist, and, even worse, encourage other countries to emulate the new U.S. procedure or process.

Process protection is most evident in antidumping and countervailing duty cases under GATT rules, which permit each country to set criteria for finding that imports have been dumped or subsidized, that the dumping or subsidy injures a domestic industry, and that the injured industry is therefore entitled to relief. It is also seen in Section 301 of the Trade Act of 1974, which permits the U.S. president to retaliate against "unjustifiable and unreasonable" foreign practices by limiting access to U.S. markets for the offender's exports. Section 301 has been used increasingly since 1985 to question trade practices in Korea and other East Asian countries, but because retaliation can breed further retaliation and even lead to trade wars, Section 301 has been used mainly to gain preferential access for U.S. firms. The result is market sharing, rather than import liberalization, and a worldwide increase in protectionism as other countries have emulated Section 301. Most important quantitatively have probably been the "voluntary" export restraints (VERs) that have curbed U.S. imports of Korean textiles, clothing, and steel, particularly the quotas on textiles established under the 1973 Multifibre Arrangement. These VERs fall outside of normal trade-relief channels under GATT or U.S. trade laws and provide windfall profits to exporters in the form of quota rents.

Other types of remedies for unfair trade practices and new VERs have sprung up recently. For instance, U.S. companies have started to file patent infringement cases against Korean competitors in semiconductors, car phones, and other products under Section 337 of the Tariff Act of 1930 (as amended). Such cases, if decided favorably, offer as remedy the exclusion of the infringing product. Also, a unilateral or true form of VER has been adopted by Korean producers of shoes, VCRs, and other products shipped to the United States in order to avoid more restrictive negotiated (bilateral) VERs and other forms of import restraint. In addition, Section 301 has been extended to trade in services, with bilateral negotiations to open insurance, cinema, advertising, and other Korean domestic service markets to U.S. firms. Moreover, a provision of the 1988 Trade Act, "Super 301," requires the U.S. government to identify "priority" countries that must demonstrate that unfair trade practices (as defined by the United States) will be reduced over the next three years or face trade sanctions. "South Korea tops the list of countries most frequently cited by U.S. corporate petitioners seeking redress under the tough new provisions [i.e., Super 301]."[6]

At a time when the United States has been running huge balance-of-payments deficits that promote protectionism, and which cannot be sustained in the long run, there should be more to trade policy than process protection and the provisions of recent trade legislation.[7] In particular, the problem calls for curbing excess demand in the United States by reducing government deficits and, with the subsequent decline in U.S. demand, taking up the slack in world demand by pursuing expansionary policies in West Germany, Japan, and the Asian NIEs, like Korea, that have all been running large balance-of-payments surpluses. Devaluation of the U.S. dollar since late 1985 and continued appreciation of the New Taiwan (N.T.) dollar and won urged on Taiwan and Korea by the United States are supplementary measures that should also act to curb the U.S. balance-of-payments deficits, but the currency realignment and macroeconomic policy actions needed appear unlikely to occur at this time. Reduction of the U.S. government deficit seems improbable after President Bush's foreswearing of tax increases while running for office in 1988, and past intrusions by U.S. policymakers in other countries' domestic demand management have fostered resentment and political backlash as well as the economic results desired.[8] Currency realignment, in turn, can be a treacherous policy instrument because the elasticities of exports and imports, and hence current-account balance with respect to devaluation or revaluation, are uncertain. Such uncertainty, the phasing out of the export subsidies that might be used to cushion the effects of won appreciation, and the recent labor unrest with its consequent wage escalation all argue against substantial appreciation for Korea, particularly since higher labor costs are likely to raise the real effective won exchange rate anyway.[9] This leaves trade policy alone to overcome the deficit problem, though trade policy was never designed to do this.

As it is perhaps more fruitful to assess U.S. trade policy according to what it was intended to do rather than according to its ability to reduce large deficits, performance can be rated by success in achieving the three major goals: liberalization, multilateralism, and reciprocity. The increase in U.S. process protection (import relief under the trade laws) in the 1980s has probably offset or more than offset liberalization elsewhere under threat of Section 301 relief. Increasing protectionism may follow from shifts in world economic power that favor protection rather than liberalization, from erosion of the U.S. trade policymaking system, or from changes in the nature of U.S. commercial policy itself, but the fact that the U.S. market is now more protected than it was in the 1960s and 1970s shows that U.S. policy has failed the liberalization test.[10] Similarly, the unilateral judgments of foreign trade practices under Section 301 and the rise of VERs that fall outside U.S. trade law and GATT provisions undermine multilateralism. U.S. policy has probably been most successful—or least unsuccessful—in achieving reciprocity. Korea, for instance, recently announced a three-year plan to open its market to agricultural and fishery products in response to U.S. complaints about Korean trading practices. However, reciprocity backed by threats of retaliation has probably been less effective than reciprocity that rewards appropriate behavior with market opening. Demands for reciprocity have already created political backlash: Some 15,000 farmers in 300 buses traveled to Seoul this past February to protest U.S. agricultural imports. Their demands for reciprocity undermine the credibility of liberal forces elsewhere because they deflect attention away from the economic merits of their case and raise the political costs of unpopular but economically appropriate behavior.

A summary assessment of U.S. trade policy cannot do justice to the full range of issues involved or to all of the options facing policymakers. Nor can poor performance be attributed to trade policy itself when external events, macroeconomic policy failures, and interest-group politics have hurt the policymaking system. Nevertheless, U.S. trade policy and the policymaking system are significant per se (because they affect relations with other countries) and therefore merit attention here. Recent trade friction with Korea, for instance, raises issues that bear on the central themes of U.S. policy. U.S. demands for reciprocity require large changes in Korean policies and shift the burdens of adjustment to Korean producers. This may level the playing field insofar as Korean markets are more restricted than U.S. markets, but the demands—backed by threats of U.S. market closure—look like bullying when reciprocity involves access that is of vastly different importance to the two countries. Also, the coincidence of restrictive trade policy and good economic performance in countries like Korea seems to have raised doubts in the United States about the efficacy of liberalization. Many economists are now familiar with the new, more realistic trade theories that show that import restriction and export subsidy can—under certain conditions—promote the national interest, but not all seem to appreciate that real-world policy—and game theory—still make liberalization and free trade worthy goals.[11] Similarly, recent trade friction and political considerations indicate that a renewal of the multilateral theme in U.S. trade policy is needed. Although GATT and other international institutions have been weakened in recent years by the unilateral and bilateral actions of the United States and other major trading nations, the benefits of multilateralism in limiting political backlash and reducing protectionist pressure by domestic economic interest groups may well outweigh the costs of restoring GATT or building new multilateral trade institutions.

Korean Trade Policy

Trade policy in Korea, as in the United States, is a creature of macroeconomic considerations, but unlike the United States, in Korea trade policy coexists with industrial policy and has been directed by an interventionist government. Before the mid-1960s Korea suffered from inept policies and weak implementation similar to those found in many developing countries. Exports lagged and inward-looking or import-substituting policies caused the proliferation of controls that diverted entrepreneurial incentives away from productive activity. Import substitution was becoming increasingly difficult as opportunities were exhausted for the easy substitution that suited domestic factor proportions and used simple technology. Slow growth, political upheaval, and a new regime (the Park government) were followed by stabilization and export-promotion programs in the mid-1960s that were designed to reduce currency overvaluation and government deficits, increase savings, and expand exports. These programs unleashed substantial comparative advantage in producing textiles, apparel, and other labor-intensive manufactures. Korea's exports soared and the pace of growth accelerated.

Korea's export expansion, growth acceleration, and subsequent economic success can be traced to real factors, such as the low wage costs associated with a large supply of hardworking and increasingly skilled workers and the supply of entrepreneurial talent, particularly talent for "initiating change" and for starting new enterprises or new types of production. This success can also be traced to increased political stability, to the establishment of trade and marketing institutions like KOTRA (the Korea Trade Promotion Corporation), and to trade policies that altered the structure of incentives to favor export rather than import-substitution activity.

Besides tax breaks and maintaining generally favorable real effective exchange rates, several quite ingenious export-promotion devices have been utilized in Korea. One of these, for example, is the domestic L/C (letter of credit), which extends incentives of the direct exporter to his domestic suppliers and thus provides an essentially free-trade setting for exports that would otherwise be stifled by the high input costs that result from Korea's import restrictions. Perhaps most significant has been the exporter's preferred access to bank credit at times when such credit has been rationed (because it is too cheap) and the only alternative to bank credit is borrowing at high cost in the unorganized money market. Exporting also has been encouraged by monthly national trade promotion meetings designed to set export targets, facilitate their achievement, and reward outstanding performance. Although export-promotion devices were important instruments of trade policy in the late 1960s and 1970s, many were eliminated or reduced so that in the 1980s the major means of encouraging export activity was exchange-rate manipulation. Real exchange rates (estimated by adjusting nominal rates to reflect differences in domestic and export-market inflation) increased substantially after a major devaluation of the won in 1980; as a result, Korean exports have become increasingly competitive. In fact, Korea's real effective exchange rate increased more between 1981 and 1987 than that of any other East Asian NIE.[12]

Trade policy has been associated with industrial policy and the targeting of new industries to be developed. This is because the targeting criteria not only include the appropriateness of factor proportions and opportunities for technology acquisition but also the new industry's export potential. For example, when comparative advantage shifted because Korea's capital inputs were increasing faster than its labor inputs, heavy industry and chemical plants were targeted for development in the 1970s. More recent targeting of skill-intensive industries, like machinery and electronics in the Fifth Plan and automobiles in the Sixth Plan, has not only utilized the rapidly expanding stock of human capital but has also provided new products that are already sufficiently competitive to be exported. Targeting, like export promotion, has been implemented by granting access to low-cost "policy" loans and through technology licensing. (Domestic firms must obtain permission before purchasing new technology.) In addition, local content requirements and other forms of infant-industry protection have been instituted in order to strengthen targeted industries. The effects of industrial policy and targeting are controversial, if only because the relations between means and ends are not as explicit or clear cut as with fiscal policy, for example, but Korea's industrial policy has probably served "to prepare the way for future factor proportions" and to launch new exports before they would have otherwise appeared.[13]

Trade and trade policy have also been important elements of an overall macroeconomic strategy that has stressed rapid growth. The focus on "growth-first" reduced emphasis on other targets, such as price stability, external balance, and unemployment reduction, until the early 1980s when inflation threatened growth and the planners' concern for rising unemployment was first expressed in Korea's Fifth Plan.[14] Evidence of emphasis on growth can be seen in spartan government budgets that include relatively little for housing, welfare and social services. It can also be seen in Korea's unusually high investment ratios. Gross fixed capital formation in 1982–1987, for example, averaged almost 32 percent of gross domestic product. Much capital formation has been required to expand the productive capacity needed for rapid output growth; until the mid-1980s a significant portion of this new capacity was financed by foreign loans.[15] Foreign savers and lenders covered a long series of current-account balance-of-payments deficits before Korea's external debt reached $47 billion in 1985, and subsequent surpluses were then used (in part) to reduce external debt. Foreign lenders were willing to lend to Korean firms not only because the government's loan guarantees reduced the risks of default and loss from a depreciating won, but also because rapid export growth promised that Korean borrowers would have the foreign exchange needed for repayment when the loans came due. On the Korean side, foreign borrowing was encouraged by tight domestic credit, high rates of return on investments, and an overvalued won; as a result, real interest rates on foreign loans were negative during much of the period before the 1980s.[16]

Policies directed toward promoting exports and restricting imports have other functions in Korea's growth-first strategy besides encouraging foreign lenders. One is to husband foreign-exchange earnings for high-priority uses, such as the purchase of materials and equipment, rather than using them to purchase "unnecessary and luxurious imports." This has been done by a customs service that is exhorted to "conserve foreign exchange for national prosperity," according to wall posters hanging in customs offices. This objective has also been facilitated by "the very strong moral prejudice against imports that the government has long cultivated."[17] Such austerity, as well as increased domestic savings and export expansion, can be credited at least in part for the recent shift from deficits to surpluses in Korea's balance of payments, for the reduction in foreign debt, and for maintaining creditworthiness in an era when many major debtors have had to reschedule their debts. Another function of trade policy, to promote exports, contributes directly to growth because any increase in exports necessarily increases GNP. Exports may also contribute indirectly to growth, because export production tends to follow comparative advantage and hence suit a country's factor endowments, because export industries are necessarily competitive and thus tend to be efficient, and because export-promotion policies typically distort markets less than import-substitution policies since the costs of subsidy are more apparent than the costs of protection.[18]

Policies that stress export expansion and import restriction have contributed to Korea's economic success and would appear to have served Korea well. However, such policies increasingly have come under attack in trade negotiations with the United States, particularly since 1982 when Korea's bilateral trade with the United States shifted from deficit to surplus, and even more since 1985 when substantial dollar devaluation increased the competitiveness of Korean exports against Japanese exports in third markets like the United States (as the won, tied to the U.S. dollar, depreciated against the yen). Import restrictions, particularly infant-industry protection and localization requirements, have sparked growing criticism from the United States. In addition, industrial targeting and sudden, disruptive expansion of exports have increased demands for voluntary export restraints.

Since Korea has become a major supplier of U.S. imports, Korean trade policy has been scrutinized and judged to be unsatisfactory because "Korea is not reciprocating adequately for the market access that it enjoys in the United States." Accordingly, the U.S. government "has employed the provisions of its trade law to pry open the Korean market further."[19]

The Korean response to U.S. market-opening efforts has been to liberalize imports, increase public investment to expand aggregate demand, employ buying missions to reduce its bilateral trade surplus with the United States, and appreciate the won.[20] Negotiators have formed sector-specific discussion groups and accepted export restraints to forestall new quotas. Such responses have satisfied neither side. The Koreans, who have to make the major adjustments, have argued for gradualism and for U.S. policymakers to "take into account the political and emotional factors" that make liberalization difficult.[21] The Americans, in turn, see this as footdragging; they step up their demands for market opening, and then they encounter an anti-American, anti-liberalization backlash from Koreans who feel that such demands are unreasonable and unfair.[22]

Bilateral and Global Options

Bilateral and global (GATT) options are examined here because brief surveys of U.S. and Korean trade policy indicate that existing options have not been particularly satisfactory. U.S. policy has departed from long-standing goals of liberalization and multilateralism, and piecemeal process protection and aggressive reciprocity have not only failed on occasion to open foreign markets but also have increased protection in U.S. markets and invited retaliatory escalation. Korean policy has featured buying missions, won appreciation, limited market opening, and other palliatives mainly designed to satisfy specific U.S. demands. The lists of U.S. requests get longer, partial results satisfy neither side, and evidence mounts that attempts to "muddle through" are not working. Also, the costs of policy failure or greater protection than might otherwise prevail have been substantial. For instance, during the 1977–1981 period, when orderly marketing agreements restricted U.S. nonrubber footwear imports from Taiwan and Korea, the annual costs to U.S. consumers (in 1982 dollars) of each job "saved" in the domestic footwear industry averaged $52,000. The costs of subsidies to farmers and agricultural products exporters in the United States in 1984–1986 have been estimated at almost $80 billion.[23] Possible reasons for such costly failures merit attention. Among these reasons are the partial nature of trade negotiations, the drawbacks of the new reciprocity, and the excessive influence of special interest groups on trade policy.

Recent trade negotiations between the United States and Korea have featured submission by the United States of long lists of requests for Korea to open markets for particular goods and services. The rationale for choosing particular items is often unclear, though one observer has suggested that the lists include goods and services of special interest at the time to certain members of Congress and industry representatives. What is significant about the lists, besides the ad hoc nature of their preparation, is that attempts to achieve partial or limited opening are likely to arouse stronger resistance from the industries singled out for opening than if all industries were affected by across-the-board market opening. Across-the-board negotiations could hardly be slower and more cumbersome than current negotiations and might well be more efficient, both in saving time and in shielding negotiators from political attacks after each round of partial negotiations.[24] Also, long lists indicate that items are of equal importance and, possibly, that the different items can be dealt with in similar fashion, which is not true. In particular, market opening for agriculture and banking is likely to be unusually difficult and protracted. Korea's commercial banks have been saddled with nonperforming policy loans that are likely to "drag them under in a competitive environment."[25] In agriculture, incomes have lagged despite protection and subsidy because attempts to preserve family farming have restricted plot size and hence labor productivity, and because spatial concentration of industry has limited off-farm incomes. Retraining and off-farm migration offer little hope for short-term solution because one-third of the population still lives in rural areas and more than one-half of agricultural workers are now forty-five years of age and older. Demand for market opening conflicts, in this case, with "mounting public pressure for more equitable distribution of income and wealth."[26]

The new reciprocity initiated in 1985 by the Reagan administration under Section 301 of the Trade Act of 1974 has featured aggressive action to open particular foreign markets. This "aggressive" reciprocity calls for unilateral imposition of new protection measures by the United States if the offending country does not provide market access comparable to that it already receives from the United States. Such usage violates the most-favored-nation (MFN) principle that the United States has long favored and is unlike past market-opening policies, which sought liberalization with major trading partners for all products considered together. It also requires the United States to renege on previously negotiated agreements and forces other countries either to default on their own MFN obligations or to give up bargaining power by offering the new concessions to all. Though there have been deviations from the MFN principle in the past for GSP (the generalized system of preferences offered to developing countries), customs unions, and free-trade areas, these have promised to liberalize trade. The new reciprocity, in contrast, would suppress trade if the U.S. threat has to be enforced or if there is retaliation. If the goal is to open foreign markets, then any country can either seek compensation for impairment of past concessions under Article XXIII of the GATT or rescind previous concessions, either by agreement (in which case the country must provide compensatory liberalization elsewhere) or unilaterally (in which case the other country could withdraw its own concessions) under GATT Article XXVIII. Although GATT actions can be cumbersome when other GATT members must authorize action, they publicize the complaint and, unlike aggressive reciprocity, they bear the GATT imprimatur.[27]

Perhaps the major reason for trade-policy failure has been the pressure from economic interest groups for protection. Despite attempts to reform campaign financing, the influence of interest groups in the United States on legislation and administration has increased so much that the public or general interest is often sacrificed to special interests. The rise of economic interest groups has not only fostered mistrust of government and declining voter participation but has also combined with huge trade deficits and large bilateral imbalances to warp trade policy. The liberal and multilateral themes of earlier years have been replaced by process protection, the negotiators' long market-opening lists, and aggressive reciprocity. In Korea, the recent democratic revolution has unleashed the economic interest-group phenomenon; economic favors are the currency of competition in the struggle for political support between the Roh regime and the opposition-dominated National Assembly. If trade-policy failure follows from interest-group pressures, then any remedy must either reduce the demand for protection or shield the policy process from pressure.

One way to reduce protectionist demands is to provide trade adjustment assistance (TAA), which was inaugurated in the United States in the Trade Expansion Act of 1962 to compensate workers injured by trade policies based on general welfare considerations. Goals of TAA, besides providing equity for workers in trade-impacted industries, were to reallocate resources by retraining workers and to buy off interest groups that could block desirable policy. The act offered little relief until benefits were expanded in 1974, and President Carter escalated the TAA budget to compensate laid-off auto workers just before the 1980 election. Such politically expedient use of TAA and doubts that it had fulfilled its adjustment goal led the Reagan regime to cut the program; as a result, the effects of TAA were negligible during most of the 1980s.[28] Whatever the shortcomings of TAA in the past, comparative advantage will continue to shift from one country to another, the shifts will create excess capacity and idle resources, and market adjustment will be hampered by uncertainty, imperfect information, factor immobility, wage-price rigidities, and insufficient investment in human capital. When the Ministry of Agriculture recently announced a three-year plan to open the Korean market to a broad range of foreign agricultural and fishery products by 1991, it also announced that $755 million would be allocated to compensate farmers for losses that might follow.[29] Some such assistance is needed in any country where trade policy is to serve the general welfare rather than particular economic interests.

The shielding remedy for policy failure would remove trade negotiation from national governments to international institutions like the GATT. The GATT, however, is neither a juridical system nor an enforcement institution but, rather, a set of rights and obligations based on mutual concessions and national agreements among the contracting parties. The GATT operates by consensus and has no mandate to initiate studies of compliance by members or to find and publicize violations. Also, proceedings have been dominated by the United States and the European Community (EC), each of which has increasingly negotiated disputes outside the GATT framework. In addition, recent attempts during the Uruguay Round to reduce agricultural subsidies sparked a U.S.-EC conflict over beef that has yet to be settled. The GATT's history suggests that the GATT, like other international organizations, functions only as well as its least enthusiastic member permits and that self-interest is likely to block rational action.

Other Policy Options

Existing policy mechanisms—bilateral bargaining and multilateral negotiations under GATT auspices—are inadequate mainly because neither has provided sufficient shielding from domestic protectionist interests. Two other possibilities—(1) a shift in U.S. macroeconomic policy to eliminate or significantly reduce the budget deficit, and (2) adoption of industrial policies to enhance the competitiveness of U.S. firms—are not considered here. Eliminating budget deficits would reduce but not eliminate trade deficits, while the same economic interest groups that now weaken trade policy would most probably weaken industrial policy as well. This leaves other options that have been raised recently, particularly the trading bloc or free-trade area (FTA), managed trade, and creation of a new institution to deal with Asia-Pacific economic issues.

Suggestions to expand the sort of free-trade-area agreement that the United States now has with Canada to all the countries of the Asia-Pacific region have cropped up in response to EC plans to reduce intra-European trade restrictions. The fundamental idea behind the suggestion seems to be that EC integration will restrict trade between the EC and the rest of the world; thus, other countries must form their own large trading blocs or FTAs in order to compete in a world that will be dominated by such blocs. Such a world lacks appeal because it exchanges one set of restrictions for another and, worse, shrinks each country's trade horizons from the rest of the world to the boundaries of its bloc. Also, there is no reason to believe that the sort of trade friction that now exists between Korea and the United States, the United States and Japan, Japan and Korea, and other pairs of Asian Pacific countries would not persist within an Asia-Pacific FTA.

The concept of "managed" trade is not well established but seems to be a policy response stemming from the work of revisionists like Chalmers Johnson and Clyde Prestowitz, who hold that conventional free-trade and comparative-advantage theses do not apply when dealing with the mercantilistic policies, institutions, and cultures of countries like Japan, or possibly Korea. Because standard market considerations do not always prevail in such countries, orthodox policy prescriptions have worked poorly. What is needed, the argument goes, is a system of market-share guarantees, or managed trade, in which Japan's exports to the United States, for instance, would depend on U.S. exports to Japan, and any failure to reciprocate would be followed by retaliation. In effect, the sort of VERs now imposed by the United States on Japanese steel and auto imports would be extended to all Japanese imports, and these VERs would be revised according to the performance of U.S. exports to Japan. While the revisionist thesis itself may help to explain Japan's or Korea's imperviousness to foreign goods and services, managed trade policies would greatly expand government intervention in export markets to "manage" export quotas. Such intervention is anathema in the United States and, given recent political upheavals, may no longer be as feasible in Japan or in Korea as it once was. Also, management would most likely reduce trade by offering protection to domestic industries that now face import competition but that are not yet protected by VERs.

A new institution or organization to deal with trade and other economic issues of regional interest offers a less radical and therefore more feasible means of improving economic relations than that presented by the FTA or trading bloc. Also, it would probably be less interventionist than the managed trade option. However, the Asia-Pacific region includes countries whose economic relations are competitive as well as complementary, and there is no reason to expect that regional cooperation will reduce the trade friction that arises from such competition. In addition, new institutional arrangements no longer appear to be the panacea for international economic problems that they seemed when the World Bank, IMF, and GATT were established.

Nevertheless, at least two considerations favor establishment of a new Asia-Pacific body to deal with regional economic issues, and these might be sufficient to outweigh the costs of creating another new organization. One is that bilateral trade negotiations are duplicative if negotiation involves an issue raised by trade between other country pairs. The United States, for example, may find that copyright practices in Taiwan are the same as in Korea and that in each case the practice has reduced U.S. book exports. Insofar as an issue is regional as well as bilateral, an Asia-Pacific organization might reduce negotiating costs. The other consideration is that an Asia-

Pacific institution could reduce protectionism and policy distortion if it shielded the trade policies of member countries from attack by domestic economic interest groups. The amount of shielding would depend on the willingness of members to yield power to the regional body in return for trade arrangements that are more in the national interest than current arrangements.

Notes

1. Korea Exchange Bank, *Monthly Review*, vol. 20, no. 12 (December 1986), p. 4.

2. Richard Luedde-Neurath, *Import Controls and Export-Oriented Development: A Reassessment of the South Korean Case* (Boulder, Colo.: Westview Press, 1986), pp. 142–143.

3. Ibid., pp. 151–154.

4. Peter A. Petri, "Korea's Export Niche: Origins and Prospects," *World Development*, vol. 16, no. 1 (January 1988), pp. 47–63.

5. Ibid., p. 30. Petri shows 1986 indices of protection from tariff and nontariff barriers (NTB) in developed countries for Korea, the United States, Japan, and other world "regions." The overall (world) NTB index, using 1985 weights, was 20.9; the tariff index was 4.3. Comparable figures for Korea, higher than those of any other region, were 35.2 and 6.6, respectively.

6. Eduardo Lachica, "Koreans Making a Pre-emptive Strike to Ward Off New U.S. Trade Sanctions," *Wall Street Journal*, April 14, 1989, p. A-10.

7. Large deficits are unsustainable because "foreign investors will . . . not finance U.S. deficits of this magnitude indefinitely" and because a stoppage of capital inflows or capital outflows would raise real interest rates in the United States and cause recession. See C. Fred Bergston, "U.S. International Macroeconomic Policy," in Thomas O. Bayard and Soo-Gil Young, eds., *Economic Relations Between the United States and Korea: Conflict or Cooperation?* (Washington, D.C.: Institute for International Economics, Korea Development Institute, January 1989), pp. 23, 25.

8. For example, when U.S. officials negotiated with Japan in 1977-1978 to stimulate Japanese domestic demand, "it generated a severe backlash." See I. M. Destler and Hideo Sato, *Coping with U.S.-Japanese Conflicts* (Lexington, Mass.: Lexington Books, 1983), p. 281.

9. See Mahn Je Kim and Sung-Tae Ro, "Korean International Macroeconomic Policy," in Bayard and Young, *Economic Relations*, pp. 57–60, and comment by John Williamson on p. 75.

10. Increasing protectionism is found among other developed countries besides the United States, and was clearly noticeable by the late 1970s. See Gary P. Sampson, "Contemporary Protectionism and Exports of Developing Countries," *World Development*, vol. 8, no. 2 (February 1980), pp. 113–127. See also I. M. Destler, *American Trade Politics: System Under Stress* (New York, N.Y., and Washington, D.C.: Twentieth Century Fund—Institute for International Economics, 1986), especially Chapter 8 on the erosion of the U.S. policymaking system.

11. See Paul R. Krugman, "Is Free Trade Passé?" *Economic Perspectives*, vol. 1, no. 2 (Fall 1987), pp. 131-144.

12. Bela Balassa and John Williamson, *Adjusting to Success: Balance of Payments Policy in the East Asian NICs* (Washington, D.C.: Institute for International Economics, 1987), p. 18. Despite minor revaluation from the fall of 1985, competitiveness increased—especially against Japanese producers—as the won fell against the yen.

13. The term "future factor proportions" was used to explain the adoption of more capital-intensive technology in Japan than was justified by current factor proportions but might, with equal force, have been applied to Korea. See Tuvia Blumenthal, "Factor Proportions and the Choice of Technology: The Japanese Experience," *Economic Development and Cultural Change*, vol. 28, no. 3 (April 1980), p. 559.

14. For example, "whenever any conflicts have arisen between the growth target and the management of external debt, Korean planners have not hesitated to sacrifice the balance-of-payments and price stability objectives." See Yung Chul Park, "Foreign Debt, Balance of Payments, and Growth Prospects: The Case of the Republic of Korea, 1965-1988," *World Development*, vol. 14, no. 8 (August 1986), p. 1044.

15. Where Sd = domestic saving, Sf = foreign saving, I = investment, X = exports, and M = imports, $I - Sd = M - X = Sf$.

16. Wontack Hong found, for example, that real rates of return on manufacturing capital rose from 17 percent in 1962-1966 to 26 percent in 1967-1971 and 27 percent in 1972-1975, and concluded that "borrowed capital has yielded extremely high rates of return . . . in Korean industry." See Wontack Hong, "Export Promotion and Employment Growth in South Korea," in Anne O. Krueger, et al., eds., *Trade and Employment in Developing Countries*, vol. 1 (Chicago, Ill.: National Bureau of Economic Research, University of Chicago, 1981), p. 374.

17. Soo-Gil Young, "Korean Trade Policy: Implications for Korea-U.S. Cooperation," in Bayard and Young, *Economic Relations*, p. 133.

18. There is a large and growing literature on the contribution of exports to growth and the virtues of outward-oriented as opposed to inward-oriented trade policies. See, for instance, Bela Balassa, "Industrial Policies in Taiwan and Korea," *Weltwirtschaftliches Archiv*, B. 106, H.1 (1971), pp. 55-76, and R. Ram, "Exports and Economic Growth in Developing Countries: Evidence from Time-Series and Cross-Section Data," *Economic Development and Cultural Change*, vol. 36, no. 1 (October 1987), pp. 51-72.

19. See Peter F. Allgeier, "Korean Trade Policy in the Next Decade: Dealing with Reciprocity," *World Development*, vol. 16, no. 1 (January 1988), p. 91.

20. Bon Ho Koo, "Trade Policy Issues: A Korean Perspective," in Robert A. Scalapino and Hongkoo Lee, eds., *Korea-U.S. Relations: The Politics of Trade and Security*, Research Papers and Policy Studies No. 25, Institute of East Asian Studies (Berkeley, Calif.: University of California, 1988), pp. 87-88.

21. Ibid., p. 90.

22. For instance, "in recent years there has been an overwhelming increase in . . . 'resentful forces' . . . composed of students, farmers, and intellectuals—against . . . the United States which is largely attributable to unrelenting U.S. pressure for complete agricultural liberalization." See Sung-Hoon Kim, comment on Soo-Gil Young, "Korean Trade Policy," in Bayard and Young, *Economic Relations*, p. 168.

23. See Eric Youngkoo Lee and Michael Szenberg, "The Price, Quantity and Welfare Effects of U.S. Trade Protection," *International Economic Journal*, vol. 2, no. 4 (Winter 1988), pp. 107-108, and OECD, *Agricultural Policies, Markets and Trade: Monitoring and Outlook, 1988* (Paris: OECD, 1988), p. 58.

24. These points were made by Kim Kihwan in a speech sponsored by the Japan and Asia Societies in New York on June 6, 1988. See Korea Economic Institute, *For Your Information*, June 24, 1988.

25. Yoon-Je Cho and David C. Cole, "The Role of the Financial Sector in Korea's Structural Adjustment," in Vittorio Corbo and Sang-Mok Suh, eds., *Structural Adjustment in a Newly Industrialized Country: Lessons from Korea* (Washington, D.C.: World Bank, Korea Development Institute, no date), unpublished manuscript, p. 263.

26. From Bon Ho Koo, "Challenges Facing Newly Industrialized Economies: A Korean Perspective," speech before the 9th International Monetary and Trade Conference of the Global Interdependence Center, Philadelphia, Penn., December 5, 1988. See Korea Economic Institute, *For Your Information*, December 9, 1988.

27. On these issues see William R. Cline, "'Reciprocity': A New Approach to World Trade Policy?" in William R. Cline, ed., *Trade Policy in the 1980s* (Cambridge, Mass.: MIT Press, Institute for International Economics, 1982), pp. 121-158.

28. J. David Richardson discusses the U.S. experience with TAA and likely international causes of employment growth and displacement. See his "Worker Adjustment to U.S. International Trade: Programs and Prospects," in William R. Cline, ed., *Trade Policy in the 1980s*, pp. 393-424.

29. See the *Wall Street Journal*, April 10, 1989.

5

Korea's Perspectives on Asia-Pacific Economic Cooperation

Bon Ho Koo

The Asia-Pacific region has experienced the most remarkable economic changes in the world over the past two decades. The region has emerged as one of the world's major growth centers after many years of rapid economic growth and trade expansion. This dynamic growth has been accompanied by much structural adjustment and increased interdependence in the region. Unfortunately, it has also resulted in huge external imbalances and frequent economic frictions among the regional economies.

In view of these past achievements and current problems, there has been much discussion about the region's future and the potential for Asia-Pacific cooperation. In addition, recent developments in the world economic environment, such as the rise of protectionism, regionalism, and bilateralism, have provided an even stronger argument for the promotion of regional economic cooperation.

The Asian Pacific countries, however, seem to have considerably different interests in substantiating the idea of Asia-Pacific cooperation, mainly owing to the diversity in their economic situations as well as differences in sociopolitical conditions. Because of these different interests, it is unlikely that a unified framework for Asia-Pacific cooperation will be established in the near future. This, however, is not to deny the potential for organizing such cooperation in the long run.

The Republic of Korea has pursued rapid economic growth by following an outward-oriented development strategy. As a result, Korea is heavily dependent upon its external trade and investment activities with neighboring nations in the Asia-Pacific region. Korea is currently undergoing major structural adjustment of its economy in the midst of rapid political democratization. Whether Korea can successfully achieve smooth structural adjustment and continue such rapid growth will largely hinge upon the international economic environment, especially in the Asia-Pacific region. This is why Korea has a high stake in the promotion of Asia-Pacific cooperation.

In this chapter I will assess the rationale for Asia-Pacific cooperation and suggest possible scenarios for its future direction from the standpoint of Korea. For that purpose, in the following sections, I will first review the economic performance and problems of the Asia-Pacific region and then explain Korea's recent internationalization efforts.

Increased Interdependence of the Asian Pacific Economies

During the past two decades or so, the Asia-Pacific region has continuously recorded relatively rapid economic growth and trade expansion compared to other parts of the world. As a result, its shares of the world GDP and trade reached more than 50 percent and 35 percent, respectively, in recent years. (See Table 5.1.)

Among the Asian Pacific nations, major shifts in economic power have taken place. Japan and the Asian Newly Industrializing Countries (NICs) showed much higher economic growth than others, followed by the ASEAN countries in more recent years. Reflecting changes in comparative advantage, trade and industrial structure have also changed significantly.[1] The NICs emerged as major exporters of manufactured goods after upgrading their exports into human capital- and technology-intensive products. At the same time, ASEAN and other developing nations increased their exports of labor-intensive products, for which the NICs formerly enjoyed comparative advantage.

The structural adjustment described above has led to very rapid growth of intra-regional trade among the Asian Pacific economies. Table 5.2 shows that in the 1980s all of the Asian Pacific nations significantly increased their dependence on intra-regional trade. The rapid growth of intra-regional trade demonstrates ever-increasing interdependence among the economies of the Asia-Pacific region. In particular, as a result of horizontal and vertical integration of industries across borders, intra-industry trade has been on the rise, though it has not yet reached a large scale.[2] For example, developing countries in the region produce technologically standardized parts and components at low costs and export them to developed countries, where they are assembled into higher-value-added final products. Increased intra-industry trade will not only foster economies of scale and efficient division of labor but will also bring about closer economic integration in the Asia-Pacific region.

The growing interdependence among the Asian Pacific countries has been furthered by increased foreign direct investment flows into the region.

Korea's Perspectives

Table 5.1 GDP and Trade Growth of the Asia-Pacific Region (in billions of U.S. dollars)

	World (A)	Asia-Pacific[a] (B)	B/A (%)	European Community (C)	C/A (%)
GDP					
1970	3,138	1,366	43.5	680	21.7
		(1,446)[b]	(46.1)		
1980	11,790	4,360	37.0	3,037	25.8
		(4,643)	(39.4)		
1987	15,789	7,950	50.4	4,287	27.2
Trade					
1970	594	206	34.6	241	40.6
		(210)	(35.4)		
1980	3,838	1,368	35.7	1,465	38.2
		(1,406)	(36.7)		
1987	4,789	1,750	36.5	1,913	40.0
		(1,833)	38.3		

[a]"Asia-Pacific" includes the United States, Japan, Canada, Australia, New Zealand, the six ASEAN member nations, Korea, Taiwan, and Hong Kong.
[b]Numbers in parentheses represent cases in which China is included.

Source: International Monetary Fund, International Financial Statistics, Yearbook, various issues.

The United States and Japan are the two largest investing nations, together occupying almost 85 percent of total investment flows into the Asia-Pacific region. (See Table 5.3.) More recently, the NICs have also become active in investing abroad as a means of utilizing their external surpluses as well as taking advantage of cheaper labor and untapped markets. The developing

Table 5.2 The Ratio of Intra-Regional Trade to the Total of the Asia-Pacific Countries (in percentages)

Year	U.S.	Japan	Canada	Australia	New Zealand	ANICs	(Korea)	ASEAN	Total Asia-Pacific
1980	41.8	54.1	73.0	60.8	61.9	65.1	(60.4)	69.7	55.0
1987	49.9	65.4	79.3	62.2	63.7	71.9	(70.3)	72.7	62.6

Source: International Monetary Fund, Direction of Trade Statistics, Yearbook, 1988.

Table 5.3 Foreign Direct Investment Flows in the Asia-Pacific Region as of 1986 (in millions of U.S. dollars)

From:	To: U.S.	Japan	Canada	Australia	New Zealand	Asian NICs[a]	ASEAN[b]	PRC	Total
U.S.		11,333	50,178	8,384	488	7,523	8,690	199	86,795
Japan	23,433		1,951	4,502	354	9,173	11,861	513	51,787
Canada	18,312								18,312
Australia	4,862								4,862
New Zealand	92								92
Asian NICs[a]	1,173								1,173
ASEAN[b]	203								203
PRC	10								10
Total	48,085	11,333	52,129	12,886	842	16,696	20,551	712	163,234

[a]Korea, Taiwan, Hong Kong, and Singapore.
[b]Malaysia, Thailand, Indonesia, and the Philippines.

Sources: U.S. Department of Commerce, Survey of Current Business; Ministry of Finance of Japan, Reported Direct Foreign Investment Statistics.

countries often find it more appropriate to import technology from the NICs rather than from the advanced countries because the former's technology is usually more labor-intensive than the latter's and therefore better fits their needs.

On the whole, the Asia-Pacific region has emerged as the most economically dynamic region in the world, as evidenced by the rapid growth of its trade and investment. In particular, the developing countries of the region have demonstrated unparalleled dynamism by following outward-looking development strategies, which have helped them to maximize the opportunities provided by the vast world markets and the diverse and complementary relations that exist in the Asia-Pacific region.

Major Challenges for the Asia-Pacific Region

The spectacular performance of the Asian Pacific economies has, however, brought about several problems, such as trade imbalances and intensified protectionism. The huge trade imbalances among the Asian Pacific nations seem most threatening to the future prosperity of the region. The United States, Australia, and New Zealand have been suffering continuous trade deficits, while Japan and Taiwan have been accumulating large trade surpluses. Recently, Korea has also started to generate a trade surplus. The trade imbalances, however they have been caused, are certain to have many adverse effects on the regional economies, both directly and indirectly. The trading environment in the region may be worsened by protectionist pressures in the deficit nations—pressures that not only will be directed against the surplus nations but will also spill over to affect other countries in the region. In addition, the huge amount of foreign capital needed by the deficit nations, notably the United States, to finance their deficits will continue to cause much uncertainty in international capital markets concerning credit availability, interest rates, and exchange rates. Even an economic giant like the United States simply cannot support continual trade deficits of the present magnitude.

These large trade imbalances, along with intensified competition among the Asian Pacific nations, have led to the proliferation of new protectionist practices throwing Asia-Pacific trading into disarray. Protectionism has spread rapidly across countries and products and has taken various forms. In recent years, some deficit nations have started to resort to bilateral negotiation and/or exclusive regionalism instead of abiding by the multilateral framework supported by the GATT. For example, the United States threatens their trading partners with the Super 301 clause while initiating bilateral free-trade arrangements. In Europe, the Single Europe Act would establish a fortress Europe by 1992.

Table 5.4 Macroeconomic Performance of Korea (in percentages)

	1985	1986	1987	1988	1989[b]
GNP Growth	5.4	12.5	12.8	12.2	8.0
Consumption	5.1	6.7	8.2	10.0	9.5
Fixed Capital Formation	4.4	15.0	17.4	11.8	13.5
Merchandise Exports	3.6	26.3	23.7	14.7	3.0
Merchandise Imports	-0.7	19.7	20.1	11.8	13.0
GNP Deflator[a]	4.1	2.3	3.4	4.3	4.5
Wholesale Prices[a]	0.9	-2.2	0.5	2.7	3.0
Consumer Prices[a]	2.5	2.3	3.0	7.1	7.0
Current Balance[c]	-0.9	4.6	9.9	14.2	8.5
Trade Balance[c]	0.0	4.2	7.7	11.5	7.0
(Exports)[c]	26.4	33.9	46.2	59.7	67.0
(Imports)[c]	26.4	29.7	38.6	48.2	60.0
Invisible Trade Balance and Net Transfers[c]	-0.9	0.4	2.2	2.7	1.5

[a]Percentage change from the same period of the previous year.
[b]Projected estimates.
[c]In billions of U.S. dollars.

Source: Korea Development Institute, KDI Quarterly Economic Outlook, various issues.

These problems highlight the need for closer cooperation among the Asian Pacific nations in order to achieve a more compatible and efficient division of labor and thus sustain the rapid growth of trade and investment.

Internationalization of the Korean Economy

For the past quarter-century, Korea has continuously enjoyed high economic growth, together with a phenomenal expansion of trade volume. More recently, in the past three years (1986–1988), the Korean economy has recorded an annual growth of more than 10 percent with relatively stable prices. Furthermore, the chronic external deficits of the past were converted into surpluses after 1986 as a result of a successful program to pursue export-oriented industrialization along with the favorable international economic conditions that emerged in the mid-1980s. (See Table 5.4.)

The recent success of the Korean economy, however, has turned out to be a mixed blessing as it has created several new problems that may cloud future economic prospects. On the domestic front, continued economic growth and external surpluses have recently contributed to major socioeconomic changes in Korea, which is concurrently undergoing social upheaval owing to political democratization. These changes include skyrocketing demands for more equitable and balanced prosperity, which have led to severe labor disputes since 1987. Internationally, Korea's large external surpluses have triggered calls from abroad for reducing its surplus by opening its markets, rapid appreciation of the Korean won, and expansion of domestic consumption.

In view of these changes in internal and external economic conditions, the Korean government has been redirecting its policy goals toward more equitable income distribution and more balanced regional and sectoral growth. With equal emphasis, internationalization of the economy on a broader front will be pursued. Internationalization is believed to be vital for the continued economic growth as well as the smooth expansion of trade in a highly trade-dependent economy like Korea in a world that is becoming increasingly interdependent. Through internationalization, greater competitiveness will be fostered as domestic industries are exposed to open competition in the world economy. In addition, Korea will be able to assume international responsibilities that are commensurate with its recent economic development.

There are four aspects to the internationalization of the Korean economy. First, the opening of domestic markets for imports will be pursued on a broader scale, including not only manufactures but also services and agricultural products. Manufactured products are already almost all liberalized for import, and tariff rates have also been greatly lowered. In addition, restrictive measures on imports imposed by various special laws will be relaxed to a large extent. In the service sector, markets such as advertising and shipping were recently opened up to the participation of foreigners. The Korean economy will continue to proceed toward greater trade liberalization. However, as might be expected, the greatest difficulty lies in the liberalization of agricultural trade. Liberalization in this area will take relatively more time and will need to be implemented in combination with measures to help farmers to maintain their incomes.

A second important feature of internationalization is the recycling of the Korean external surpluses abroad. This factor will not only contribute to the stabilization of the domestic economy but will also help to stabilize the growth of the world economy by financing the needs of deficit nations. In this context, Korea has already recycled most of its surpluses by paying back its foreign debts and by increasing its overseas investment and foreign aid. Overseas investment will bring about a more efficient international division of labor and will also facilitate the process of technology transfer, which is vital for smooth industrial adjustment across borders.

Third, liberalization of the foreign exchange and capital markets will also be pursued. As a newly instated nation under IMF Article VIII, Korea is undertaking appropriate measures to further liberalize foreign exchange transactions and also to gradually internationalize its currency, the won. In addition, it is expected that Korea's capital markets will be opened up on a broad scale to foreigners in the not-too-distant future.

Last but not least, internationalization can be achieved through greater policy coordination with other nations. Tighter policy coordination between nations with external surpluses and nations with deficits will help to relieve the current external imbalance problem of the world economy. More specifically, surplus nations should try to increase domestic consumption while deficit nations should cut consumption and increase exports through implementing a proper combination of monetary and fiscal policies. A significant reduction in the world's external imbalances would be followed by a decline in protectionism and other unfavorable effects produced by the imbalances.

Korea has been trying to contribute to policy coordination by cutting its current account surpluses, which amounted to almost 8 percent of GNP in 1988, through opening up domestic markets to imports, rapidly appreciating the won, and increasing domestic aggregate demand. These efforts, along with the excessive wage increases in the past two to three years, led to a significant decline in the current account surplus in 1989.[3]

Having first embarked on the task of internationalization in the early 1980s, Korea has already made substantial progress in many fields. It must be understood, however, that the process of internationalization tends to invite not only severe frictions among different interest groups but also many unforeseen risks. The internal conflicts and economic disturbances resulting from internationalization can be prevented only when internationalization proceeds in a well-coordinated manner in a cooperative international environment.

Korea's Perspectives on Asia-Pacific Cooperation

Since the 1960s, there have been several different movements toward the goal of Asia-Pacific economic cooperation. For example, a Pacific Free Trade Area (PAFTA) and an Organization for Pacific Trade and Development (OPTAD) were suggested but never realized; the Pacific Basin Economic Council (PBEC) and the Pacific Economic Cooperation Conference (PECC) were established in the mid-1960s and the early 1980s, respectively, and have continued their activities at the private-sector level. More recently, various plans for more formal regional cooperation of either the OECD type or the Forum type have also been suggested, and the first Pacific Ministerial Meeting is likely to take place soon.

Table 5.5 Korea's Export and Import Share by Region (in percentages)

	1986 Exp.	1986 Imp.	1987 Exp.	1987 Imp.	1988 Exp.	1988 Imp.	1989 June Exp.	1989 June Imp.
U.S.	40.0	20.7	28.7	21.4	35.3	24.6	33.3	25.1
Japan	15.6	34.4	17.8	33.3	19.8	30.7	21.1	28.2
EC	15.1	10.1	14.0	11.2	13.4	11.7	12.4	10.9
Asian NICs[a]	5.9	3.3	7.8	3.9	9.7	4.2	10.8	4.2
ASEAN[b]	2.3	5.9	2.2	5.9	2.8	5.5	3.6	6.1
Total	100.0	100.0	100.0	100.0	100.0	100.0	100.0	100.0
	(34.7)[c]	(31.6)	(47.3)	(41.0)	(60.7)	(51.8)	(29.2)	(29.1)

[a]Hong Kong, Singapore, and Taiwan.
[b]Brunei, Malaysia, Thailand, Indonesia, and the Philippines.
[c]Figures in parentheses are values of exports and imports in billions of U.S. dollars.

Source: Foreign Trade Statistics, Office of Customs Administration, Korea, 1989.

Unlike the European Community, whose members share a relatively similar culture, history, and even economic structure, the Asia-Pacific region, composed of a majority of the world's population, has tremendous diversity, not only of culture and history but also of levels of economic development. The path toward setting up a unified framework for Asia-Pacific cooperation will surely be difficult. Furthermore, if such a cooperative mechanism is indeed established, the Asian Pacific nations will participate in it with sharply differing interests.

Nevertheless, the potential benefits from regional economic cooperation should not be underestimated, and Asia-Pacific diversity should not prevent the establishment of a less formal cooperative channel. Recent developments in the world economy, especially the rise of regionalism and bilateralism, should spur the Asia-Pacific nations to move quickly to further their own regional cooperation.

Asia-Pacific cooperation would be beneficial to the Korean economy in many ways. First of all, through such cooperation, Korea could diversify its trade relations more smoothly. Currently Korea imports most of its intermediate and capital goods from Japan and imports its raw materials from the resource-rich developing countries, including ASEAN, while exporting a major portion of its manufactured products to the United States. (See Table 5.5.) This trade structure has been a major cause of a triangular trade imbalance among Korea, the United States, and Japan, where Korea has a trade surplus with the United States while running a deficit with Japan. Through closer regional cooperation, Korea would be able to expand its trade with all Asian Pacific nations and a better international division of labor could be achieved.

Second, Korea could enjoy more favorable conditions for its overseas investment and could also contribute to the economic development of developing countries in the region. Korea's overseas investment is expected to increase as its trade surplus continues and conditions for overseas investment become more favorable. (See Table 5.6.) Through increased overseas investment, Korea could not only find more efficient methods of production and more stable supplies of resources but would also have broader markets for its products. At the same time, the receiving nations would also benefit much from acquiring technology and management skills.

Finally, through regional cooperation, Korea could improve its relations with socialist countries, such as China and the Soviet Union. The economic reforms and opening up of these countries would certainly have a significant impact on the Asian Pacific economies. It is too early to assess the full impact of these changes on the regional economies. For Korea, however, which is confronted by its hostile neighbor North Korea, reform in the socialist nations may provide an opportunity to break the long-standing political and military tension and begin to take initiatives toward reunification.

Anticipating these benefits, Korea has been and will continue to be very supportive of Asia-Pacific cooperation. In the process of cooperation, Korea could play the role of mediator between the advanced nations and the developing nations in the region. Korea is indeed unique in that it possesses characteristics of both the advanced and the developing nations as well as elements of both a Westernized and a traditional Asian socioeconomic system. Thus, Korea seems ready to contribute to the balanced prosperity and peace of the whole Asia-Pacific region.

In the forthcoming round of Asia-Pacific cooperation in whatever form, it is of utmost importance to find effective cooperative measures to resolve the external imbalances in the region.[4] First, steps must be taken to ensure that those countries with excessive trade deficits take steps to reduce domestic savings and investment gaps, further liberalize their external transactions, and speed up industrial adjustment. These steps can be taken jointly and/or unilaterally. At the same time, the other countries in the region should also make efforts to reduce the external imbalances.

Second, the Asian Pacific nations highly dependent on trade should take initiatives in the ongoing Uruguay Round of trade negotiations to lessen the growing threat of protectionism. In addition to such multilateral efforts, regional and unilateral liberalizing efforts should also be pursued.

Finally, ways should be found to recycle external surplus in a healthy and stable manner. For example, the surplus could be used to increase overseas investments, expand development aid, and increase contributions

Table 5.6 Korea's Overseas Investment (amount of investment in millions of U.S. dollars)

	Approved Investment		Actual Investment (A)		Withdrawn Investment (B)		Remaining Investment (E) (E=A-B+E-1)	
	No. of Projects	Amount of Investment	No. of Projects	Amount of Investment	No. of Projects	Amount of Investment	No. of Projects	Amount of Investment
1968-1975	125	66.8	82	55.6	12	6.0	70	49.6
1976-1980	287	207.0	281	113.3	64	21.0	287	141.9
1981-1985	280	603.6	241	457.4	85	123.2	443	476.1
1986	74	358.5	50	172.0	18	14.8	475	633.3
1987	109	356.2	91	397.2	32	64.5	534	966.0
1988	253	479.6	165	212.9	31	59.8	668	1,119.1
March 1989	165	333.0	58	92.2	4	75.5	722	1,135.9

Source: Ministry of Finance, Korea.

to international organizations and multilateral programs for carrying out productive projects in developing countries.

This is certainly not an exhaustive summary of the issues facing Asia-Pacific cooperation, nor is there anything new about the issues mentioned here. The various existing channels for cooperation, such as PECC, PBEC and PAFTA, have already made much progress in identifying major issues for cooperation, including those I have mentioned. To a certain extent, they have also succeeded in building up an Asia-Pacific consensus for the resolution of these and other issues. Our next step should be toward deriving more substantial and visible benefits from such cooperation. For this purpose, efforts should be made to strengthen the existing mechanisms so that they function more effectively. In addition, closer linkages among them should be built up so that we can eventually achieve a unified framework for Asia-Pacific cooperation.

Notes

1. See Young Sun Lee, "Changes in Asia Pacific Economic Relations and Regional Economic Cooperation: A Korean Perspective," mimeo, May 1989, and I. Yamazawa, T. Nohara, and H. Osada, "Trade and Industrial Adjustment in Pacific Asia," Institute of Developing Economies, November 1985.

2. Detailed analysis of intra-industry trade in the Asia-Pacific region can be found in Bongsung Oum, "Changing Patterns of Trade and Prospects for Economic Cooperation in the Pacific Region," Korea Development Institute, mimeo, September 1985.

3. For up-to-date information on the economic performance of Korea, see Bon Ho Koo and Taeho Bark, "Recent Macroeconomic Performance and Industrial Structural Adjustment in Korea," Korea Development Institute, mimeo, August 1989.

4. More details can be found in Bon Ho Koo, "Horizon of Regional Cooperation in the Asian-Pacific Basin," paper presented at the Tokyo Conference on the Future of the Asian-Pacific Economy, May 1988.

6

China and Asia-Pacific Economic Cooperation

Nicholas R. Lardy

In marked contrast with the situation only a decade ago, China has become a major participant in world and Asia-Pacific trade. Trade turnover in 1976 was less than $15 billion (in U.S. dollars) and China ranked thirty-fourth in the world in trade value. By 1988 trade value had climbed to more than $100 billion and China ranked fourteenth in world trade.[1]

Moreover, this extraordinary pace of trade expansion has not depended on the accumulation of an unmanageable amount of foreign debt and has been accompanied by favorable trends in the structure of exports. In 1988, when total trade grew by almost one-fourth, China's trade balance was only slightly unfavorable and the current account was in balance. Total external debt outstanding at the end of 1988 was $40 billion. Based on the current debt structure, the year of peak interest and principal repayments will be 1992, when $8 billion to $9 billion in loans must be repaid. But even if Chinese exports grow only modestly, the peak repayments in 1992 will absorb only 15 percent of export earnings, below the 20 percent ratio that international agencies sometimes use as a guideline.[2] In short, China has sustained a rapid growth of imports primarily through rapid expansion of its export earnings rather than through expansion of its foreign debt.[3]

Manufactures have made up an increasing share of exports, reducing China's dependence on the export of agricultural products and raw materials, for which international prices are more volatile. The share of manufactured goods in total exports rose from 54 percent in 1981 to fully two-thirds in 1987.[4] Thus, China has joined with the Newly Industrializing Economies (NIEs) of East Asia, particularly Taiwan, Hong Kong, and South Korea, in providing a rising share of world exports, in the process reducing the predominant role of the advanced Western economies in supplying exports to the world market.

The Asia-Pacific region has played a growing role in China's international economic relations. In 1986, 65 percent of China's trade turnover was with countries in the Asia-Pacific region. Moreover, the region was the source of more than one-half of China's direct foreign investment.[5] With the more recent above-average growth of China's trade with Taiwan, South Korea, and Indonesia, the share of China's trade with countries in the region has expanded even further since 1986.

Although China is a major economic power in the Asia-Pacific region, it is not clear whether or how China would be accommodated in any scheme of Pacific regional economic cooperation. Indeed, in early discussions of regional cooperation in the mid-1960s, there was no explicit discussion of China's participation. China at that time was an insignificant trading country on a world scale and was not a significant export market for any of the countries in the Asia-Pacific region. Discussions of Pacific economic cooperation only very gradually and belatedly took into account that by the mid-1980s China had become the second largest export market for Japan, the third or fourth largest export market for Taiwan, the second largest export market for Hong Kong, the third or fourth largest export market for South Korea, the second or third largest export market for Australia, and so forth. Thus it has become increasingly difficult to envisage a significant form of economic cooperation in the region that excludes China.

PRC Policy Toward Regional Economic Cooperation

The issue of accommodating China is made more difficult by the failure of the Chinese government to articulate clearly its views on proposals for regional economic cooperation. Statements by the Ministry of Foreign Affairs purporting to reflect China's views on Asia-Pacific regional economic cooperation are usually limited to formulistic declarations that cooperation should be based on the principles of "mutual respect, equality and mutual benefit, strengthening communication, and economic development."[6] China did become in 1986 a member of the Pacific Economic Cooperation Conference (PECC), a nongovernmental organization founded in 1980 to promote economic cooperation in the region. By June the following year, China had set up a National Committee for Pacific Economic Cooperation. Huang Xiang, the director of the International Studies Center of the State Council, was elected chairman, and Rong Yiren, the chairman of the China International Trust and Investment Corporation (CITIC), became the committee's honorary chairman.[7] The first meeting of the National Committee was in June 1987 and the second in December 1988. Outside of vague statements about increased interdependence and cooperation in the region and a reiteration of China's willingness to cooperate in the region on the basis of mutual respect and equality, little has been disclosed about what has taken place in these meetings.

Although neither official statements nor the meetings of the National Committee have thrown much light on China's official policy toward regional economic cooperation, Chinese journals and other publications carry frequent articles on various schemes of regional economic cooperation from which broad Chinese attitudes may be deduced. First, Chinese authors writing on the issue are well aware of the relatively rapid growth of both output and trade in the Asia-Pacific region. Articles document this superior economic growth; the far above average growth of trade, particularly the rising share of manufactured goods in exports; and the development of world finance and banking centers in the region that challenge traditional world financial centers.[8] There is a clearly articulated sense that China is a major economic power in the region and that the rising prosperity of the region can and should exert a powerful positive influence on China's economic development.

Criticisms of the informal proposals that have been advanced in the past provide further clues to Chinese attitudes. A Japanese proposal on Pacific Rim cooperation initially put forward in late 1979 and finalized in 1980 was criticized for its lack of specificity on how the organization would be structured, its lack of clarity on the scope of the membership, and its lack of detail on the type of authority the organization would have and what duties and obligations its members would assume. In addition, the legacy of World War II and the memory of the Japanese attempt to establish Pacific cooperation under their leadership is explicitly raised as a factor mitigating against the Japanese proposal.[9]

The most detailed article I have read sets forth five criteria that an acceptable organization for Asia-Pacific regional cooperation would fulfill. First, the organization must have purely economic objectives. The Chinese are apprehensive of any military or political dimension of cooperation and argue that these would not benefit the region. Second, the scope of membership must be based on what the author called the "geographic characteristic of the Pacific region." In short, he supports a broad, inclusive scope of membership. Specifically, he obviously opposes a scope of membership, even if only at the preliminary stages of organization, limited to market economies in the region. Third, he envisages an organization that takes as its primary goal the establishment of a structure to harmonize the economic and trade policies of countries in the region. But this structure would not include any limitation on the sovereignty of individual governments in their mutual dealings with each other. Fourth, the organization must clearly specify the duties and obligations of its members and the degree of authority invested in the organization. Finally, he envisages an organization that would actively promote the economic development of its member states via discussions on issues related to economics, trade, technology, finance, and so forth.[10]

In short, if this article reflects official policy, China appears to oppose anything remotely approaching the creation of a trade union or economic community, as among the nations of the European Community, or a free-trade area, as in the case of the free trade agreement between the United States and Canada. Indeed, according to the *Beijing Review*, which usually reflects official policy faithfully, "The actual conditions that exist in the Asia and Pacific region will strongly impede, in the remaining years of this century, the formation of contract-like economic cooperation that is being practiced in Western Europe and North America."[11]

Three factors appear to account for this ambivalence, that is, China's desire on the one hand to play a role in shaping the form of cooperation in the Asia-Pacific region but, on the other hand, to effectively rule out more significant forms of cooperation for a decade or more. The first factor entering into this attitude is the fear that Japan, because of its economic strength, would dominate any organization for regional economic cooperation. The Chinese, for historical reasons and because of their experience in economic and commercial relations in the past decade, are not interested in any organization that would augment Japan's already enormous economic power in the region.

Second, China has not yet entirely abandoned the North-South framework in which it has long viewed international economic relations. Analysis of economic trends and developments in the Pacific region frequently identifies China as part of the South.[12] Despite a decade of rapid growth, China's level of development, and particularly its level of technology, remains low. China thus welcomes the aid of advanced Pacific countries, such as Japan and the United States, in the supply of capital and technology to facilitate its own development. In short, the Chinese retain a residual of their attitude that the countries of the North have an obligation to provide assistance to those of the South. This view has been heightened more recently by Japan's emergence as the major source of development assistance, mixed credits, and commercial loans for China. The problem the Chinese face is to identify the forms of economic cooperation that maintain formal equality among its members while at the same time allowing China to benefit from a significant volume of aid and mixed credits from Japan. The EC and the U.S.-Canada free-trade area are clearly not relevant models because the participants in these forms of cooperation are far more homogeneous in terms of level of development than are the countries of the Asia-Pacific region.

Third, and most important, is that despite its far-reaching economic reforms, China remains a socialist, semi-planned economy with a degree of trade protectionism that clearly exceeds that of any other major country in the region. It is not clear how to incorporate such a large, still predominantly state-directed trading system into a scheme of regional economic cooperation in which the other members' economies are predominantly market-oriented.

Despite a major reform of its foreign trade system begun in 1984, China's trade regime continues to differ significantly from its major trading partners in several respects. First, despite some reduction in the role of central government foreign trade corporations, they still have monopoly control over specified commodities and continue to be responsible for what is referred to as the command portion of the plan, which comprises about 40 percent of all imports and 50-60 percent of all exports.[13] These foreign trade corporations do not make decisions primarily on the basis of economic criteria; rather, they are subsidized by the government to cover the losses they incur meeting quantitatively specified import and export targets. In short, they are not very sensitive to relative prices in China and the world economy. Second, licensing of both imports and exports covers a significant share of the commodities not included in the command plan. These quantitative trade restrictions provide highly variable and difficult to measure protection for many domestic industries. Third, China's tariffs, which range as high as 200 percent, provide a high degree of protection for domestic producers and result in a substantial bias against export activities. Finally, China's currency is not convertible and foreign exchange is largely allocated bureaucratically. This environment is not conducive to the kinds of trade-promotion measures usually included in various forms of regional economic cooperation.

Conclusion

China favors, in principle, some sort of Asia-Pacific economic cooperation. Cooperation is seen as facilitating enhanced economic interaction with the most dynamic economies in the world—an attractive prospect for an economy seeking to move from the autarkic development strategy of the past to a more open economic development strategy. However, China's options in participating in such an organization are constrained by historical, ideological, and economic factors. For other countries in the region, China's growing foreign trade and other forms of economic interaction, which are increasingly focused within the Asia-Pacific region, make it difficult to envisage significant forms of economic cooperation that do not include China.

The major implication of this analysis is that further reforms of China's foreign trade regime, as well as related domestic economic reforms, are a prerequisite for making significant progress toward regional economic cooperation.

Thus, China should focus on policy reforms that would assist them in reaping the advantages of specialization on a global scale. The main impediment to China's expanded participation in international as well as Asia-Pacific trade is its domestic price structure. Trade raises a country's real income and living standard through an exchange of products in which a country sells on the international market goods that can be produced relatively cheaply domestically and purchases on the international market goods that are relatively expensive to produce domestically. To rationally make this calculation, however, domestic prices must reflect production costs—a condition that does not prevail in China, where the prices of many raw materials, intermediate goods, and final products are fixed by the government. If trade is decentralized in an environment where changes in relative costs cannot be reflected in prices, profit-maximizing trade may not bring any national advantage. The risk is that Chinese firms will export noncomparative-advantage goods for which the state has fixed relatively low domestic prices. Similarly, firms may import goods that are relatively cheaper abroad only because the domestic substitute product is overpriced. To alleviate these problems China relies heavily on export subsidies to promote the sale of overpriced domestic goods and export licenses to restrict the export of underpriced domestic goods. Similarly, China uses import prohibitions and other quantitative restrictions on imports, in part to protect the production of domestic goods in which China has a comparative advantage but whose domestic prices have been fixed relatively high.

Although these administrative measures are taken in an effort to improve China's trade performance, in the long run they will hinder it and will reduce substantially the benefits that China accrues from its participation in international trade.

A second step China should take in order to reap the advantages of increased trade is to move more rapidly toward the convertibility of its currency. Despite a reduction in the value of the yuan by more than half between 1977 and 1987, it remains substantially overvalued. This was particularly true after July 1986 when the official exchange rate was pegged at about 3.72 yuan per U.S. dollar while the rate of inflation in China soared much faster than the world average.[14]

Domestic price reform and a convertible currency together would significantly enhance the volume and role of foreign trade in China's economy. Most important, it would make possible a reduction in the degree of state administration and in the amount of control of foreign trade and would make it possible for enterprises to be given greater freedom to operate directly in the international market. China could then rely more upon tariffs and less upon quantitative restrictions on imports and exports. This would create conditions under which China might more reasonably participate in Asian economic cooperation schemes.

Postscript

In the aftermath of the Tiananmen tragedy many questions have been raised concerning China's prospects for sustaining economic reforms and outward-oriented economic policies. The official line enunciated by Party General Secretary Jiang Zemin in a major speech on the fortieth anniversary of the PRC is that "the great achievements of the past ten years prove the complete correctness of the general principle and policy of reform and openness and the need to carry it forward."[15] However, conservative critics of economic reform have assumed more prominent positions, both formally and informally, which has led to a new emphasis on upholding the principles of socialism, including public ownership and limiting "unfair" wage gaps, ideological remolding, and strengthening the role of the party. These trends are obviously in conflict, and it is impossible to predict the outcome with confidence.

Deng Xiaoping, in the months following the Tiananmen tragedy, has reiterated China's outwardly oriented economic development strategy. In addition, China hosted an international meeting of government and private-sector representatives from twenty countries to discuss specifically the issues of Asia-Pacific economic cooperation.[16] Chinese foreign trade officials have reiterated the importance of the region to China's trade and investment policies, and they expected to participate in the first ministerial meeting of the Pacific Basin Forum in Canberra in November 1989. The need to amortize existing external obligations alone probably is sufficient guarantee against an absolute closure to the outside world, despite renewed exhortations to "uphold the principles of independence and self-reliance."

Although China's general policy of economic openness seems unlikely to change abruptly, the results over the longer run will depend on the character and pace of domestic economic development. As discussed above, sustaining the growth of China's exports and, in particular, increasing the efficiency of its trade, depend on further domestic economic reforms. If events of May-June 1989 lead to retrogression or to a lengthy hiatus in domestic economic reform, the prospects for further expansion of China's role in the Asia-Pacific region will be diminished significantly.

Notes

1. If Hong Kong's reexports are included in its trade value, it ranks ahead of China, dropping China into fifteenth place in world trade value in 1988.

2. China's total exports in 1992 would be $53 to $60 billion if exports grew at an average annual rate of 3 to 6 percent between 1988 and 1992. I characterize this pace as modest because export growth in the decade from 1978 to 1988 was 17.1 percent per annum.

3. China's cumulative incremental imports through 1988 over the 1976 base of $6.5 billion totaled $248.5 billion. Thus, expansion of indebtedness from approximately zero to $40 billion over the same period financed less than one-seventh of China's incremental imports. The balance of import growth was financed largely by the growth of export earnings and direct foreign investment in China. Expanding income from services, such as shipping and tourism, was also significant.

4. State Statistical Bureau, *Statistical Yearbook of China 1981* (Hong Kong: Economic Information and Agency, 1982), p. 390; *Chinese Statistical Yearbook 1988* (Beijing: Statistical Publishing House, 1988), p. 722. Comparable data for the years prior to 1981 are not available. Earlier data differ in their scope because they were compiled by the Ministry of Foreign Trade rather than by the Chinese Customs Administration. The pre-1981 commodity classification also differs. Exports were divided into three categories: industrial and mineral products; processed farm and sideline products; and farm and sideline products.

5. Shen Guijin, "Trends and Proposals with Regard to China's Policy Toward Pacific Economic Cooperation," *Social Science* (Shanghai, 1987), no. 10, pp. 12-15, reprinted in *Shijie Jingji* [World Economy], 1987, no. 12, pp. 57-60, data cited on p. 60. The geographical concept underlying these data is not specified.

6. See, for example, the statement of Foreign Minister Wu Xueqian, "China's Basic Opinion with Regard to Asia-Pacific Economic Cooperation," *People's Daily*, April 22, 1989, reprinted in *New China Monthly*, no. 4, 1987, pp. 183-184.

7. Mr. Huang died in the spring of 1989.

8. See, for example, Li Lianzhong and Zhu Yong, "Reasons Why the Asia-Pacific Region Is Becoming the Economic Center of the World," *Social Science* (Shanghai, 1987), no. 3, pp. 12-16, reprinted in *Shijie Jingji* [World Economy], 1987, no. 4, pp. 59-63.

9. Shen Guijin, "Trends and Proposals," p. 59.

10. Ibid., pp. 59-60.

11. Wang Juyi, "An Analysis of the Three Economic Rims," *Beijing Review*, March 20-26, 1989, pp. 15-17.

12. Zhu Yulin, "Prospects in the Year 2000 for North-South Relations in the Pacific Region," *Asia-Pacific Economics* (Fujian, 1987), no. 4, pp. 1-5, reprinted in *Shijie Jingji* [World Economy], 1987, no. 12, pp. 61-65. Zhu is identified as a member of the Contemporary International Relations Research Institute.

13. *China: External Trade and Capital* (Washington, D.C.: The World Bank, 1988) p. 22.

14. The State Administration of Exchange Control announced a further devaluation of the yuan to 4.72 in December 1989. Given China's high rate of inflation, especially in 1988 and 1989, this devaluation has not significantly alleviated the overvaluation of China's domestic currency.

15. "Jiang Reaffirms Policies of Reform and Openness," *China Daily*, September 30, 1989, p. 3.

16. "Trade Conference Scheduled for Beijing," *China Daily*, September 22, 1989, p. 2.

7

Economic Cooperation in the Asia-Pacific Region: The Southeast Asia Dimension

Anthony C. Albrecht

World Politics and Economy and the Economies of the Asia-Pacific Region

Four Power Relationships and Alternative Scenarios

An analysis of economic cooperation in the Asia-Pacific region, particularly with regard to the Association of Southeast Asian Nations (ASEAN) will be facilitated by first outlining the possible scenarios for ASEAN international relations.

First, in a benign scenario, U.S.-ASEAN relations would remain strong, trade tensions would be managed, and the U.S. regional role and credibility would be maintained with continued U.S.-Japan cooperation on major international issues. China and the USSR would remain preoccupied with internal problems, thus facilitating a gradual reintegration of Vietnam and Cambodia into the region.

In contrast to this is the destabilizing scenario, where U.S. protectionists control U.S. foreign policy, the GATT Uruguay Round stalls, and Japan-bashing peaks and provokes a Japanese reaction. ASEAN countries would lose market access as GSP benefits were further reduced and new restrictions were placed on textiles. Europe would follow the U.S. protectionist example, and ASEAN would lose exports to Europe. The United States would continue to subsidize agricultural exports in competition with ASEAN, and the United States and ASEAN would disagree on a Cambodian solution.

In the following sections I will summarize ASEAN relations with four powers—the United States, Japan, the USSR, and the PRC. Benign factors dominate at present in these relationships, but destabilizing factors are clearly present.

U.S.-ASEAN Relations. Relations between the United States and ASEAN are good at present; they are based on close cooperation on political issues and shared confidence in the benefits of open markets, but they are also threatened by strong, protectionist lobbies that have a disproportionate influence on U.S. foreign policy. This negative impact on U.S. national security interests in Southeast Asia can be seen in the case of textiles, where ASEAN's growth potential has been severely limited by the U.S. textile lobby; in the case of rice, where considerable damage was done to U.S.-Thai relations by the U.S. rice lobby; and, more recently, by the American Soybean Association's attack on tropical oils, a crucial export of Malaysia and the Philippines.

This protectionist tendency, combined with U.S. government budgetary constraints, makes the United States a less credible partner than it was in the past. One area where the United States can show political support and solidarity with ASEAN is in foreign assistance. This should be increased to certain ASEAN members despite the severe U.S. budgetary constraints. Currently, total U.S. assistance to ASEAN represents less than 5 percent of total U.S. assistance worldwide. The United States would gain some political credit by increasing the absolute amount of its aid to Indonesia, the Philippines, and Thailand. Such an increase would not be easy to achieve, but it would serve to counterbalance some of the negative developments on the trade side of the equation.

ASEAN also bears some of the responsibility for trade tensions. It still has major protectionist barriers against U.S. exports of goods and services. In addition, its failure to protect intellectual property remains a major issue despite recent progress in a number of countries.

ASEAN-Japanese Relations. Japan's economic success and its massive capital surplus, combined with more skillful Japanese diplomacy, means greater Japanese influence in ASEAN now and in the future. Resentment of Japan is still strong in ASEAN, but it seems to be lessening as Japanese aid and investment increase and, most recently, as Japan imports more from the ASEAN countries. As Japan's role grows, ASEAN friends of the United States hope to see Americans meet the challenge with increased trade and investment. They also worry about congressional demands that Japan carry a larger defense burden. Based on history, they do not want to see Japanese rearmament.

ASEAN-USSR Relations. There have been recent moves toward increased trade between ASEAN and the Soviet Union, but the major issue between them has been Soviet support of Vietnam's occupation of Cambodia. As the Soviet role becomes more constructive and a Cambodian solution seems more likely, Vietnam once again becomes a major element in the Southeast Asian dimension of economic cooperation in the Pacific. As it is unlikely that ASEAN will be able to build a major trading relationship with the USSR, the major significance of the change in Soviet policy toward Vietnam is not bilateral but regional—Vietnam is again part of the equation.

The implications of this regional change are interesting. Both ASEAN and Japan are well positioned to play a key role in reintegrating Vietnam into the region. ASEAN has the political influence and private sector, and Japan has the capital and experience to rebuild the Vietnamese economy. U.S. companies are in danger of being left behind and are further handicapped by U.S. budgetary constraints, which translate into a minor role for U.S. aid programs in the Vietnam reconstruction effort. The key for U.S. companies may well be joint ventures with Japanese companies in aid projects financed by Japan.

One caveat here is the possible U.S. public and congressional resistance to major U.S. participation in rebuilding Vietnam. This obstacle may limit any U.S. budgetary outlay, but U.S. export companies should begin preparing public opinion now by stressing the important role that U.S. exports can play in creating jobs in U.S. manufacturing industries.

ASEAN companies are already active in Vietnam while U.S. companies are forced to wait on the sidelines. Japanese companies are also going slowly in response to guidance from the Japanese government, which shares the view of the U.S. government that leverage on the Vietnamese must be maintained if a Cambodia settlement is to be reached.

ASEAN-PRC Relations. As with the Soviet Union, China's short-term relevance to ASEAN hinges on the impending solution to the Cambodian question. Fear of the Khmer Rouge seems to be holding up a settlement, and the Chinese role is becoming even more critical. The prospect of warring factions within Cambodia is real, and China is sure to be involved, as will ASEAN. In this situation it is likely that the economic and trade relations between ASEAN and China may not reach their full potential.

Several years ago the PRC took pains to assuage ASEAN fears that China might take away ASEAN markets in the developed countries. China has done just that in the case of textiles and apparel, but ASEAN can blame the United States rather than China. The fact is that the U.S. textile lobby has more leverage over the smaller ASEAN countries than it does over a major power like China, which has demonstrated that it will fight back on trade issues. Prior to the Tiananmen Square tragedy, it appeared that China wanted to import more consumer goods in order to meet the rising expectations of the population and that it did not wish to present a major threat to ASEAN competitors in third country markets. The hardline forces now in control in Beijing are damaging the Chinese economy, making it even less of a threat to ASEAN on the export side, but also less of a market for ASEAN products.

U.S.-Japanese Relations

A dangerous new idea is being pushed by protectionist/isolationist forces in Washington, i.e., that competition with the Soviets is of less concern now than in the past, that foreign economic competition is the new threat to our security, and that Japan is the new enemy. This idea is being pushed by the U.S. Department of Commerce in the context of the FSX debate as a means toward greater bureaucratic power. The FSX is Japan's new fighter plane, which hardliners in the United States want Japan to buy off the shelf from U.S. manufacturers in order to maximize U.S. exports and avoid technology transfer, which might help Japan build a commercial airplane industry. Protectionist forces in Congress see this case as a way to further weaken the internationalist approach of the executive branch and the State Department. The message to Japan and others in the region is clear—not only is the United States a less powerful ally than it was, but its policies are dominated by Congress, which sees only short-term parochial interests rather than broad, long-term objectives. The FSX example shows once again that the U.S. Congress acts out its frustrations most easily against U.S. allies. On top of the FSX case, which has fueled rancorous debate in Congress, the administration decided on May 30 that Japan should be listed under the Super 301 section of the 1988 Omnibus Trade and Competitiveness Act as an "unfair" trading partner.

The FSX deal finally went through because its opponents lacked the votes to block it. The fact that Japan is in political disarray over the Recruit scandal may have moderated an immediate Japanese response to the 301 designation. The sophisticated managers of the U.S. relationship with the Japanese establishment may proceed on the basis that Congress is just letting off steam and that restraint and accommodation constitute the best course of action. After all, Super 301 designation carries with it the requirement for further negotiations to open up the Japanese market—this is nothing new for Japan.

The question of U.S. credibility will remain. Whatever Japan decides to do, others in the region will see that the U.S. is lashing out at its friends because it will not face up to difficult domestic issues such as the budget deficit. In particular, ASEAN is unlikely to accept crude congressional attacks on its economic interests without a political backlash. The damage done to U.S.-Thai relations by U.S. rice subsidies is ample evidence of ASEAN sensitivity. The U.S. soybean lobby, not content with its public relations campaign denigrating palm and coconut oil, is now seeking subsidies for sales of soybean oil to the Soviet Union, thus further exacerbating U.S.-ASEAN trade tensions.

The World Economy

On balance, ASEAN seems to be benefiting from the current state of the world economy. U.S. demand for imports remains strong despite the recent slowing of the U.S. economy. Japan is investing in ASEAN and importing more ASEAN goods. Europe also remains a good market and source of investment. The long-term prospects for the world economy are less satisfactory for ASEAN. A recession in the United States still appears likely to many analysts, and this could stimulate protectionist actions and a trade war. At best it is likely to trigger a slowing of other OECD economies. Japan might be able to take up some of the slack, but a bias toward imports similar to that in the United States is unlikely. In a growing market atmosphere of world economic expansion, Korea and Taiwan would be buying more from ASEAN, but in a shrinking market they would not earn enough to do so. One key factor, however, is that ASEAN has diversified its exports and is likely to survive a world economic slowdown better than other developing regions.

Outlook for the Economies of the Asia-Pacific Region

Benign Scenario

Under current conditions, which are essentially the same as the benign scenario outlined above, the costs and risks to ASEAN would remain high. Even the benign scenario assumes that individual U.S. lobbies and their congressional supporters will, in many cases, be able to force the administration into actions detrimental to ASEAN interests. Congressional attacks on Japan could also unleash forces that would hurt ASEAN. Such attacks make foreigners the scapegoat and divert attention away from domestic economic problems that the United States must solve in order to maintain steady economic growth without unmanageable inflation. The "blame the foreigners" mentality in Congress also encourages stronger action under the 1988 Trade Act on such issues as intellectual property and workers' rights, where ASEAN countries will have little room for maneuver to avoid retaliation.

In addition to these general difficulties inherent in the current situation, there are a number of specific sectors where ASEAN faces strong U.S. lobbies, which have already damaged ASEAN interests and are likely to continue to do so unless ASEAN takes strong action to oppose them. The rice, textile, and steel lobbies have already done considerable damage. The soybean lobby has devastated ASEAN sales of coconut and palm oil in the U.S. market by portraying these products as dangerous to one's health.

Their high-powered PR campaign has featured such slogans as "Tropical products will kill you," and full-page ads about the "poisoning of America." This despite the fact that the FDA has stated that palm and coconut oil represent only 8 percent of the U.S. consumption of saturated fat. The ASEAN producers and their governments were helpless before the onslaught of the attack ads. More dangerous than the potential loss of the U.S. market is the prospect that the reputation of their product in world markets is also being undermined. In recent months a new danger has emerged—subsidized sales of U.S. soybean oil to the USSR. ASEAN has protested to the U.S. State Department, but it remains to be seen whether these sales can be turned off.

The current scenario assumes continued Japanese economic dominance in East Asia and growing ASEAN dependence on Japan for aid, investment, and trade. Much of the Japanese investment surge was caused by the strong yen. Many Japanese factories were set up to produce for the Japanese market, but if conditions change they could move to other countries. The key question will be whether they leave behind a legacy of useful technology transfer and improved technical and managerial skills. It may be prudent for ASEAN to strengthen its efforts to maintain and increase the flow of U.S. and European investment. Protection of intellectual property may turn out to be a crucial factor in the promotion of such investment. ASEAN has made great improvements in this area, but it may cut itself off from the transfer of important technology unless further steps are taken.

Even under the current (benign) scenario the United States has a major problem in its relations with ASEAN. Simply put, the United States is rapidly losing its credibility as a reliable economic partner. The actions of U.S. lobbies and their congressional supporters, which attack vital ASEAN interests, also undermine U.S. national security interests in Southeast Asia. The administration has been unable to head off many of these initiatives, and in the case of GSP, it was rogue action by the Treasury Department within the administration itself that cut off Singapore's benefits. The soybean lobby's campaign against ASEAN is the latest example of the type of action that must be controlled if the United States is to restore its credibility as a reliable economic partner.

Destabilizing Scenario

In the destabilizing scenario, ASEAN would be hurt by a major U.S. shift toward protectionism and isolationism. In essence, the United States would retreat from an economic war that it convinced itself it could not win. U.S. economic self-confidence would be shattered by Japan much as U.S. military confidence was lost in Vietnam. The protectionists of today would fill the role of the protest marchers of the Vietnam era. U.S. protectionism would be imitated by Europe, and Japan would have a pretext to look at the Pacific as its private lake. Japan would exercise more control over all ASEAN interests; the danger of renewed conflict in Southeast Asia would grow as the U.S. isolationist trend gained strength; increased Soviet and PRC influence over ASEAN interests would increase; likely ASEAN cohesion and internal political stability would weaken as economic growth slowed and unemployment increased.

Conditions for Economic Growth

The ASEAN economies meet the conditions for continued strong economic growth—with one key exception. They have the raw materials, the educated work force, and the economic leadership, but they do not have the markets. ASEAN is not only vulnerable to blatant protectionism or economic recession in developed countries but could also experience problems if it fails to attract investment and technology transfer or if the heavy hand of government continues to restrain the full energies of the private sector. In other words, ASEAN is in as much danger from its own protectionists and defenders of the status quo as is the United States or the European Community (EC). If ASEAN is to continue its successful economic performance, it must continue to increase its involvement in the world economy by opening its markets to new technology and business services that will increase its competitiveness. It must also recognize its environmental problems and be willing to take greater leadership in international fora. Economic issues should be given equal priority with political issues at the annual Post-Ministerial meetings. While ASEAN may not be able to participate directly in the seven-nation Economic Summit, it should make its views known to all the participants in advance rather than relying on Japan to represent its interests, as seems to have been the case in the past.

Given the many important factors that contribute to economic growth, ASEAN cannot go it alone. Given the deep and pervasive interdependence of the world economy and ASEAN's need for markets, ASEAN cannot afford to turn over its destiny to a Pacific economic bloc competing with other economic blocs. Competing in an open world economy is one thing; competing with Japan, Korea, and Taiwan in a closed bloc would be quite another. One ASEAN leader put it this way: "[R]ecent experience thus teaches us that national policies alone are incapable of solving our domestic economic problems. The reality has changed: the world economy drives us, not the other way round."

The Need for Regional Cooperation

International Coordination of Macro Policies

For ASEAN, with its commitments to world markets and an open international economic system in which it can prosper, regional macroeconomic cooperation must be approached cautiously. Macro policy is dominated by Japan on the financial side and by the United States in trade. ASEAN needs the EC and other markets too much to adopt a narrow or confrontational regional position.

Singapore's recent participation in the OECD seminar with the Newly Industrializing Countries (NICs) raises the interesting possibility of ASEAN's gradual involvement in serious international coordination of macroeconomic policy. Thailand and Malaysia are participating in the workshops that were planned as a follow-up to the OECD seminar.

Another major forum for international economic coordination is the seven-nation Economic Summit. In the past, Japan has consulted with ASEAN and then suggested that it was representing ASEAN interests at the Summit. It would be prudent for ASEAN to communicate its views directly to the other players, especially the United States.

The critical issue in any regional discussion of macroeconomic policy issues is whether they can be dealt with effectively without the participation of the Europeans. The ASEAN countries have long-standing ties with Europe and active trade and investment relations. As the world economy becomes more and more competitive and interdependent, ASEAN must seek new market niches. What benefits from regional macroeconomic coordination would compensate for the loss of commercial ties with Europe?

Trade Liberalization and the Resolution of Problems of Trade Imbalance

ASEAN must proceed cautiously on the idea of regional trade liberalization for the same reasons it must go slow on macroeconomic coordination—it cannot afford to become part of a confrontational bloc. ASEAN officials have made clear that they do not want the gradual movement toward closer Pacific Basin cooperation to result in a closed bloc or regional institution that could undermine ASEAN strength and unity. These officials are also concerned that a regional bloc could undermine the multilateral trading system. Although they share concerns that Europe could become more protectionist as a result of the EC 1992 process, they have not yet subscribed to the notion that the Pacific Basin countries should "send a message to the EC" that there is a Pacific alternative to a protectionist EC bloc.

ASEAN's cautious approach is also reflected in the language of a recent study of the ASEAN-U.S. Initiative. In recommending an umbrella agreement, the authors stated that:

> The complementary nature of U.S. and ASEAN economies and the extensive economic interchange suggest that bilateral agreements under the umbrella designed to resolve any disagreements or seize important opportunities would

be welfare-enhancing, without contradicting multilateralist ideals. Indeed, all actions would be consistent with GATT.

The initial umbrella should consist of the following components. First, it should establish a set of basic guiding principles for the conduct of trade and other economic relations between the United States and ASEAN, based on GATT compatibility and affirming the primacy of multilateral liberalization. It should be grounded on the presumption that trade and investment flows are determined by market forces as much as possible; the nature of government intervention should be strictly defined and temporary. Most basically, the United States and ASEAN should commit themselves to the principle of "stand-still and roll-back" of trade barriers. Moreover, measures harming other trading partners should be avoided.[1]

Enhancement of Security and Stability Within the Region

Security issues are a sensitive topic for ASEAN. While security cooperation with the United States has been excellent in the broad context of peace and stability in Southeast Asia, the notion of Pacific-wide security would be troublesome. U.S. cooperation with ASEAN in resisting Vietnamese aggression succeeded because ASEAN took the lead and the United States provided political and material support. In fact, ASEAN's economic success is an excellent example of what can be achieved if security interests are met and basic political stability is maintained. The threat to ASEAN was clear and present and close to home, and it provoked cooperation and unity. It would be difficult for ASEAN to agree that another threat was so great that it would require some type of regional security arrangement for the Pacific. This type of agreement would be all the more difficult in view of the new policies and soft line adopted by the Soviet Union.

ASEAN sensitivity regarding security questions has been quite apparent in its reaction to the possibility of a larger military role for Japan. When the United States was pressing Japan to spend more on defense, ASEAN strongly objected to U.S. officials that this could lead to Japanese rearmament and present a danger to ASEAN, which had suffered under Japanese military rule.

While ASEAN certainly would agree, based on its own experience, that security is a prerequisite for economic growth, it would probably view formal Pacific regional security ties as unnecessary and perhaps even detrimental. The underlying assumption, of course, would be that whatever happens, the United States would continue to support ASEAN politically and would cooperate with ASEAN should any threats to ASEAN security develop.

Another aspect of the regional security question is how to remove future threats. Vietnam might return to its aggressive ways if it cannot be reintegrated into the regional and world economy. ASEAN companies are already exploring opportunities in Vietnam. Japanese economic assistance can play a key role, and U.S. companies could benefit from cooperation with Japan. These potential benefits could be lost if Congress and the Commerce Department persist in treating Japan as the enemy. Thailand in particular has tried to interest the U.S. in cooperating on future projects in Vietnam.

Factors Affecting Cooperation

ASEAN unity and cooperation have already moderated some intra-ASEAN conflicts. The ASEAN spirit of cooperation has been expressed in the Post-Ministerial Dialogue with other countries and regions outside the Pacific, such as the European Community. ASEAN has also been supportive of a successful new GATT round. This not only indicates a preference for settling disputes but also a basic understanding of the wisdom of openness and dialogue with all parties. This attitude would militate against ASEAN support for an exclusive Pacific Basin organization to confront Europe. This wisdom also recognizes the benefits of diversifying markets in an interdependent world, where political or protectionist shocks could be damaging if ASEAN depended too much on any one market.

ASEAN representatives have also made clear that ASEAN recognizes that it is also engaged in fierce economic competition. It clearly sees that ASEAN has a greater say in the world economy when it speaks with one voice. Therefore, it will not enter into any agreements or cooperative ventures that could weaken or divide ASEAN. This fundamental tension—between regional Pacific goals and ASEAN domestic goals—is likely to endure. It is exacerbated by conflicts between the goals of individual member states of ASEAN and larger Pacific regional goals. ASEAN works by consensus, and if one member state has strong objections to Pacific Basin regional cooperation, the other member states will not break ASEAN unity and proceed without it. This makes for a slow process toward new initiatives, but it is balanced by ASEAN's basic policy of openness and consultation in its relations with other countries.

One example of the complexity and delicate nature of the ASEAN decision-making process can be found in the evolution of the ASEAN position regarding the proposal of Australian Prime Minister Robert Hawke for a Pacific OECD. ASEAN was quick to agree on a long-standing element of its position—that no efforts at Pacific Basin economic cooperation should be allowed to denigrate or undermine ASEAN. But when it came to the question of who would be invited to Hawke's November 1989 meeting to discuss the idea, ASEAN unity showed some cracks over the question whether to invite the PRC, Taiwan, and Hong Kong. In the end, none of the three was invited, even though the absence of Hong Kong will deal a sharp blow to its hopes of maintaining autonomy on trade matters after 1997. Other countries wanted to see Hong Kong participate, but without a clear signal from ASEAN they reluctantly accepted a PRC veto of Hong Kong on the basis that this was a ministerial meeting and Hong Kong could not attend because it was not a "country." ASEAN, however, is trying to keep its options open by insisting that Hawke's November meeting be no more than an exploratory session.

Another major factor affecting cooperation is ASEAN's desire to maintain close ties with the United States, or at a minimum, a strong U.S. presence in the region. From a political and security point of view, the United States can help offset PRC and Soviet influence. On the economic side, the United States can offset Japan's growing influence in a number of areas. The U.S. market remains a top priority for ASEAN, and U.S. investment is valuable not only as a means to developing U.S. marketing relationships but also as a source of technology transfer. This ASEAN desire to keep the United States engaged in the region appears to be the underlying reason for ASEAN's renewed interest in the so-called ASEAN-U.S. Initiative, now known as the AUI. ASEAN and U.S. officials are now working toward a framework agreement for economic cooperation that will provide a statement of principles designed to guide a consultative mechanism and a specific work program. This closer cooperation is a natural outgrowth of the ongoing U.S.-ASEAN economic dialogue, which has provided a forum for government-to-government consultation since 1977.

The ASEAN members can see that the movement toward a Pacific Basin economic organization could erode ASEAN's influence and importance. They were perplexed when the United States moved to support Hawke's plan to accelerate government-to-government consideration of such an organization. It remains to be seen whether ASEAN can accept the U.S. argument that the Pacific Basin talks are on a slow policy-level track that need not interfere with progress on the specific bilateral goals of greater U.S.-ASEAN cooperation that could be achieved through the AUI.

Alternative Forms of Asia-Pacific Cooperation

PBEC. The Pacific Basin Economic Council (PBEC) is a private-sector group of business leaders that has been encouraging government leaders and academics to focus on the practical realities that must be confronted in the everyday world of business. They have correctly emphasized that in today's interdependent global economy, any government effort toward cooperation could become ineffectual or counterproductive if the private sector is not fully engaged from the outset. PBEC is composed of member committees from Australia, New Zealand, Canada, Chile, Japan, Korea, New Zealand, Mexico, Taiwan, and the United States. Unfortunately, ASEAN business interests are not well represented, although some key business leaders attend the International General meetings.

PECC. The Pacific Economic Cooperation Conference (PECC) is a good forum for continued discussion of possible Pacific Basin economic cooperation because it includes business leaders and academics as well as government officials in their private capacities. Its informal, nonofficial character has facilitated broad participation from countries in the Pacific. ASEAN has played a role in the group, but its representatives have clearly questioned whether PECC activities would be in the interests of a stronger ASEAN.

Consultations. A cogent case can be made that existing institutions and consultative mechanisms are adequate. One powerful argument is the fact that the dynamic growth in the Pacific region is the envy of the world and it has occurred without a Pacific-wide organization of government officials directing and controlling it. Problems in trade and investment have been overcome either directly by the private sector or through bilateral or multilateral government-to-government negotiations and consultations. The World Bank and the Asian Development Bank have played a major role in the region's development, as have European aid donors. Pacific Basin nations are active in the GATT and the OECD. Bilateral consultative mechanisms are strong and effective. In fact, most of the practical trade and investment problems are best resolved bilaterally, with governments encouraging solutions that are mutually beneficial and that reduce barriers to private-sector cooperation.

One can also question the need for a regional cooperation institution by asking what the substantive contribution of such an organization might be. What stands out when viewed from this perspective is the fact that there appears to be little urgent need for a regional institution because the problems to be addressed—trade, finance, investment, the environment, communications, technology transfer, and education—are global problems.

Indeed, if one looks at the most successful model of economic cooperation, namely ASEAN, we see that it has placed high priority on maintaining an open, consultative position toward non-ASEAN and even nonregional countries. This is epitomized by the fact that the European Community is not only a regular dialogue partner throughout the year but is also invited to the ASEAN Post-Ministerial meetings, where all of ASEAN's dialogue partners discuss regional and global issues. ASEAN can be expected to urge that a similar open and nonpreferential approach be taken by any Pacific Basin consultative group that may emerge, or at a minimum, that such a group not create a preferential trade bloc.

Given the political costs of selecting or rejecting members of a new regional organization, a case can be made for using existing organizations to promote improved consultation. This is particularly true at a time of global political change and interdependence when exclusion from a new group can create needless tensions and resentment. In keeping with this spirit of global cooperation, an alternative approach using existing institutions might include the following steps: (1) the opening of the existing regional consultative mechanism (i.e., the ASEAN Post-Ministerial meeting) to full participation by other regional partners, such as Korea, which currently has second-class status; (2) the introduction of more Pacific Basin countries into existing coordinating groups, such as the OECD, where, for example, Korean and Singapore membership would make sense; and (3) ASEAN and Korea should be encouraged to present their views to the seven-nation Economic Summit.

Free-Trade Area. A free-trade area for the Pacific would almost by definition result in a preferential trading bloc. Both ASEAN and the United States have strongly opposed any concrete steps toward such a goal, although some have suggested that discussion of such an idea would be useful in inducing the European Community to keep the EC market open after 1992. The idea of free-trade areas is useful as an analytical tool. Studying how a free-trade area would work helps to reveal the current barriers to competition, which interest groups and lobbies are being subsidized, and how much this is costing taxpayers and consumers. In fact, such a study might be considered a prerequisite to taking further steps toward creating some mechanism for Pacific Basin economic cooperation.

Asia-Pacific OECD. This idea has been given a strong push forward by Australian Prime Minister Hawke. ASEAN has been extremely cautious about this initiative, which it sees as having the potential to weaken ASEAN and undermine an open trading system. ASEAN's many objections have been met by promises that nothing would be done to damage ASEAN and reassurances that there are no plans to set up a preferential trading bloc. ASEAN remains wary of creating another institution but has gone as far as offering to host the next meeting to discuss the idea. This is being interpreted as an attempt to preempt the leadership role in order to prevent this effort from undermining ASEAN. The U.S. position toward the Hawke initiative was laid out in testimony before the Senate Foreign Relations Committee by Assistant Secretary of State Richard H. Solomon on September 21, 1989. Many of the points made in that statement coincide with concerns expressed by ASEAN over the need to avoid a preferential trading bloc in the Pacific. Solomon stated: "It is imperative that any mechanism that evolves from current consultations complement existing institutions and processes such as the Uruguay Round of the GATT, the OECD, and ASEAN. It must help, not hinder, efforts to keep the global trading system as open as possible. We seek to create neither a regional superbloc nor a new international bureaucracy."

The U.S. support for ASEAN and its concerns over the Hawke initiative are clear in the following paragraph of Solomon's testimony: "Mr. Chairman, while seeing great promise in this effort, we also are clear-eyed about the difficulties inherent in forging a new institution. Building a consensus requires, among other things, assuring the ASEAN countries that a new mechanism will not weaken their collective efforts or dilute their identity as a regional association."

Other Approaches. Consistent with ASEAN's basic wisdom of consensus and open dialogue with all parties, as symbolized by the Post-Ministerial Dialogue, the new approach would be one of total openness and flexibility—in essence, a fundamental and revolutionary rejection of the regional institutional approach in favor of global cooperation based on mutual benefit with whichever partners are prepared to cooperate.

Measures to Be Taken

Short-term Measures. ASEAN could take the lead in ongoing Pacific economic cooperation discussions to ensure that the 1990 ASEAN Post-Ministerial meeting clearly rejects a preferential regional approach. Instead, it should make the Pacific a symbol of peace and worldwide cooperation. The meeting should also declare full support for the success of the Uruguay Round as essential to the success of an interdependent world economy.

Medium-term Measures. The Post-Ministerial participants should also be urged to ensure that Europe 1992 does not turn inward, that the U.S. Congress does not make Japan the new enemy, and that Japan continues to open up to the world with cooperation in trade and aid.

Long-term Measures. The 1991 Post-Ministerial meeting could be regarded as the head-of-state-level meeting that could usher in a new era of international cooperation between East and West, North and South, Atlantic and Pacific that fully recognizes the benefits of global economic interdependence.

Notes

1. Seiji Naya, Kernial S. Sandhu, Michael Plummer, and Narongchai Akrasanee, "ASEAN-U.S. Initiative Joint Final Report," East-West Center, Honolulu, Hawaii, and Institute of Southeast Asian Studies, Singapore (Singapore: Kinkeong Printing Co., PPE, Ltd., April 12, 1989).

8

Taiwan's Future Role in International and Regional Economic Cooperation

Yuan-li Wu

What role will Taiwan be capable of playing in the future economic and overall development of the Asia-Pacific region? What is that role likely to be in reality? Economic cooperation between different countries can be understood in two different ways. Apart from specific projects jointly financed or operated by the nationals of more than one country, or functional cooperation, such as in foreign aid by two countries to a third country, the term "economic cooperation" may be understood more broadly. For instance, agreement among the central banks of certain countries to keep a reserve currency and internationally used unit of account like the U.S. dollar within a certain range of fluctuation relative to their own currencies requires that the monetary policies of these countries be "coordinated." This requirement is, of course, far from being easily accomplished. Or, if one regional power tries to promote exports and, therefore, to increase exports to another, while the other wishes to reduce imports in general and, therefore, to reduce imports from the first country, policy conflict can easily arise. To speak of such "policy conflict" in turn presupposes the existence of national economic and perhaps also "industrial policies" as well as the ability of national governments to enforce them. Hence, possibilities for regional economic cooperation are more easily mentioned rhetorically in international forums than planned in practice. As long as we have nation-states that are also free-market economies, the role of any country in a region's economic future cannot be fully understood before we know how its economy will develop, what that country's economic policy is, how the unfolding of the policy might impact others, and how both the country's economic policy and development have taken the corresponding factors of other nations into account. The last point is of course especially true for a trade-oriented economy like Taiwan.

To answer the questions posed in the preceding paragraph I shall begin by describing the economic policy of the Republic of China (ROC) government on Taiwan. Implementation of its economic policy is predicated upon the ongoing, extremely active process of domestic political restructuring taking place in Taiwan as well as changes occurring in the international environment. Although the domestic political process is still fraught with uncertainties, a few clear indications became quite discernible during the late 1980s. At the same time, circumstances outside of Taiwan also have been changing. Not the least important of these changes are the unstable domestic political and economic conditions of the PRC; Taiwan's relationship is being gradually adjusted, on the whole, in the latter's favor. Other major external factors that can have a vital impact on Taiwan are the trade and investment policies of the United States, the EC, and Japan. Taiwan will have to make the best of the interactions among these three; the issues involved include (1) U.S. policies on the U.S. trade and federal budget deficits, the popular call in the United States to enhance the competitiveness of U.S. enterprises, and the vigorous prosecution of trade talks, (2) the energetic policy drives of Japan in all directions, modified by the country's new domestic politics, and (3) the pressures posed by the 1992 target date for European economic integration. Every one of these global developments will present serious challenges to Taiwan as it tries to become a global player. But how does Taiwan perceive these problems, and what are the public and private sectors trying to do about them?

Taiwan's Overall Economic Policy

Lack of space precludes a discussion of Taiwan's economic development during the post–World War II period. Those who are interested in the background of this topic may wish to look at some other accounts in a very rich literature.[1] Suffice it to say for our purposes that after three decades of sustained, rapid growth, the economy of Taiwan was characterized in 1989 by an unusually equitable income distribution, a high official foreign exchange reserve predicated on years of export surplus (which is now being threatened by exchange appreciation at the behest of the United States), relatively high wages and rising labor costs, a high rate of domestic savings in excess of domestic investment, and far too much money and liquidity in the hands of the public—which presents the real threat of price inflation, which the central bank is trying to defuse. This domestic scene is complicated by external pressures, coming almost entirely from the United States, to reduce exports—and increase imports—and to appreciate the New Taiwan (NT) dollar (see Table 8.1). Both Taiwanese economists and Americans also

Table 8.1 Exchange Rate of the U.S. Dollar in Selected Asian Countries (per U.S. dollar)

End of Month	China (yuan)	Hong Kong (dollar)	Japan (yen)	Singapore (dollar)	South Korea (won)	Taiwan (dollar)
1985						
Jan.	2.8027	7.7985	254.47	2.2065	830.10	39.10
Feb.	2.8446	7.7950	258.70	2.2300	836.90	39.15
Mar.	2.8129	7.7950	252.85	2.2200	850.60	39.60
Apr.	2.8536	7.7780	252.55	2.2220	859.80	39.86
May	2.8366	7.7715	251.55	2.2200	869.00	39.75
June	2.8707	7.7610	248.80	2.2400	872.90	39.77
July	2.8706	7.7450	237.40	2.1910	872.80	39.99
Aug.	2.9022	7.8015	237.08	2.2555	883.40	40.45
Sept.	2.9607	7.7800	221.25	2.1375	891.90	40.36
Oct.	3.1935	7.7920	212.60	2.1320	892.90	40.05
Nov.	3.1935	7.7980	201.05	2.0910	890.80	39.90
Dec.	3.1935	7.8050	201.95	2.1150	891.50	39.91
1986						
Jan.	3.1935	7.8025	192.65	2.1450	891.30	39.53
Feb.	3.1999	7.7970	181.30	2.1450	885.60	39.16
Mar.	3.2031	7.8150	179.55	2.1720	883.60	38.94
Apr.	3.3175	7.7860	167.70	2.1890	884.50	38.57
May	3.1935	7.8050	171.95	2.2260	887.60	38.33
June	3.1935	7.8095	165.30	2.1982	888.30	38.10
July	3.7040	7.8075	155.30	2.1790	884.10	38.07
Aug.	3.6943	7.8030	155.95	2.1575	880.07	37.75
Sept.	3.7150	7.8007	153.40	2.1705	879.20	36.76
Oct.	3.7150	7.7985	161.30	2.1885	874.00	36.55
Nov.	3.7128	7.7850	162.95	2.1910	868.90	36.41
Dec.	3.7128	7.7900	159.85	2.1770	861.60	35.69
1987						
Jan.	3.7220	7.7690	152.25	2.1280	857.90	35.14
Feb.	3.7128	7.7935	153.08	2.1315	855.90	34.98
Mar.	3.7128	7.7975	146.10	2.1335	848.50	34.36
Apr.	3.7220	7.8020	139.20	2.1285	838.60	33.53
May	3.7220	7.8065	143.15	2.1175	825.80	31.59
June	3.7220	7.8065	146.65	2.1205	811.70	31.02
July	3.7220	7.8000	150.70	2.1105	808.10	30.98
Aug.	3.7220	7.8070	141.95	2.1050	807.70	30.05
Sept.	3.7220	7.8065	146.35	2.0930	806.10	30.05
Oct.	3.7218	7.8060	138.40	2.0685	804.40	29.93
Nov.	3.7220	7.7875	134.85	2.0365	798.40	29.54
Dec.	3.7220	7.7580	123.30	1.9925	795.10	28.50

Table 8.1 (Continued)

1988						
Jan.	3.7220	7.8000	127.00	2.0180	789.50	28.46
Feb.	3.7220	7.7970	128.35	2.0110	771.60	28.57
Mar.	3.7220	7.8030	124.75	2.0050	750.80	28.59
Apr.	3.7221	7.8150	124.50	2.0015	740.30	28.60
May	3.7127	7.8148	124.86	2.0165	734.40	28.57
June	3.7221	7.8015	132.90	20.470	728.70	28.82
July	3.7220	7.8095	132.38	2.0360	724.30	28.58
Aug.	3.7221	7.8032	134.95	2.0385	721.70	28.72
Sept.	3.7220	7.8089	134.35	2.0403	716.25	28.93
Oct.	3.7220	7.8115	125.67	2.0010	704.10	28.58
Nov.	3.7187	7.8065	121.92	1.9424	688.00	28.10
Dec.	3.7220	7.8090	125.80	1.9460	684.90	28.19
1989						
Jan.	3.7220	7.8000	129.25	1.9350	682.70	27.65
Feb.	3.7227	7.8000	126.60	1.9255	673.00	27.75
Mar.	3.7220	7.7875	133.40	1.9600	672.80	27.20
Apr.	3.7220	7.7810	132.10	1.9468	666.00	26.91
May	3.7227	7.7765	142.90	1.9545	666.00	25.90
June	3.7214	7.7950	143.65	1.9590	658.72	25.72
July	3.7214	7.8050	139.55	1.9560	659.71	25.53
Aug.	3.7214	7.8075	144.25	1.9650	670.70	25.42
Sept.	3.7220	7.8040	140.34	1.9665	667.80	25.38
Oct.	3.7221	7.8080	141.90	1.9550	671.60	25.70
Nov.	3.7214	7.8135	142.85	1.9510	674.00	25.96
Dec.	4.7214	7.8085	144.00	1.8900	677.40	25.96
1990						
Jan.	4.7216	7.8110	145.30	1.8625	685.70	25.95
Feb.	4.7225	7.8075	148.65	1.8645	687.30	25.98
Mar.	4.7250	7.8140	156.45	1.8855	691.57	26.40
1st Q 85	2.8201	7.7962	255.34	2.2188	839.20	39.28
1st Q 86	3.1988	7.8048	184.50	2.1540	886.80	39.21
1st Q 87	3.7159	7.7869	150.48	2.1310	854.10	34.83
1st Q 88	3.7220	7.8000	126.70	2.0113	770.63	28.54
1st Q 89	3.7222	7.7958	129.75	1.9402	676.17	27.53
1st Q 90	4.7230	7.8108	150.13	1.8708	688.19	26.11
1st Q 85 to						
1st Q 86	+13.4	+0.1	-27.8	- 2.9	+ 5.7	- 0.2
1st Q 86 to						
1st Q 87	+16.2	-0.2	-18.4	- 1.1	- 3.7	-11.2

Table 8.1 (Continued)

1st Q 87 to 1st Q 88	+0.2	+0.2	-15.8	-5.6	-9.8	-18.0
1st Q 88 to 1st Q 89	neg.	+0.05	+2.4	-3.5	-12.2	-3.5
1st Q 88 to 1st Q 90	+26.9	+0.2	+15.7	-3.6	+1.8	-5.1
1st Q 85 to 1st Q 89	+32.0	-0.005	-49.2	-12.5	-19.4	-30.0
1st Q 85 to 1st Q 90	+67.5	+0.2	-41.2	-15.7	-18.0	-33.5

Source: The Wall Street Journal, various issues, January 1985-March 1990.

have called upon the ROC government to restructure aggregate demand toward the domestic market. The U.S. pressures on Taiwan are similar to those applied to Japan.

Restructuring of Foreign Trade

Given these conditions, Taiwan has tried for the past several years, especially since 1987, when the NT dollar began to appreciate against the U.S. dollar, to reorient its exports, and especially real export growth, away from the U.S. market and to reduce import tariffs and nontariff restrictions. Together with other measures deliberately aimed at increasing imports from the United States, this policy has brought about a gradual shift in the market structure of export demand.

The restructuring of the current account balance and market orientation in external trade has been slower than it might have been for several reasons. As imports from the United States became cheaper for Taiwan's buyers, EC and at times even some Japanese exports to Taiwan, in spite of the appreciation of their currencies, also became cheaper and their sales to Taiwan often expanded faster than U.S. sales (see Table 8.2). Somehow, they have been more competitive. As for Taiwan's exports, appreciation of its currency reduced the price competitiveness of Taiwan products simultaneously to European, U.S., and other buyers in comparison with the products of Taiwan's competitors (see Table 8.3 and 8.4). The U.S. policy to talk non-U.S. currencies up was targeted successively in Asia, first at Japan, then at Taiwan, and finally at Korea; it did not increase the

Table 8.2 Taiwan's Merchandise Imports from Selected Developed Countries (in thousands of U.S. dollars)

	1984 Average Value	Index	December 1986 Value	Index	December 1987 Value	Index	November 1988 Value	Index
France	18,537	100	26,078	141	40,642	219	60,284	325
UK	24,530	100	30,096	123	57,969	236	157,997	644
FRG	64,002	100	108,180	169	150,894	235	217,502	340
Netherlands	20,729	100	37,714	182	49,432	238	48,354	233
U.S.	420,137	100	502,520	120	875,887	208	1,032,877	246
Japan	536,821	100	818,692	152	1,084,274	202	1,370,016	255
World	1,829,924	100	2,273,900	124	3,335,948	182	4,310,777	235
*	127,798	100	202,068	158	298,937	234	484,137	379

* = France + UK + FRG + Netherlands.

Source: ROC Ministry of Finance, <u>Chung-hua-min-kuo Chin-ch'u-k'ou Mou-yi T'ung-chi yueh-pao</u> (Monthly Statistics of Exports and Imports, ROC, November 1988), January 20, 1989.

competitiveness of U.S. products in terms of quality or the dollar supply prices.

The reorientation of Taiwan's exports to non-U.S. markets has been slow for the additional reason that Taiwan exporters have long neglected these markets—because many U.S. buyers come directly to look for suppliers and the U.S. market has been more open while direct buyer contacts with Europeans and distributional channels in Europe take time to build. In this regard, Taiwan recently has opened exhibition centers in Dusseldorf, Hamburg, and Rotterdam. Other export promotion efforts have led to the removal of restrictions for direct commerce with Eastern Europe and for indirect trade with both the PRC and the Soviet Union, which can now take place legally. Visa restrictions and delays imposed by many of Taiwan's trading partners for fear of offending the PRC also have been falling away.

Product restructuring on the supply side, which started earlier, has now been superimposed on the restructuring of export markets. Although recognition of these twin developments as a prerequisite of the continuation of economic growth dates well over a decade ago, the shift in emphasis toward "technology-intensive" products began in earnest in the late 1970s. The U.S. diplomatic derecognition of Taiwan supplied a powerful impetus. The establishment of the Hsinchu Science Park in July 1979, which followed closely upon the diplomatic blow, may be regarded as the benchmark of this all-out effort. With nearly a decade of history behind it, 103 firms had

Table 8.3 U.S. Trade Balance with Selected Asian Countries

	U.S. Trade Deficit in 1st Q 1985[a]	Increase in U.S. Trade Deficit Between 1st Q 1985 and 1st Q 1987 In Value[a]	Increase in U.S. Trade Deficit Between 1st Q 1985 and 1st Q 1987 In Percent (1st Q 1985 = 100)	Increase in U.S. Trade Deficit Between 1st Q 1985 and 1st Q 1988 In Value[a]	Increase in U.S. Trade Deficit Between 1st Q 1985 and 1st Q 1988 In Percent (1st Q 1985 = 100)	% Change in Value of One U.S. Dollar in Local Currency (−) = $ down (+) = Local down 1st Q 1985 to 1st Q 1986	1st Q 1986 to 1st Q 1987	1st Q 1987 to 1st Q 1988
Two Asian NICs:								
S. Korea	822	+1,130	+137.5	+1,482	+180.3	+5.7	−3.7	−9.8
Singapore	149	+256	+171.8	+410	+275.2	−2.9	−1.1	−5.6
	971	+1,386	+142.7	+1,892	+194.8			
Hong Kong	1,116	+131	+11.7	−36	−3.2	+0.1	−0.2	+0.17
PRC	59	+683	+1,157.6	+754	+1,278.0	+13.4	+16.2	+0.16
PRC + Hong Kong	1,175	+814		+69.3	+718	+61.1		
All Four Above	2,146	+2,200	+102.5	+2,610	+121.6			
Taiwan	2,531	+1,826	+72.1	+338	+13.3	−0.2	−11.2	−18.0
Japan	9,378	+5,227	+55.7	+3,535	+37.7	−27.8	−18.4	−15.8

[a] in millions of U.S. dollars.

Source: U.S. Department of Commerce, Survey of Current Business, June 1987, vol. 67, no. 6, pp. 61-63; December 1988, vol. 68, no. 12, p. 26.

Table 8.4 U.S. Trade Balance with the PRC and Taiwan, 1981-1988 (in millions of U.S. dollars)

Year	U.S. Imports from Taiwan	U.S. Exports to Taiwan	Balance	U.S. Imports from China	U.S. Exports to China	Balance
1981	8,048	4,263	-3,785	1,892	3,599	+1,707
1982	8,893	4,366	-4,527	2,284	2,912	+628
1983	11,205	4,561	-6,644	2,244	2,163	-81
1984	14,768	4,840	-9,928	3,065	2,989	-76
1985	16,396	4,571	-11,825	3,862	3,800	-62
1986	19,791	5,389	-14,402	4,771	3,077	-1,694
1987	24,622	7,246	-17,376	6,294	3,468	-2,826
1988	24,804	12,131	-12,673	8,512	5,039	-3,473
1989	24,326	11,323	-13,481	11,988	5,807	-6,181

(-) = U.S. trade deficit.
(+) = U.S. trade surplus.

Source: U.S. Department of Commerce, customs value for imports, f.a.s. value for exports.

been approved for establishment inside the Park by early December 1988[2] and were expected to account for $2 billion of Taiwan's $60 billion annual exports in 1989. While the Hsinchu Science Park member firms as a group may lead the way in product upgrading, the effort to do so in terms of embodied technology and higher value-added has touched Taiwan's manufacturing industry as a whole. Thus, during the first nine months of 1988, of the $18.7 billion in U.S. imports from Taiwan, the top twenty items (in terms of seven-digit tariff schedule of the U.S. [TSUS] numbers) accounted for $3.9 billion (20.7 percent), and of these twenty, nine (9.8 percent of the $18.7 billion) were electronic and electrical products (excluding such simple devices as ceiling fans), having replaced textiles, footwear, and the like of earlier years.

External Political Factors in Economic Restructuring

Two political obstacles to the restructuring of Taiwan's external markets have been (1) the lack of formal diplomatic relations between the ROC and the majority of Taiwan's trading partners, and (2) the ROC's absence from most international organizations and agreements like the IMF, the World Bank, and GATT. This unfavorable diplomatic situation started initially as an exercise in the Hallstein Doctrine by the ROC government. This doctrine espouses the principle that "there is only one China and the ROC government is its only legitimate government," so that the ROC would cut off relations with any country upon the latter's formal recognition of the PRC. But the same doctrine has progressively worked against Taiwan since the PRC's entry into the UN in 1971 and the switch of formal U.S. recognition to the PRC in 1979.

This diplomatic disability has created numerous annoying problems that make the expansion of trade and other contacts by Taiwan with other countries sometimes unnecessarily difficult. The desired resumption of participation by Taiwan as a signatory to GATT, for example, has become a political issue of some sensitivity because of PRC objection and the PRC's current application; the seating of Taiwan, a founding member, at the Asian Development Bank's meetings has for years been a matter of speculation, also because of PRC maneuvering among the bank's members.[3] However, as the phenomenal expansion of the Taiwan economy and its foreign trade since 1971 amply demonstrates, these diplomatic disabilities have not been able to put a real brake on Taiwan's economic growth. Instead, they have exacted a more strenuous effort.

Domestic Political Restructuring and Liberalization

On the domestic scene, political restructuring has been taking place rapidly in Taiwan. Skipping details, it has involved the process of giving birth to a functioning democracy, beginning with the step-by-step legalization since late 1986 of an opposition political party—now rapidly becoming several opposition parties—and the process of learning by all parties to disagree peacefully with mutual respect and to accommodate competing ideas according to generally accepted rules.

Planning for political restructuring and liberalization began in the government party (the Nationalist Party or Kuomintang, abbreviated as KMT) and was very much the handiwork of Chiang Ching-kuo, who died in January 1988. On the thirty-eighth anniversary of the 1947 Constitution in December 1985, Chiang, then rounding off the second year of his second six-year term as president, declared that upon finishing his term, he would neither permit a member of his family to try to succeed him nor allow the emergence of military rule.[4] In the following spring (1986), in his capacity as KMT chairman, he appointed a special task force to draw up a strategy of party reform. The task force's report covered six points:

1. Removing martial law and replacing it with new laws safeguarding national security;
2. Legalizing the formation of new political parties under new laws governing civic associations and revised election and recall laws;

3. Overhauling the memberships of the three elected bodies in the central government (the National Assembly, which elects the president and the vice-president, the Legislative Yuan, and the Control Yuan);
4. Further reforming Taiwan's local government;
5. Reforming the KMT internally regarding its own role, structure, and leadership;
6. Strengthening the deteriorating public order and social morals that had come with economic prosperity and social liberalization.

As one looks back, the first two tasks were essentially completed or nearly completed by the time of Chiang's death. President Lee Teng-hui, who was Chiang's vice president, was sworn in within four hours after Chiang's death, thus fulfilling Chiang's announcement of December 1985. Items 3, 4, and 5 have been the principal preoccupation of the KMT and the ROC government under President Lee and his premiers (Yu Kuo-hua and, since June 1, 1989, Lee Huan). All these vigorous activities revolve around Taiwan's new democratic party politics as reported by a highly competitive and liberated press.

With a free and expanding press, which has yet to develop its own distinction between unbridled free expression and responsible and truthful reporting, the year of 1988, after the death of Chiang Ching-kuo, witnessed numerous street demonstrations and many brawls in the legislature by ambitious politicians engaged in testing the boundaries of their newly gained political freedom as against good taste and civility. The ostensible argument of the opposition, the essence of which cannot be faulted, is that, above all, many members of the Legislative Yuan, which enacts laws, and the National Assembly, which functions as an "electoral college," have long lost their constituencies on the Chinese mainland. After long wrangling and many demonstrations and arguments, the legislature finally agreed to encourage the members of these two institutions to retire voluntarily. As most of the members are well advanced in years, the final date of their removal from the active political scene is likely to come well within a decade, perhaps in only a very few years.[5]

But the real political questions are who will replace them and what will be the political inclinations of the new members? The opposition, which has learned much from parliamentary tactics of various radical groups outside Taiwan, apparently hopes to remove as many of these incumbents as possible—immediately and in toto if it had its way—by making it hard, if not impossible, for the KMT government to govern and the legislature in the meantime to pass laws. The KMT government, on the other hand, has successfully refused to be goaded into acts that might be interpreted by the media as unconstitutional or repressive, but it has done so, however, at the cost of being criticized by the man on the street as being indecisive, weak, and rudderless. After the reelection of Lee Teng-hui as president in his own right in March 1990, retirement of all the mainland-elected legislators now promises to take place in about two years.

Thus, until recently, while the government could truthfully claim that it had weathered the worst initial stages of the transition to a more democratic governance and that orderly government might soon be forthcoming, there were a number of items on the debit side. Institutional reform, e.g., in banking, has been delayed but remains on track. Insufficient care, according to some, has been exercised in handling new labor demands and ad hoc concessions to environmentalists. A tendency of overindulgence in social welfare measures has also been observed. All these are at the cost of Taiwan's international competitiveness. Yet the controversies are essentially matters of judgment; whether any decision is correct depends upon the rate of real growth of the national product and its distribution, and so far a real growth of nearly 7 percent still appears possible in 1989. Perhaps, after all is said and done, the adverse economic effects of the new politics of 1988–1989 will soon dissipate. At any rate, after the 1989 year-end votes and the March 1990 election for the next president and vice president, Taiwan is finally able to return to its more normal economic concerns.

Diplomatic Shifts

A new turn on the agenda of the ROC government, then headed by Yu Kuo-hua in the Executive Yuan and President Lee Teng-hui took place in the late spring of 1989 when, following a widely acclaimed presidential visit to Singapore, the ROC government sent an official delegation headed by its minister of finance to the regular annual meeting of the Asian Development Bank (ADB) holding forth in Beijing in May. The minister in question, Professor Shirley W. Y. Kuo, is a highly respected economist in Taiwan who had first shown her mettle by reimposing a capital gains tax on the wildly gyrating stock market. The ADB move is another indication of Taiwan's fearless but carefully planned steps to assert its position in the international society. Yet at the same time, it is a faint but unmistakable gesture, by virtue of the nature of the meeting and its locale, to the PRC, and the mainland Chinese, of Taiwan's friendly and peaceful attitude and potential helpfulness to the PRC, if only the circumstances were right. In addition, the ROC has now semi-officially floated the slogan of "one Chinese nation but two governments" against the 1979 PRC offer of "one country, two systems." As Premier Yu had earlier visited Singapore and the Caribbean, these official visits constituted a coordinated effort by the successor team to Chiang Ching-kuo. Boldness and a steady hand on the external front have inevitably had an offsetting effect on the domestic policy of patience and caution.

A second major development foreshadowing future changes in Taiwan-mainland relations took place in mid-summer (August) 1989, two months after the June 3-4 massacre of students and civilians in Beijing by Communist troops under the direct orders of Beijing's top leaders. The event, establishment of formal diplomatic relations between Grenada and the Republic of China, which passed unnoticed by most Western readers, was significant for two reasons: At the time, Grenada and the PRC had already recognized each other diplomatically; the event, therefore, constituted one of the first open cases of "dual recognition" of "two Chinas" on the part of a third country. Second, on the Chinese side, following a delay, Beijing responded by "suspending," but not "breaking," diplomatic relations with Grenada.[6] Taiwan, on the other hand, claims that this was merely an exercise of diplomatic "flexibility." As long as the ROC has not recognized Beijing, none of the "taint" of the acceptance of the "two China" concept is with Taiwan. In this case, it was first a result of action by Grenada and, later, at least provisionally, an action initiated by Beijing. Taiwan simply does not acknowledge the existence of a diplomatic relationship (suspended) between Grenada and Beijing as equivalent to its own recognition of "two Chinas."

An even more far-reaching development of long-term consequence was the massacre ordered by Deng Xiaoping (as supreme party "helmsman"), Yang Shangkuen (as PRC president), and Li Peng (as premier) of thousands of pro-democracy demonstrators in Beijing during the early hours of the night of June 3-4, 1989 (Beijing time). This violent suppression of dissent took place in the open view of an army of television and news reporters who had gathered in unprecedented numbers to report on the May 15-18 Deng-Gorbachev Summit to normalize Sino-Soviet relations after a quarter-century's estrangement.

The violent suppression all over the Chinese mainland has had its effect on the PRC's image in foreign eyes and on the economic prospects of the PRC and its future domestic political developments. In contrast, it has enhanced Taiwan's image and made the ROC's efforts to play a larger role in the world community even more credible and welcome.[7]

Political Restructuring and Relations with the Mainland

In the context of Taiwan's domestic politics, a small group in the opposition Democratic Progressive Party (DPP) is both militant and separatist; it desires to declare immediate independence for Taiwan, seemingly in complete disregard of the possible consequences in view of the PRC's repeated statements that such a declaration would constitute one of three separate circumstances that would trigger its use of force against Taiwan.[8] Some members of the public, including businesspeople in both the KMT and the opposition, in their turn have come to view the PRC almost solely as a potential foreign market that has been barely explored. Ignorance about the nature and present chaotic condition of the PRC's economy, plus wishful thinking, characterize many in this group. Still others desire to see a softening of mutual hostility between the two sides of the Taiwan Strait, believing perhaps that trade on a larger scale might be an opening wedge for this purpose, without, however, thinking through how the process should evolve.

On its part, the PRC has for a long time waved as inducements to Taiwan the slogans of trade, postal exchange, and shipping contacts. Until recently, this gesture was interpreted by official Taiwan as a deliberate effort to undermine the island nation's domestic political cohesion. The interpretation was probably quite correct at the time. However, to the surprise of almost all in Taiwan, and perhaps in the PRC, Chiang Ching-kuo himself took the initiative toward the end of 1987 by removing the ban on visits by Taiwan residents (except government employees) to the mainland. This measure was taken against the background of the many complex motives and public attitudes described in the preceding sections. By taking the initiative himself, Chiang preempted his mainland opponents, initiated, as it were, a direct dialogue with people on the mainland, and placated those in Taiwan who desired such contacts. Since trade is likely to expand with increasing visits, the development of increasing economic contacts between Taiwan and the mainland would seem to be inevitable.

As Chiang died in mid-January 1988, no one knows how he would have tried to manage the emerging new relations with the mainland. With his death and the removal of an undisputed authoritative voice in the KMT, and in light of the complex, conflicting, and often inchoate ideas of the opposition and the electorate, "mainland policy" became a major topic of the government's preoccupations in 1988 and, until Taiwan's latest diplomatic coups, competed with election politics for top place on the government's timetable. The political impact of the June 1989 massacre and the repression campaign it unleashed have had the effect of calming down Taiwan's mainland fever and reinjecting a sense of caution and realism.

Taiwan's Mainland Politics and Economic Restructuring

Economically, the restructuring of aggregate demand toward domestic public and private expenditures in Taiwan calls for an increase in spending on the social infrastructure. This calls for a reexamination of local government finance, which cannot be separated from the long-recognized need to revamp the economy's banking institutions and the capital as well as money markets. These items of institutional change are part and parcel of the necessary economic restructuring the island economy must undergo. They are tied to measures impacting on the distribution of income and economic opportunities. But the place of local government finance in the overall structure of revenue and expenditure cannot be fully settled without reexamining the relationship between Taiwan's central and provincial governments. The latter issue in turn calls for a clearer definition by the ROC government of Taiwan in relation to the mainland. If an approach to the latter issue[9] cannot be resolved—one cannot realistically expect a quick resolution of the issue itself, and most people on both sides of the Taiwan Strait probably do not have such expectations—the role of the PRC in Taiwan' s economic future cannot be fully defined in the minds of many businesspeople and investors. Economic relations between Taiwan and the mainland are therefore a major factor in discussions on Taiwan's economic future. Fortunately, in view of the events of 1987-1989, this uncertainty will not preclude us from developing some alternative scenarios and from discussing their relative probability. Depending upon domestic developments in Beijing and the eventual Chinese Communist response to Taiwan's moves, a reduction of these uncertainties by the end of this century is no longer entirely out of reach.

Economic Orientation: Facing the World, Not Just Mainland China

In summary, as of 1989, the Taiwan economy had made more progress in reorienting its foreign trade (excluding trade with the PRC) by redirecting exports away from the United States than in stimulating domestic investment. It had also accelerated its drive toward producing more "technology-intensive" products and upgrading product quality. The expansion of domestic investment may catch up once the political changes that are expected after the 1989-1990 elections have been completed, but a certain time lag cannot be avoided. In the meantime, however, several developments can be anticipated.

First, as of this writing (August 1989), the PRC has begun a period of economic retrenchment in investment as well as in expenditures of foreign exchange for all purposes. The country under Li Peng as premier is slowing down the pace of reform toward a market economy and is moving again toward greater centralization and repression. These readjustments begun after the summer of 1988, however, are by no means unheralded policy shifts taking place for the first time since the beginning of Deng Xiaoping's return to power nearly a decade ago. Additional twists and turns can be expected, at a frequency of perhaps once every two years or so, if the Deng-Yang-Li regime lasts.

In view of the PRC's economic volatility, its long-standing balance-of-payments difficulties, and its associated political instability, one can plausibly assume that the PRC will not offer Taiwan a greatly expanded market or sphere of investment in the next few years.[10] In the longer run, different scenarios can be developed according to the degree of the PRC's political liberalization and its stalled economic reform and growth. Suffice it to point out that the longer run will also present the PRC with immense new uncertainties, including the passing of Deng's relatively firm but diminishing leadership, which may be well before 1997 or even 1992, the crucial dates for Hong Kong and the EC respectively, and the uncertain future of a reformist Soviet Union and its emerging new relationship with the PRC.

Hence, for Taiwan, the most probable element of all possible scenarios focusing on the PRC does not envisage the latter's emergence as an overwhelmingly important economic partner of Taiwan. Of Taiwan's $60 billion annual exports at the current level, perhaps up to 5 percent will be accounted for by the PRC—possibly less.

Second, if the PRC is for all practical purposes not a real contender for Taiwan's expanding economic relations with the rest of the world, the latter developments will no doubt be based upon:

1. Taiwan's drive to reorient exports toward some old but neglected markets outside the United States, especially the EC member countries and other regional economies, e.g., members of ASEAN.
2. Taiwan's increasing interest in investing abroad: portfolio investment centered on territories familiar to its exporters and, second, direct investments, especially in Southeast Asia.
3. Technology, both imported and developed at home, which is becoming available in increasing volume and sophistication, supported by increasing numbers of production engineers and technicians.
4. A new foreign aid program, for which funding has already begun.

During 1987-1988, Taiwan had already become the main source of foreign investment in the Philippines. Taiwan investors have flocked into Thailand and Malaysia. This development of intraregional ties is aided by the presence of Chinese communities possessing historical ties in Southeast Asia in the mercantile, financial, mining, agricultural, and, more recently, manufacturing fields.

Given the availability of both technology and surplus savings for export, Taiwan is in a particularly good position to develop closer ties with prospective new industrializing countries of the second wave; namely, members of ASEAN other than Singapore, which had led the first wave of Asian Newly Industrializing Countries (NICs).

Finally, two intriguing aspects of the expansion of Taiwan's economic role should be mentioned. Taiwan's exports to and investment in some of the Southeast Asian countries can be carried out in cooperation with some of the high-tech and other enterprising firms of the EC and the United

States. Taiwan can serve for these firms as a gateway to the Pacific region. Private Western firms that have difficulty in competing with Japan in this geographical area, especially for after-sale service, maintenance, and parts supply, may wish to join hands with Taiwan. Taiwan, with its technical personnel, proximity to the markets (even closer than Japan), lower wages for technical personnel, and manufacturing capacity, and the available marketing channels provided by Chinese businesspeople on the spot, can support Western firms possessing know-how and vision.

Perhaps some Westerners can be so bold as to think of competing with Japan in the latter's home market. Already Japanese investors and importers are producing goods in Taiwan for export to Japan. Perhaps Western firms can cooperate with their partners in Taiwan for export to Japan as well. The Dutch Philips Company apparently has chosen precisely for these reasons to use Taiwan as such a base in the Far East. This strategy has the potential of being emulated by other Western firms.[11]

In addition, it seems to me that Taiwan's economic role can play an active part in providing technical human resources for the region through the export of both technical services and training. As such, Taiwan must orient itself to other regional powers even as it must also strengthen its ties with the rest of the world. In doing so, it can only hope that the PRC can eventually be convinced that the more successfully Taiwan can develop within the world economy, the more it can eventually be helpful to the Chinese mainland in the latter's much longer march toward development.

Notes

1. See, for instance, Yuan-li Wu, "Taiwan's Open Economy in the Twenty-First Century," in Wolfgang Klenner (ed.), *Trends of Economic Development in East Asia*, (New York: Springer Verlag, 1989), pp. 111–129.

2. Of the 103 firms, 91 were already resident and 80 were in operation. Twenty-eight were foreign firms.

3. See the discussion in the section below entitled "Political Restructuring and Relations with the Mainland."

4. For a succinct report see Yin-mao Kau, "Political Challenges of the Post-Chiang Ching-kuo Era," prepared for the Hearing on Political Development in Taiwan Since the Death of Chiang Ching-kuo, Committee on Foreign Affairs, U.S. House of Representatives, Washington, D.C., May 26, 1988.

5. As of the end of December 1988, the Legislative Yuan (parliament) and the National Assembly (electoral college) were constituted as shown in Table 8.5.

According to the ROC Information Office, a bill was passed January 26, 1989, to allow the older members of these institutions to retire. The numbers of members of the two bodies are expected to be adjusted as shown in Table 8.6.

Table 8.5 Number of Members of the Legislative Yuan and the National Assembly in Taiwan, 1988 Yearend

	Legislative Yuan	National Assembly
Members of Mainland Origin	220	779
Members of Taiwan Origin	78	101
Total	298	880

Since the incumbent members' uncontested seats will pass from the scene, the entire body is likely to be elected and will effectively represent Taiwan by 1992.

6. Indonesia "suspended" diplomatic relations with the PRC in 1964 after the local Communist party's abortive coup to take over control from a group of generals, including then Defense Minister Abdul Haris Nasution. Indonesia promised at the time of Hirohito's funeral to resume formal relations with the PRC. Beijing's decision to "suspend" formal relations with Grenada was commented upon by a PRC diplomat in Hong Kong. See the Central News Daily (international edition), August 13, 1989, p. 1.

7. An unexpected outcome of the massacre of June 3-4, 1989, was the worldwide recognition of the Beijing leaders' lack of confidence in themselves to govern the country without open coercion and the internal divisions within the leadership. The emergence of a pro-democracy front in exile has created an open opposition to the PRC government other than Taiwan, a fact that can open up new political opportunities. The ROC's present policy of giving aid to the PRC students and intellectuals in exile in an effective but low-key manner is well outlined by Yu-ming Shaw, the official spokesman for the ROC government before the San Francisco World Affairs Council on August 3, 1989. Text from the ROC Government Information Office, Taipei.

8. The other two contingencies for the possible use of force would be Taiwan's siding with the Soviet Union and internal unrest in Taiwan. Given the normalization

Table 8.6 Membership Adjustment in the Legislative Yuan and National Assembly (Seats Open to Election in 1989 and 1992)

Year	Legislative Seats Open to Election in Taiwan	Year	National Assembly Seats Open to Election in Taiwan
December 1989			
Before Adjustment	96	1986	82
After Adjustment	130	1992	230
1992	150	1998	375

of PRC-Soviet relations in May 1989 and the opening of Taiwan-Soviet trade, these conditions can not long remain as they now stand.

9. By "approach" we mean the creation of circumstances conducive to mutual agreement rather than negotiations, which are useless and even counterproductive if the favorable conditions and mutual understanding necessary for possible agreement are absent.

10. See Chapter 9 in this book.

11. Such cases can be found in reports of the Council on External Trade, Taiwan's principal trade promotion organization.

9

The Future Role of Hong Kong in the International and Regional Economy

Yuan-li Wu

The Future of the Hong Kong Economy

How will the Hong Kong economy develop during the next decade? In the first years of the twenty-first century? How will Hong Kong as a trading community expand commercial relations with its neighbors in the region and with the rest of the world? What role will and can Hong Kong play both as a source and as a recipient in the international flow of capital and enterprise? And in the transfer of technology, especially in the prosperous market economies of the Asia-Pacific rim? What specific cooperative economic measures can be envisaged in which Hong Kong might play a part?

All of the above and many others are normal economic questions to ask in discussing international economic policy and the future economic prospects of nations. If a country's past economic success has been based upon certain specific favorable conditions, one asks whether these conditions will continue and how they might change. But in the case of Hong Kong in the 1990s, we are faced with abnormal times. Normal economic discussions presuppose certain constant institutional and behavioral parameters. The system of entrepreneurial and business decisions is generally taken for granted in a market economy. The role of private property rights and the judicial system in settling contract performance disputes and defining relations between the government and the private sector are usually assumed to be given. But the 1990s may see radical changes in all of these areas in the case of Hong Kong. To what extent and how they will change the situation for Hong Kong cannot even be speculated upon at this writing (summer 1989). Those who read an earlier draft of this chapter, before June 4, 1989, might have been inclined to think that I was exaggerating the degree of these uncertainties. Some may now begin to think differently. If such a change has come about on the part of observers, this would in itself confirm the gross uncertainty facing Hong Kong's economic future. Hence, no economic discussion on Hong Kong makes real practical sense without a prior discussion and understanding of the ways in which the noneconomic parameters might evolve. Yet the latter changes may well continue throughout the forthcoming decade and longer. Consequently, answers to the many normal economic questions raised in the preceding paragraph would have to be regarded as tentative and applicable only under interim speculative conditions.

Mutual Economic Dependence Between Hong Kong and the PRC

As of the beginning of 1989, Hong Kong's economic condition still appears rosy on the surface. Long known to economists as the epitome of the free market, Hong Kong since the 1970s has become one of the four Asian Newly Industrializing Countries (NICs),[1] that have set new records of sustained, rapid, and steady economic growth. According to preliminary official estimates, Hong Kong registered a gross domestic product, at current prices, of HK$425.6 billion (US$54.6 billion) in 1988—equivalent to HK$74,917 (US$9,604) per capita[2]—which in Asia was second only to the corresponding figures for Japan and Singapore, the latter being another Asian NIC and likewise a city-state. During 1988, Hong Kong's total exports, including both domestic exports and reexports, amounted to HK$493.1 billion (US$63.2 billion); imports were HK$501.2 billion (US$64.3 billion). These magnitudes, comparable to the corresponding statistics of giant China next door (which is about 200 times more populous), testify unmistakably to the vital importance of foreign trade to Hong Kong's everyday life and to that of its neighbors. Reexports from Hong Kong of imported goods amounted to HK$275.4 billion (US$35.3 billion) in 1988, 55.1 percent of total exports, which in turn highlights the historical role of Hong Kong as an entrepôt. But the size of Hong Kong's domestic exports shows that it is a great deal more than an entrepôt or a distribution center for regional commerce. Hong Kong is in fact a light manufacturing center in East Asia in its own right (see Table 9.1).

At a time when businesspeople, politicians, and publicists are all talking about the "Pacific century," another set of vital facts should be mentioned before discussing the future of Hong Kong in the 1990s and beyond. First, the PRC is the destination of a significant portion of Hong Kong's reexports (18 percent in 1988). In the opposite direction, 48 percent of Hong Kong's reexports in the same year originated from mainland China.[3] (See Table 9.2.) Thus, for the world's traders, Hong Kong still is a gateway to China

Table 9.1 The Gross Domestic Product, Foreign Trade, Population, and Basic Financial Statistics of Hong Kong

		1983	1987	1988
GDP (1980 market prices)	HK$billion	164.6	229.1*	246.0**
(current prices)		207.6	368.2	425.6**
Total Domestic Exports (f.o.b.)	HK$billion	104.4	195.3	217.7
Reexports (f.o.b.)	HK$billion	56.3	182.8	275.4
Total Domestic and Reexports	HK$billion	160.7	378.0+	493.1
Total Imports (c.i.f.)	HK$billion	175.4	377.9	498.8
Population (mid-year)	Million Persons	5.34	5.61	5.68
Labor Force++	Million Persons	2.60	2.78	2.79
Per Capita GDP	HK$			
1980 Market Prices		30,785	40,813*	43,308**
Current Market Prices		38,832	65,602*	74,917**
Basic Money Supply (M1)	HK$billion	30.9	81.9	88.8
Prices				
GDP Deflator	1980=100	126.1	160.7	173.0
Urban Consumer Price Index	Oct. 84–Sept. 85 x 100	90	109	118

* Provisional estimate.
** Preliminary estimate.
+ Rounding error included.
++ Based on general household surveys in August-October each year.

Source: Census and Statistics Department, General Statistics Section, Government of Hong Kong, Hong Kong in Figures, 1989.

in both directions, as it was in the nineteenth century. Second, the same Hong Kong trade statistics show that the U.S. market accounted for 34 percent of Hong Kong's total reexports in 1988; a sizable portion of these goods imported by the United States, including textiles, apparel, and other manufactures from Hong Kong firms located in China, was produced in mainland China.[4] Finally, in 1988, 31.2 percent of Hong Kong's total imports came from the PRC, including fresh produce, other food stuffs, water, and energy; the latter will increase after the completion of the nuclear power plant at Daiyawan, which is still under construction. These statistics should suffice to convince anyone that the Hong Kong economy is highly dependent on China both as a market and as a supplier.

However, this economic dependence is more mutual than one-sided. First, Hong Kong is not only the largest single market of the PRC's exports (35 percent in 1987), but these Chinese exports include a large degree of

Table 9.2 Hong Kong's Direction of Foreign Trade (value in billions of HK dollars)

	1983 Value	1983 Percent	1987 Value	1987 Percent	1988 Value	1988 Percent
Domestic exports (f.o.b.)						
EC	23.1	22.1	42.1	21.5	47.8	21.9
Commonwealth Countries	20.1	19.2	31.2	16.0	36.0	16.5
United States	43.8	41.9	72.8	37.3	72.9	33.5
China	6.2	5.9	27.9	14.3	38.0	17.4
F.R.G.	8.0	7.7	14.9	7.6	16.2	7.4
UK	8.5	8.1	12.9	6.6	15.5	7.1
Japan	3.9	3.7	9.5	4.9	11.4	5.2
Total	104.4	100.0	195.3	100.0	217.7	100.0
Reexports (f.o.b.)						
EC	3.0	5.3	17.8	9.7	29.6	10.7
Commonwealth Countries	9.7	17.2	22.0	12.0	30.8	11.2
United States	8.0	14.2	32.5	17.8	49.5	18.0
China	12.2	21.7	60.2	32.9	94.9	34.4
Taiwan	3.5	6.2	9.7	5.3	14.1	5.1
Republic of Korea	2.4	4.3	9.0	4.9	11.8	4.3
Japan	3.2	5.7	9.8	5.4	17.4	6.3
Total	56.3	100.0	182.8	100.0	275.4	100.0
Imports (c.i.f.)						
EC	20.4	11.6	41.7	11.0	51.7	10.4
Commonwealth Countries	25.4	14.5	40.6	10.7	51.7	10.4
China	42.8	24.2	117.4	31.1	155.6	31.2
Japan	40.3	23.0	71.9	19.0	93.0	18.6
Taiwan	12.4	7.1	33.3	8.8	44.4	8.9
United States	19.2	10.9	32.2	8.5	41.3	8.3
Republic of Korea	5.0	2.8	17.0	4.5	26.3	5.3
Total	175.4	100.0	377.9	100.0	498.8	100.0

Source: Census and Statistics Department, General Statistics Section, Government of Hong Kong, Hong Kong in Figures, 1989.

goods and services that are indistinguishable from those produced for China's domestic consumption. Because of Hong Kong's ethnic Chinese population, sale of these goods in Hong Kong does not present the problem of market acceptance that would appear if a shift to other markets were to be attempted. Second, apart from merchandise exports to Hong Kong, the PRC earns dividends, interest, and financial and other service income from Hong Kong. Many Chinese-owned investments in Hong Kong are really PRC state investments. Many, including, for instance, the group of Chinese banks,[5] were originally private Chinese investments with head offices in mainland China that were expropriated after 1949. In terms of the PRC's total foreign exchange income and net foreign assets, Hong Kong accounts for a much larger share than its foreign trade dependence on China alone would show.

The economic relations between Hong Kong and China described above have been true for many years, and the facts are well known to both sides. Rational behavior would seem to suggest that both sides should wish to see the same relations continue. Since the inauguration of Deng Xiaoping's policy at the beginning of the 1980s to modernize China through economic reform and expanding contacts with the West and Japan, importation of capital and technology has played and must necessarily play an increasing role. It follows that PRC–Hong Kong economic relations should be strengthened to promote such a development. For the uninitiated, this was precisely what was assumed when the PRC and the United Kingdom chose to begin negotiations at this juncture. Agreement was reached in 1984 to return all of Hong Kong—including the Kowloon Peninsula and the New Territories—to Chinese sovereignty in 1997. In return, the PRC promised not to interfere with the economy of Hong Kong for at least fifty years after the transfer.

In this respect, Hong Kong businesspeople took some encouraging initiatives. Hong Kong investors have become a major source of foreign capital in the Shenzhen Special Economic Zone (SEZ) on the border between the PRC and Hong Kong. Elsewhere in China and in other SEZs, Hong Kong capitalists and entrepreneurs soon joined the most active group in China, either independently or in joint ventures with others (frequently with ethnic Chinese businesspeople from the United States and Southeast Asia). However, transfers of high technology have been far less prominent than the infusion of management methods—for instance, in hotel management and other service industries. The principal factors motivating Hong Kong investors were the cheap labor available in the PRC and the export quotas available to China for goods subject to quantitative restrictions on the importing side, such as in textiles. On the other hand, a project to establish an Institute of Science and Technology, financed by Hong Kong interests, suggests official support for the idea of making Hong Kong technologically more useful to China later on.

But all was not well. Subsequent and overlapping developments have shown that the resultant changes in the parameters of the Hong Kong economy may be far more than Hong Kong can stand. The effect on the PRC is equally uncertain and potentially could be more than just a little damaging, depending upon what otherwise transpires in the PRC. Since these actual and potential damages are all self-inflicted, one wonders what has accounted for these unwitting as well as knowingly committed mistakes.

The Impetus to Negotiate

The British desire to reach a long-term settlement with the Beijing authorities on matters related to Hong Kong can be readily explained. Historically, the island of Hong Kong was ceded to Great Britain in 1842 at the end of the Opium War, but the New Territories were acquired by the British under a ninety-nine-year lease expiring in mid-1997. Leases of public land in the New Territories to private parties are limited to fifteen years. Legally, such leases, which are a source of government revenue, may not be extended beyond mid-1997. Furthermore, long-term investments of great expense would be needed for the further development of industrial land and Hong Kong's infrastructure. Thus the British wanted to know how secure their tenure of the solitary remaining Crown Colony was. After all, Hong Kong has been an exceptionally paying proposition. The U.K. apparently took the initiative to sound out the Chinese on negotiations, hoping to exchange administrative rights over Hong Kong for the nominal return to China of sovereignty over the colony.[6]

On the Communist China side, Deng Xiaoping was anxious to change the political and legal status of Hong Kong during his "reign" in China, for he was already advanced in years.[7] Deng had previously made a nine-point offer to Taiwan calling for the latter's incorporation into the People's Republic as a Special Administrative Region. The offer included a promise of "autonomy" to a high degree, except in the vital areas of defense and foreign policy.[8] Deng apparently wanted to go down in history as the author of China's reunification and the recovery of "lost territories" under "unequal treaties." In PRC thinking, the successful incorporation of Hong Kong into the PRC as a Special Administrative Region would set a good example to precede the absorption of Taiwan. Unfortunately, the need to set a precedent for Taiwan requires, politically, the reversion of Hong Kong to PRC sovereignty in toto. No part of the colony could be held back. There could not be an exchange of Chinese sovereignty for British administrative rights, as the U.K. and the local Hong Kong population apparently would have preferred.

To a degree, Deng Xiaoping probably could appreciate the complementary and mutually supportive relationship between the Hong Kong and PRC economies. A devastated Hong Kong economy would be contrary to Beijing's vital interest. But Deng and those who shared his views also believed that the transfer of sovereignty to China—a swapping of flags and emblems as it were—did not have to make any real difference to Hong Kong's ability to serve China's economic interest. Their reasoning is very simple and logical—except that it is fatally flawed in a few details.

Under present conditions, Hong Kong's greatest service to China lies in the relative ease with which the PRC government, as well as PRC enterprises and nationals, can earn hard currencies in Hong Kong. Nowhere else within China's reach in the world of convertible currencies is this true. But the Hong Kong currency, floating on its own since November 1974, was, until October 15, 1983, convertible into other hard currencies only at rates permitted by market demand and supply. A long period of decline of the Hong Kong dollar began in March 1977 and reached a crisis stage as negotiations between the United Kingdom and Beijing went through their paces in 1982–1983. Finally, as of October 1983, the authorities replaced the floating exchange system by pegging the Hong Kong dollar at 7.8 to one U.S. dollar, because the accelerating drop of the Hong Kong dollar in an economy dependent on imports threatened total economic chaos.

But the freely convertible Hong Kong dollar pegged at a fixed rate is, in the ultimate analysis, still based on the relative stability of demand-supply relations on the foreign currency market. Stability can be maintained only through the periodic intervention of a Foreign Exchange Fund administered by the British. Given the possible fluctuations of demand for foreign exchange, which could be greatly augmented by capital flight, and the limited size of all Exchange Funds of this nature (or British willingness to draw upon what is available), the stability of the Hong Kong dollar on the free market and its ultimate convertibility are therefore predicated upon the capacity of Hong Kong's export industry to sell goods and services and the extent to which money supply and prosperity in Hong Kong can be reduced. At first glance, it would appear that all this has nothing to do with the color or design of the flag flying over the governor's mansion. The fatal flaw of this line of thinking lies in glossing over the fact that such incomes must be earned by Hong Kong's workers, entrepreneurs, investors, and public officials, who must continue to behave under a new PRC flag or a Hong Kong SAR flag precisely as they do under another. Will they do so after 1997? Will they even do so in anticipation of 1997? How have they behaved so far? Will they and their capital remain in Hong Kong?

Hong Kong's Economic Role as a Free-Market Economy

In a historical context, the roles currently played by the free-market economy of Hong Kong, both regionally and on the global scene, evolved in several stages. First, Hong Kong began to play the part of a transit port when it was first ceded to Britain by Imperial China. Its geographical area of distribution for imports of non-Chinese products and collection of Chinese goods for export was initially concentrated in South China, from which its reach then spread to the Far East as a whole. After the outbreak of the Korean War, Hong Kong served as a conduit for imports to the PRC, which was then besieged by the U.S.-sponsored UN embargo. Geographical location and the natural excellence of the deep water harbor were the original advantages endowed by nature. As long as the market areas it serves cannot offer other equally attractive docking, warehousing, exhibition, repackaging, reprocessing, and other facilities, this entrepôt's role can be Hong Kong's indefinitely, as it has been in the entire postwar period.

When the Communist takeover of mainland China began in 1947-1949, large numbers of Chinese entrepreneurs, capitalists, and professionals, many from the Shanghai area, migrated to Hong Kong—some with their machinery, most with their capital, and all with their skills. The relocated and new enterprises attracted a continuous flow of immigrant refugees—at times reaching a crescendo, as in 1962—willing to work hard at a pittance. Many probably thought that even a meager livelihood in Hong Kong was better than what they left behind on the Communist mainland, which was wrecked unceasingly by political campaigns for more than three decades. Their spirits were bolstered by the hope of eventual emigration to a more permanent home, which, for many, was the United States. The global economic expansion that came during the period between the Korean and Vietnam wars saw the steady rise of Hong Kong as a center of light manufacturing industry, exporting goods produced locally with imported materials and intermediate inputs.

From the 1950s on, the growth of transit and direct trade, as well as local manufacturing, nurtured the demand for finance and thus spurred the growth of Hong Kong's banking industry. Earlier in this century, during the period between the two world wars, modern banks in mainland China had sought to use Hong Kong as a post for their branches to serve trade in Southeast Asia and the South China ports. "Overseas remittance" grew to become a source of bank earnings. During the period of hyperinflation in post–World War II China, banks in Hong Kong serviced the requirements of foreign exchange transactions in the only adjacent free market to mainland China in a sea of exchange controls, which were partially offset and enormously complicated by a variety of private measures designed to bypass them. During the 1970s and later, the recycling of petro-dollars and the emergence of large numbers of independently wealthy groups and individuals created an increasing demand for offshore financial institutions not subjected to sovereign state regulations of banks. With such a long and colorful history, it is not surprising that Hong Kong has developed in our time into an international financial and Asian currency center.[9]

All the preceding economic functions are mutually supporting. Together they have contributed to making Hong Kong a hub of air and sea transportation that feeds on tourism. For wealthy individuals in Southeast Asia, Hong Kong then became the place to have a second home in normal times. It also serves as a haven for others who for one reason or another are obliged to leave their homes in less normal times. This function Hong Kong has most recently provided for the escapees of the June 4, 1989, Tiananmen Square massacre.

From the time of the Communist takeover of China until the year of the UK-PRC Agreement of 1984, a whole generation of Hong Kong–born residents grew up. They were themselves not refugees and most probably never thought that they might one day face the prospect of becoming refugees. But this prospect is now eminently possible unless Hong Kong can somehow preserve at least the one prerequisite of its economic prowess— an honest, noninterventionist government that maintains order, administers justice evenly, taxes lightly, and provides a free, safe, and competitive environment for business but does not poke its nose into financial and other matters that Hong Kong citizens prefer to regard as entirely their own personal affairs.

In recent times, Hong Kong has expanded its social welfare benefits to the public in view of its burgeoning population. But the British administration is not in Hong Kong for charitable purposes. Many British citizens and enterprises from outside Hong Kong make a good living and profit there. Apart from taxes, Hong Kong also sells and leases public land as a source of revenue. Land development companies in turn raise the market value of land through resale, with or without further development, as well as speculative transactions.

But, all in all, under the British administration, law and fairly administered justice have prevailed and, in spite of occasional lapses, there has been honest government for all private business operations. There is freedom to travel—which means the readiness of other countries to admit Hong Kong residents. There are speed and privacy in those offshore banking facilities we mentioned. The basic human rights, secure under British law, are guaranteed for all. Hong Kong being what it is to all non–Hong Kong peoples, no country has any reason to threaten its security. But, apparently, in the minds of many Hong Kong residents, all this may change when a different flag is flying over the governor's mansion. These fears are evidenced by both capital flight and emigration. The 1989 massacre in China, under the order of Deng Xiaoping the "reformist," has accelerated both.

The 1983 Collapse of the Hong Kong Dollar

As reported by an experienced and knowledgeable expert observer of Hong Kong's financial scene, the Chinese demand for the retrocession of all of Hong Kong and the threat to announce a unilateral plan for Hong Kong produced shock waves so big that

> the stock market and the property market collapsed; the prices of shares, land, and real properties in 1982 fell by 50-70 percent from their peaks in 1981. The erosion in asset values and the escalation of bad debts in turn caused a severe liquidity squeeze for many property firms and financial institutions, particularly the less prudent deposit-taking companies (DTCs) that resulted in many failures and bankruptcies. . . . The real growth rate of the economy dropped sharply to 1.1 percent from 9.4 percent a year earlier. Finally, the Hong Kong dollar came under heavy pressure from two sources: outright capital flight and internal portfolio shift from domestic currency to foreign currency-dominated deposits. The exchange rate against the U.S. dollar fell relentlessly from US$1.00 = HK$5.69 at the end of 1981 to US$1.00 = HK$8.00 on September 17, 1983. The next few days saw wild and seemingly uncontrollable speculation against the Hong Kong dollar. The final crunch came on Saturday, September 24, 1983. As news was received that the Beijing talks ended in a stalemate, panic selling of the Hong Kong dollar pushed the exchange rate to US$1.00 = HK$9.60, a record for Hong Kong. Many shops began to quote prices in U.S. dollars and refused to accept Hong Kong legal tender notes. Panic buying of staples and imported items also broke out. More ominously, rumors spread quickly about the solvency of banks and DTC.[10]

The 1983 collapse of the Hong Kong dollar led promptly to the adoption on October 15, 1983, of a new stabilization scheme pegging the Hong Kong dollar at HK$7.80 to US$1.00. Under this scheme the Exchange Fund was pledged to supply dollars at this rate to the banks that were charged with the responsibility of selling U.S. dollars at the pegged rate to the public. The two banks given this responsibility must in turn pay Hong Kong dollars in full value for the U.S. dollars acquired. In effect, this means that henceforth capital outflow will have to be financed by contracting the money supply at the potential cost of deflation.

The panic selling of the Hong Kong dollar in 1983 was a result of capital flight, aggravated no doubt by speculation on the part of opportunists. It soon calmed down. But there are other forms of capital flight. Multinational firms of Hong Kong registry that shift their registration outside of Hong

Kong automatically make their businesses into non-Hong Kong, foreign enterprises with investments in Hong Kong. This act could make such firms come under the protection of those foreign countries that have investment treaties with the PRC, assuming of course the latter's faithfulness in keeping treaty obligations covering risks of expropriation, repatriation, and loan servicing and other outward payments.[11]

The Hong Kong Emigrant

Another indicator of popular response to the outcome of the Sino-British agreement and, more recently, to the 1989 massacre in Beijing, is emigration. Since emigration from British Hong Kong is free, no comprehensive official study came to light until 1989.[12] An indirect indicator is the number of applications submitted for the official Hong Kong policy statement certifying that the applicant has no criminal record on file. This certification is required prior to the issuance of passports in Hong Kong and is often needed by the immigration authorities of the country to which the person wishes to emigrate. However, over the years—that is, long before 1984—many Hong Kong residents acquired the entry visas, or even citizenship or resident status, for many countries. In the minds of a number of first-generation immigrants who came to Hong Kong as mainland refugees, their stay in Hong Kong has always been regarded as a transitional phase. The prospect of 1997 and the knowledge that they can no longer count on leaving for the United Kingdom at the last minute[13] have speeded up preparations for departure, though not necessarily the departure date itself. Any attempt to compute the outflow of Hong Kong's valuable human resources is made more difficult by those emigrants who return to Hong Kong after having established their residence or citizenship status in a foreign country. These returnees are among the careful planners—mostly professionals and business entrepreneurs of means—who have made sure of their family's security and long-term prospects and have returned temporarily either for financial reasons or for the Hong Kong "life-style."[14] There are of course the super-rich, who possess the wherewithal to leave for multiple destinations, including the UK, at any time. Thus, the number of persons who can and probably will leave when Hong Kong is seized by panic is likely to be a great deal larger than is indicated by the rising number of new applications. The latter figure is said to be about 50,000 at the current annual rate in mid-1989,[15] about 1 percent of the total population, but the ratio is higher among professionals and skilled workers.

The proverbial nimbleness and alacrity of businesspeople in Hong Kong has asserted itself even in the area of preparing to abandon their operational base and habitat. Shortly after the publication of the 1984 Sino-British Joint Declaration, immigration visas to different foreign shores became items of rising demand, commanding varying market quotations, and emigration consultation services began to gain prominence. By late 1988, after the texts of the Basic Law draft had become a subject of public debate, a local monthly journal specializing in discussion and information on emigration, *The Emigrant*, made its debut. At the receiving end of the potential flow, countries interested in receiving Hong Kong capital and, in some cases, Hong Kong residents, have also joined in the act and are extolling the merits of their respective environments for investment and residence.

The 1984 Agreement: "There Are Promises to Keep"

The British negotiators must not be blamed for failing to stress the necessary conditions that must be upheld in order to assure Hong Kong's economic viability, the continuation of which would also benefit the PRC's modernization and all Hong Kong businesspeople, including existing British and foreign interests. Nor is it true that the PRC representatives failed to promise as much. What upset the optimistic facade of the initial agreement were Britain's failure to develop an effective leverage on Chinese behavior after 1997 and the events that followed the 1984 agreement, at first mostly in connection with the drafting of Hong Kong's Basic Law.

An examination of three documents—the Joint Declaration of December 1984, the April 1988 first draft of the Basic Law, and the February 1989 second draft of the same law—will bring out the crux of the PRC's handling of the Hong Kong question up to this writing. One round of "consultation" on the first draft took place in Hong Kong during the interval between the two drafts, and a second round of consultation was scheduled to be finished in August 1989 but was later delayed to October because of the Tiananmen massacre. The final version of the Basic Law, which really will be a PRC-proclaimed constitution for the Hong Kong Special Administrative Region (SAR) as of July 1, 1997, is scheduled to be issued by the PRC National People's Congress (NPC) sometime in spring 1990. As the NPC can change the PRC Constitution (i.e., currently the 1982 version) at any time by a simple vote—even the establishment of the SAR can be wiped out any time the Chinese Communist party chooses to do so—it is quite legitimate to ask why anyone should worry about the content of the Basic Law. Of course, the law will offer no guarantee of any kind whatsoever. But if the Basic Law itself allows the PRC a totally free hand, it will give Beijing's leaders even more latitude to do as they please without hindrance, protest, and, above all, even prior public knowledge. From this point of view, one can see that the Joint Declaration is a PRC promise and the two drafts of the Basic Law are the latter's second thoughts.[16] The drafting of the law is extremely revealing of PRC thinking and behavior; the law itself offers little guarantee of value.

The Future Role of Hong Kong 153

The Joint Declaration contains the following promises:

1. Hong Kong will remain a free-market and capitalistic economy after 1997. Toward this end, the following rights will be "ensured" by law: freedoms of person, speech, press, assembly, association, travel, movement, correspondence, strike, choice of occupation, academic research, and religion. Private property ownership of enterprises, legitimate right of ownership, and foreign investment will be "protected" by law (Section 5, Art. 3 in the Declaration).
2. Hong Kong will remain a free international economic center. The free port, a separate customs territory, securities, gold and futures markets, free flow of capital, and a convertible Hong Kong dollar will continue (Sections 6 and 7, Art. 3). These conditions presuppose the agreement of foreign governments and international institutions.
3. Hong Kong will be "autonomous" and will be endowed with "independent judicial power" and a government of "local inhabitants" (Section 3, Art. 3). There will be a legislature "constituted by elections" and executive authorities "accountable to the legislature" (Section I in the PRC's elaboration of "basic policies" regarding Hong Kong, Annex I to the Joint Declaration).
4. The PRC central government will not levy taxes on Hong Kong (Section 8, Art. 3). Note that this does not preclude payments by Hong Kong to the central government other than taxes or to other PRC government agencies, such as local or provincial government taxes, special levies for water and electricity, involuntary "donations," etc.
5. Hong Kong will not have to pay for the PRC military sent to Hong Kong for the latter's defense (Section XII, Annex I. Note that Chinese forces will be stationed in Hong Kong).
6. Until July 1, 1997, the UK government "will be responsible for the administration of Hong Kong with the object of maintaining and preserving its economic prosperity and social stability" while the PRC government "will give its cooperation in this connection" (Art. 4).
7. Annex I also states that the Exchange Fund "shall be managed and controlled by the Hong Kong SAR government primarily for regulating the exchange value of the Hong Kong dollar."

The 1988 and 1989 Basic Law Drafts: Some Second Thoughts

Already buried in the 1984 texts of the Joint Declaration and the PRC policy statements in Annex I were certain hints of potential trouble for the people of Hong Kong.

First, both the Joint Declaration (Section 4, Art. 3) and Annex I (Section I) stated that the chief executive of the Hong Kong SAR would be selected "by election or through consultations held locally and appointed by the Central People's Government." The Joint Declaration used the term "election" in the plural. The texts in both places neglected to say in more precise terms how many elections would be held, how the elections and consultations would be conducted, or what "constituted by elections" would actually mean. As subsequent developments proved, the PRC fully intended to implement the elections and consultations in a manner and on a timetable that would assure its own control and deny the Hong Kong population real autonomy.

A second hint of trouble was buried initially in Section 2, Article 3, of the Joint Declaration, which states that the contents of the Declaration and the attached PRC Elaboration on Policies would be "stipulated, in a Basic Law . . . by the National People's Congress . . . and they will remain unchanged for 50 years." Section II in Annex I declared further: "The legislature may on its own authority enact laws . . . and report them to the Standing Committee of the NPC for the record. Laws enacted by the Legislature that are in accordance with the Basic Law and legal procedures shall be regarded as valid." These passages do not say what happens to the laws if the NPC does not find the enactments from Hong Kong to be in consonance with the Basic Law. Nor do they explain whether the NPC has the power to pass laws for Hong Kong on its own.

While the passages on economics were left substantially alone in 1985–1989 during the drafting of and consultation on the Basic Law, the process of election and consultation and the relative powers of the future Hong Kong SAR legislature and the NPC, as well as Hong Kong's status regarding its own court of final appeal, became the focus of dispute. The PRC's behavior during the dispute also revealed rather openly that the Hong Kong SAR was never intended to be as autonomous as local optimists had hoped. Six basic issues seem to be at the heart of the dispute.

First, Article 17 of the second draft (January 1989) of the Basic Law now stipulates that the Standing Committee of the NPC can return a law enacted by the Hong Kong legislature that it regards as not conforming to the Basic Law in regard to Central-Regional relations, and the returned law will thereupon cease to have force. Thus the NPC Standing Committee possesses in effect the right to veto Hong Kong legislation.

Second, under Article 18 of the 1989 draft, the NPC Standing Committee may modify the general rule that national laws not a part of the Basic Law are not applicable to Hong Kong by adding a list (Annex III to the second draft) of specific PRC national laws that are applicable locally. "Laws listed in Annex III . . . shall be confined to those relating to *defense and foreign affairs as well as other laws outside the limits of the autonomy of the*

Region as specified by this law" (italics added). In effect, the NPC can do virtually anything not specified word for word in the Basic Law. The earlier April 1988 draft would have given the PRC State Council the authority to decree the application of any national law. But the State Council can still exercise its authority by decree in the event of war or a state of emergency in Hong Kong. The latter condition could apply in the case of a riot, or even a large-scale student demonstration similar to those in Beijing in April–May 1989. For example, the PRC could crush student protests in Hong Kong.

Third, the April 1988 draft excluded, in addition to defense and foreign affairs, cases relating to the "executive acts of the Central People's Government" from the jurisdiction of the SAR court system. The second draft changed the exclusion to "acts of state" that must be certified by the chief executive, as certified by the Central People's Government. This provision (Art. 19 in the second draft) was, however, not adopted at the Drafting Committee's final session as the required minimum number of affirmative votes was then missing.

Fourth, Article 22 in the first draft required the Hong Kong SAR to prohibit by law any act designed to undermine national unity or subvert the Central People's Government. The 1989 draft called upon the SAR to enact laws *on its own*" (Art. 23, italics added) to prohibit acts of "treason, secession, sedition or *theft of state secrets*" (italics added). Press freedom and freedom of expression may well be given up!

Fifth, who is to interpret the Basic Law? Article 157 of the second draft gives the final right of interpretation to the NPC Standing Committee for cases of concern to the Central Government or regarding Central-Regional relations. The first draft openly leaves the power of interpretation in all cases up to the NPC Standing Committee. Unfortunately, all matters relating to the autonomy of the SAR would seem to apply to Central-Regional relations.

Finally, a very complex mainstream "model" for the selection of the chief executive for Hong Kong provides that with the then chief executive's consent and with the approval of the NPC Standing Committee during the term of the third chief executive, the then Legislative Council will decide whether a referendum will be held to determine whether the chief executives of the future will be elected. Even if the chief executive is to be selected through popular election, this might not happen until the fifth term, which would begin in 2017. Each term of a chief executive is five years, so the decision on a referendum (not the referendum itself) would not be voted on until perhaps the year 2007 at the earliest. The first three chief executives will be selected by Election Committees, which, except for the first time, will themselves be constituted under an electoral law presumably to be formulated by the first SAR government. The first Election

Committee, which will select the first chief executive, will be constituted by the NPC through a special appointed SAR Preparatory Committee. The Preparatory Committee will also have authority in selecting the first Legislative Council.

The PRC has devoted considerable care to the transition of Hong Kong into its control. "Autonomy" is to be granted only as long as it is within permissible limits. But what is permissible cannot yet be defined. This is true especially after the Tiananmen massacre. Since the political and economic stakes are very high for the PRC, and opposition and distrust on the part of some Hong Kong residents are more strenuous than Beijing had seemingly expected, the PRC has tried to assume full control of the process of development of the Basic Law. The many changes from the first to the second draft reflect this concern.

The main source of the opposition consists of those Hong Kong professionals who are not themselves first-generation mainland refugees. These Hong Kong-born residents regard Hong Kong as their real home and are reluctant to leave; they wish to propel Hong Kong onto a democratic path. Through procedural amendments to the original draft of the Basic Law and by advocating a speeding up of the process of instituting local and general elections, they hope to erect a democratic framework in Hong Kong before 1997 so that, following the PRC takeover, Beijing would face a more difficult choice if it tried to lower the degree of autonomy Hong Kong is supposed to enjoy. The strikes against this nascent democratic movement are (1) its late start, (2) the fact that local nationalism is missing as a galvanizing force, (3) the lack of international governmental support and, at the root, even of an understanding of the realities of Hong Kong, and (4) the ambivalent attitude of the British and their lack of both the power and the will to solve these problems during the rapidly diminishing number of years left.

Economic Realities

One of the economic realities in 1985-1989 has been the growing realization on the part of Hong Kong-born professionals that, while PRC negotiators may be woefully ignorant of Western economic ideas and institutions, they are unbelievably crafty, deceitful, and manipulative, being survivors of forty years of Chinese communism and schooled in its work style. They might be genuinely anxious to preserve Hong Kong's economic vitality, but they cannot help but behave in a manner that destroys confidence and sows distrust. The increasing outflow of professional and younger entrepreneurial talents from Hong Kong in the past few years has been a logical outcome. The appearance of more Hong Kong enterprises and investments all over North America and in Commonwealth countries elsewhere is just the tip of an iceberg. The "brain drain" that the Hong Kong government must finally admit to is reducing Hong Kong's competitiveness. This loss cannot be quickly reversed or offset by labor supply of equal caliber and initiative from other sources.

The same lack of confidence in PRC conduct once the Communist Chinese hold on Hong Kong is secure is already undermining outsiders' demands for Hong Kong's financial services as an offshore banking center. Reports of numerous new mainland immigrants being brought in under official PRC sponsorship in order to increase the ranks of Hong Kong residents for the governing of Hong Kong do not induce confidence that business in Hong Kong will be as usual. Both privacy and efficiency will unavoidably suffer.[17]

Stories of widespread corruption in the PRC and the unfair competition of specially privileged groups suggest that rumors about the PRC style of doing business have preceded PRC bureaucrats, arriving in Hong Kong nearly a decade before the official transfer of sovereignty is to occur. The notorious Kanghua affair of 1988 offers a good illustration of special privilege and corruption run amok, just as the peremptory solution, allegedly ordered by the highest authority in Beijing, is a clear example of the PRC's style of arbitrary intervention and of the "extraterritoriality" now exercised by Beijing in Hong Kong.[18] Repressive and arbitrary intervention in Hong Kong-registered enterprises after June 3-4 strengthened such fears.

Yet, because much capital flight took place earlier, partly through re-registration under non-Hong Kong ownership, there may be little overt evidence of such fears except in the form of trade surpluses and lower new fixed investments in construction. High daily stock exchange transactions since the October 1987 global collapse may be explained by speculative buying by outsiders, including perhaps some from Taiwan. These contradictory movements further cloud the issue, so that some innocents—if they still exist—may be attracted to the China market even at this late date, and therefore to Hong Kong.

The real economic future of Hong Kong depends on the economic future of China. Unfortunately for Hong Kong, after several years of inflationary expansion, in the fall of 1988 the PRC entered a phase of economic contraction. Economic liberalization was largely reversed after the Tiananmen massacre. By 1991, the Basic Law will have been promulgated; the Liaison Group will have been ensconced in Hong Kong and may try to act as a shadow government. In China, Deng Xiaoping may no longer be at the helm. The degree of political stability, the kind of national economic policy, and the impact of the particular post-Deng politico-economic combination on Hong Kong defies a quick prognostication, and statistical extrapolations of economic development would not be meaningful.

Exogenous Developments and a Speculation

One purely exogenous development affecting Hong Kong favorably has been its growth as an intermediary in indirect trade between the PRC and Taiwan and, to a lesser degree, between the PRC and South Korea.[19] Lack of mutual political understanding between Taipei and Beijing, and of diplomatic relations between Beijing and Seoul, have made indirect trade in Hong Kong attractive, and the volume might expand further for a while.

Second, as Indonesia and Singapore reportedly are considering the prospect of resuming and establishing diplomatic relations with the PRC, some expansion of trade through Hong Kong is conceivable, though this is unlikely to be significant.

Finally, the wealthy in the PRC who enjoy special privileges in the Dengist regime are using Hong Kong as an offshore banking center and trade post before 1997. After 1997, if the same or similar groups in China continue to function in the same manner, they might develop a vested interest in maintaining the Hong Kong SAR's autonomy. Already today Hong Kong is said to have become a hub of the PRC's arms trade. This could well be associated with a demand for financial services. But none of these new activities can be expected to offset the effect of the loss of professional and entrepreneurial talents from Hong Kong. The future of Hong Kong as a Newly Industrializing Economy (NIE) is seriously in jeopardy, and the victims are both Hong Kong and China.[20]

Only one thing seems certain after 1997 for outsiders (excluding the PRC and the Hong Kong SAR), that is, the use of Hong Kong as an outpost for trading with China, however large or small that trade might then be. Hong Kong may revert to a transit trade center and possibly an "R&R" outpost for the elite of China (or of Guangdong) where deals that might not be so above-board in the more "puritanical" PRC proper could be transacted more openly. All this presupposes that the 1997 transfer of sovereignty will take place on schedule in spite of the uncertainties in China itself.

After Tiananmen, it is difficult to say when the mainland Chinese economy will regain a semblance of stability and return to steady development. Some hope the time will be soon; few, however, dare to predict that. If this happens before 1997 or not too long afterward, the minimum usefulness of Hong Kong as an SAR, or a more integrated part of China, or just a part of China—as a base for "China traders" because of its better physical infrastructure—will remain, even though the volume of business may be reduced. Beyond this minimal level, the Hong Kong economy and part of the adjacent mainland economy could develop some amorphous, ill-defined political association. But such a state of affairs can only be imagined in a post-Deng Xiaoping, and post-Li Peng, "restabilized" (partially at least)

Chinese economy on the reformist track. These conditions presuppose that the status of Hong Kong will not be upset before or shortly after 1997 in the maelstrom of a post-Tiananmen and post-Deng turmoil.

Turning at last to the issues raised at the beginning of this chapter, the normal questions one can pose about an economy's future cannot really be applied to Hong Kong. The institutional parameters are all in the process of being uprooted. Perhaps a clearer reexamination should be made in another three to five years. In the meantime, Hong Kong's emigrants and capital outflow are factors that innovative entrepreneurs elsewhere (in Singapore, Taiwan, or Manila, in that order) can perhaps find useful, if they can be as nimble as those leaving Hong Kong.

Notes

1. Some prefer to use the term "NIE" for "Newly Industrializing Economies" out of deference to those who wish to reserve the word "country" for a "sovereign state" recognized by many other "sovereign states."

2. The implied Hong Kong population was about 5.7 million people. The GDP and trade statistics are taken from the Census and Statistics Department, Hong Kong, *Hong Kong Annual Digest of Statistics*, 1988, pp. 2–14 and 96–101. For details, see also Table 9.1.

3. Ibid.

4. This is why U.S. import statistics grouped by "country of origin" regard these goods as imports from the PRC.

5. The "Chinese banks" in Hong Kong are headed by the Bank of China, which controlled twelve "sister banks," including six since April 1989, as fully owned subsidiaries. The twelve consist of eight incorporated in China (the Bank of Communications; Kwangtung Provincial Bank; Sin Hua Trust, Saving and Commercial Bank Ltd.; Kincheng Banking Corporation; China and South Sea Bank Ltd.; China State Bank Ltd.; National Commercial Bank; and Yien Yieh Commercial Bank Ltd.) and four incorporated in Hong Kong (Chiyu Banking Corporation, Hua Chiao Commercial Bank Ltd., Nanyang Commercial Bank, and Po Sang Bank Ltd.). These are all formerly private banks that were expropriated by the PRC.

6. See especially the introductory chapter of *The Future of Hong Kong: Toward 1997 and Beyond*, edited by Hungdah Chiu, Y. C. Jao, and Yuan-li Wu (New York: Quorum Books, 1987), and "Background to the Negotiations," pp. 196–212 in the same volume. See also George Hicks, *Chiu-ch'i Tao-su* (Counting Back from 97), (Hong Kong: Chi-hsien She, 1989), p. 20.

7. Deng was seventy-seven years old in 1982, when the negotiations started.

8. This is what PRC public relations announcements have continuously trumpeted as the generous and innovative formula for the reunification of Taiwan and the mainland—"one state but two systems" (socialism and capitalism).

9. The author wishes to thank Dr. Y. C. Jao of the University of Hong Kong for allowing him to read an until then unpublished paper entitled "Financial Reform

in China and Hong Kong 1978-88: A Comparative System," which included his comments on Hong Kong financial institutions.

10. Hungdah Chiu, Y. C. Jao, and Yuan-li Wu, eds., *The Future of Hong Kong*, pp. 58-59.

11. This point raises an unresolved question about the scope of the investment treaties Beijing has signed or may still be negotiating with foreign countries. The PRC's record in this area is not unequivocal. See Yuan-li Wu, "The Future of Hong Kong Before and After 1997," by this author in *American Asian Review*, vol. 2, no. 4 (St. John's University, Winter 1986), pp. 13-23. The HuKwang Railway Bond case in the United States suggests that Beijing wishes to pick and choose in honoring former foreign obligations not contracted by itself.

12. See George Hicks, *Chiu-ch'i Tao-su*, p. 9.

13. Under the current British law governing citizenship, persons born or naturalized in Hong Kong are classified as either "British Dependent Territory Citizens" or "British Overseas Citizens"; neither group enjoys the automatic right of entry to Great Britain.

14. The December 19, 1984, Sino-British Joint Declaration stated, "The current *social* and economic systems in Hong Kong will remain unchanged [after 1997], and so will the life-style." (Art. 3, Point 5; italics added.)

15. See George Hicks, *Chiu-Ch'i Tao-su*, p. 9.

16. The texts of the first two documents are contained in Chiu, Jao, and Wu, eds., *The Future of Hong Kong*, Appendix. The second draft of the law is available in pamphlet form printed by C. & C. Offset Printing Co., Ltd., 75 Pau Chung St., Takawan, Kowloon, Hong Kong. Both the Chiu et al. volume and George Hicks's *Chiu-ch'i Tao-su* contain chronologies of the major relevant events leading up to the first quarter of 1989. On the issue of leverage in negotiation with Beijing, reference may be made to my testimony before the Human Rights Caucus, U.S. House of Representatives, June 23, 1989.

17. See Y. L. Wu and Y. C. Jao, "Economic Consequences of 1997," *Journal of International Law*, (Case Western Reserve, vol. 20, Winter 1988), pp. 17-41.

18. George Hicks, *Chiu-ch'i Tao-su*, p. 9.

19. In 1988, Hong Kong's reexports to Taiwan and South Korea increased by HK$4.5 billion and HK$2.8 billion respectively (US$577 million and US$359 million respectively), which was amply covered by the increase in reexports originating from China. Similarly, reexports originating from Taiwan and South Korea increased by HK$4.5 billion and HK$6.9 billion respectively, (US$577 million and US$885 million respectively), which also was more than covered by the increase in reexported goods originating from China). The bulk of reexports coming from the PRC went to the United States.

20. The PRC has already had to bail out its subsidiaries and associates. See Y. L. Wu and Y. C. Jao, "Economic Consequences," and George Hicks, *Chiu-ch'i Tao-su*.

10

U.S. Economic Policy in a World of Regional Trading Blocs

Richard S. Belous

Serious Tensions

In this chapter I will first examine the basics of current U.S. macroeconomic policy. I will then place several issues involving the U.S. economy into the context of a global economy. Given this macro-environment, the chapter will conclude with recent research conducted by the National Planning Association on the growth of regional trading blocs in the international economy. While U.S. public policymakers have given little thought to these prospects, the U.S. business community has been very concerned by these trends on the international trading front.

The major conclusions of this chapter are as follows:

1. The current situation of the United States, which is generating a federal budget deficit of more than $100 billion per year and a current account deficit of more than $120 billion per year, is not sustainable into the early 1990s unless the United States is willing to endure major devaluations of the dollar and face significant increases in the rate of domestic inflation. This situation would also require a high level of direct foreign investment.

2. The major question that faces U.S. economic policymakers is: Will the U.S. economy experience a "soft landing" or a "hard landing" in the early 1990s? While a majority of leading economists seem to favor predictions of a soft landing, there are currently several serious signs being posted that a hard landing is more likely.

3. The United States, in general, will find it easier to blame others for its problems than to blame itself. The desire to "blame" Japan and the Newly Industrializing Economies (NIEs) for our difficulties will be particularly strong in the near future. So-called U.S. Super 301 activities will continue.

4. Many segments of the U.S. business community have lost faith in the General Agreement on Tariffs and Trade (GATT). In general, U.S. business leaders seem to believe that the international economy is shifting in the direction of regional trading blocs. U.S. business leaders seem to feel that the United States must start positioning itself now in a fragmented trading system.

5. U.S. business leaders seem to believe that most of the NIEs would rather form a regional trading bloc with the United States than with Japan. If U.S. private-sector and government leaders act in this belief, it could result in some serious U.S.-Japanese tensions over the direction and development of Asian and Pacific markets in the 1990s.

While it may be nicer to talk about the spirit of cooperation, the near-term reality may instead be fraught with serious frictions and tensions. If policymakers in both North American and Asian countries can brace themselves for this expected turbulence, then we may be able to get through the next few years with a minimum of long-term damage. Thus, the spirit behind this chapter is not one of flowering cooperation; rather, the muse behind this chapter is the spirit of damage control.

Deficits, Devaluations, and Direct Investment

While some international economists may like to believe that international economic factors are first in the hearts and minds of U.S. political, business, and labor leaders, such is not the case. U.S. international economic policies are still driven by domestic considerations more than domestic economic policies are driven by international considerations. This being the case, a short review of the U.S. macroeconomics playing field is in order.

As is often mentioned in the financial press, the United States faces large twin deficits. As indicated in Table 10.1, the federal budget deficit represented less than 1 percent of the U.S. Gross National Product in 1979. However, by 1986, the federal budget was close to 5 percent of the U.S. GNP.

It proved easier to cut tax rates than it did to reduce government budget expenditures. America's adventure with supply-side economics did many things to the U.S. economy. However, the supply-side measures did not prove to be self-financing as many supply siders had predicted.

The projections presented in Table 10.1 indicate that the federal budget deficit will decrease only slightly in the near future. For example, the 1991 deficit estimates are above the $64 billion target mandated by the Gramm-Rudman Act. If these estimates are correct, then radical changes will have to be made on the expenditure side, the revenue side, or both sides to meet Gramm-Rudman targets. Even by the year 2000, the federal budget

Table 10.1 U.S. Federal Government Receipts, Expenditures, and Deficits (in billions of 1982 U.S. dollars)

Year	Total Receipts	Total Expenditures	Deficit
1979	636.8	656.3	-19.4
1982	635.3	780.7	-145.4
1986	713.4	894.8	-181.4
1988	806.7	910.5	-103.8
1991	1,004.8	1,072.2	-67.5
1995	1,144.7	1,191.9	-47.2

Source: Nestor E. Terleckyj and Charles D. Coleman, National Economic Projections Series: Prospects for U.S. Economic Growth, 1988-2010 (Washington, D.C.: NPA Data Services, Inc., 1988); and Nestor E. Terleckyj, David M. Levy, and Charles D. Coleman, Model of U.S. Economic Growth (Washington, D.C.: NPA Data Services, Inc., 1988).

deficit would still represent a larger relative share of GNP than the federal budget deficit realized in 1979.

Beyond the federal budget deficit, other variables indicate a period of moderate long-term economic growth in the 1990s. As shown in Table 10.2, real U.S. GNP should be growing at an annual rate of roughly 2.6 percent in the 1990s. This rate of growth is somewhat slower than in the 1987-1990 period and is even more modest than the rate garnered in the 1969-1979 period.

On the labor front, the rate of growth of civilian employment will be somewhat greater than the rate of growth of the labor force in the 1990s. This trend would indicate tight labor markets in the 1990s and relatively low unemployment rates. Given these conditions, one might expect significant wage-push inflation in the U.S. economy. However, there will be other

Table 10.2 U.S. Economic Indicators (annual growth rates based on constant 1982 U.S. dollars)

	GNP	Labor Force	Civilian Employment	Productivity	Earnings Per Employed Person
1950-1969	3.8%	1.5%	1.5%	2.8	2.8
1969-1979	2.8	2.4	2.4	1.3	0.1
1979-1987	2.3	1.4	1.6	1.3	0.2
1987-1990	2.9	1.6	2.0	0.8	1.6
1990-2000	2.6	1.2	1.3	1.4	1.3

Source: U.S. Department of Commerce, U.S. Bureau of Labor Statistics, and NPA Data Services, Inc.

Table 10.3 The U.S. Contingent Work Force (millions of workers)

	1988	1980	Percent Change
A. Parts of the Contingent Work Force			
Temporary Workers	1.1	0.4	175%
Part-Timers	19.8	16.3	22
Business Services	5.7	3.3	70
Self-Employed	10.0	8.5	19
B. Total U.S. Labor Force	121.7	106.9	14

Source: NPA estimates based on U.S. Bureau of Labor Statistics data.

forces that could work to moderate U.S. compensation growth in the 1990s despite tight labor markets. For example, productivity could be growing at an annual rate of 1.4 percent in the 1990s while earnings per employed person could be growing at only 1.3 percent. If these projections are correct, then the U.S. economy would not see a return to annual double-digit growth in labor costs.

If labor markets are going to be very tight, how will U.S. employers hold down labor cost growth? Probably by using several key human resource strategies.

First, many U.S. employers have tied their compensation policies to firm-specific productivity and profitability and have based them less on norms, traditions, and industry patterns.[1] This approach has increased labor cost flexibility and has helped moderate wage growth, even in times of low unemployment.

Second, many U.S. employers have reduced their full-time core work force and replaced many *core workers* with so-called *contingent workers* (i.e., part-time, temporary, and subcontracted workers). These changes have resulted in a major institutional shift in U.S. labor markets. As indicated in Table 10.3, all parts of the U.S. contingent work force have been growing at a faster rate than the total U.S. labor force.[2] A liberal estimate of the size of the contingent work force would place it at 36.6 million people in 1988. A conservative estimate would place the contingent work force at 29.9 million people in 1988. Thus, roughly one-quarter or more of all U.S. workers are now contingents. Contingents tend to get paid less and receive fewer employee benefits compared to core workers. This shift has helped U.S. employers hold down labor cost growth.

Third, declines in unionization, the globalization of markets, and deregulation have also helped to hold down labor cost growth.[3] These forces,

Table 10.4 U.S. and Foreign Relative Labor Costs for Manufacturing Production Workers (U.S. labor costs equal 100 percent)

	1980	1985	1988
United States	100%	100%	100%
OECD	83	65	99
Canada	85	83	98
Japan	57	50	95
Europe	103	63	105
Asian NICs	12	13	19

Source: U.S. Bureau of Labor Statistics.

in conjunction with shifts in the value of the dollar, have moderated the former position of the United States as a high-labor cost market. As shown in Table 10.4, U.S. labor costs are even lower than many European labor costs. However, the labor costs for employers in Newly Industrializing Countries (NICs) still remain much lower than U.S. labor costs.

In a period of moderate long-term growth and moderate increases in U.S. labor costs, the U.S. economy should sustain respectable levels of gross investment and of public and private spending on research and development. Projections in Table 10.5 indicate that the growth in investment and research and development in the 1990s will be at a slower pace than in 1987-1990.

One way the United States could run major government budget deficits and keep domestic investment rates high would be to have high savings rates. U.S. savings rates are very low by international standards, and the

Table 10.5 U.S. Investment and Research and Development Spending (annual growth rates based on constant 1982 U.S. dollars)

	Gross Investment	Private R&D Expenditures	Government Expenditures for R&D Performed in Industry
1950-1969	4.2%	9.6%	10.3%
1969-1979	3.7	2.7	-2.8
1979-1987	1.8	5.8	6.8
1987-1990	5.3	7.1	2.5
1990-2000	3.0	4.4	2.5

Source: U.S. Department of Commerce, National Science Foundation, and NPA Data Services.

United States has been using foreign capital to finance its public and private consumption patterns. Standard national income accounting techniques show that a country's private-sector net savings and government net savings plus foreign net savings will sum identically to zero. If the United States decides to have negative net savings in both the public and private sectors, then positive net savings will result in the foreign sector.

In the 1980s, the massive trade deficit of the United States was combined with foreign capital inflows and, in effect, "financed" negative net savings in the U.S. public and private sectors. Table 10.6 shows that U.S. household savings experienced a major relative decline and were a smaller percentage of GNP compared to all of the so-called "G-7" countries except the United Kingdom. Meanwhile, in the 1980s Japan and West Germany have seen very strong positive net savings rates in their household and noncorporate sector and in their foreign sector.

Italy provides a very interesting example of why there is no simple "one-to-one" relationship between government budget deficits and trade deficits. Italy runs a very large relative government budget deficit. But savings are so high in the household and noncorporate sector that Italy's foreign sector in essence has been roughly in balance.

A key factor of Table 10.6 can be seen in the figures for the foreign sector of each country. In general, the relative size of net foreign savings has grown in almost all nations. Thus, for some nations the relative foreign deficit is larger than in the pre-1979 period, while for other nations the relative size of the foreign surplus is larger than in the pre-1979 period. In the 1980s the world economy had to deal with larger relative global imbalances than it did prior to 1980.

If the United States continues to run large budget and trade deficits, there will be downward pressures on the dollar. Given the tight capacity in the U.S. economy, this pressure could lead to higher levels of U.S. inflation. Also, the United States will require more capital inflows in a period of intense global imbalances.

The major irony of the so-called "supply-side" macro-revolution of the 1980s is that during this period the rate of net household savings has *declined* (see Table 10.7). While the U.S. household savings rate was 10.6 percentage points behind the Japanese rate in 1980, it was 12.7 percentage points behind the Japanese rate in 1987. The low rates of U.S. net private- and public-sector savings will be a key variable in U.S. relationships with nations in the Asia-Pacific region in the 1990s.

Based on these realities, the main question seems to be this: As the United States unwinds from its current position, will we see a soft or a hard landing in the 1990s?

Table 10.6 Net Savings of Various Sectors Within Different Countries (percent of GNP/GDP)

	Pre 1973[a]	1974-1979	1980	1988
UNITED STATES				
Household and Noncorporate	1.8	3.1	3.7	1.5
Government	-0.6	-1.4	-1.5	-3.0
Corporate	-0.6	-1.5	-1.9	-1.2
Foreign	0.5	0.2	0.5	-2.7
JAPAN				
Household and Noncorporate	8.3	10.2	8.8	8.2
Government	1.0	-3.4	-4.4	-0.3
Corporate	-8.2	-7.0	-5.7	-5.2
Foreign	1.4	0.3	-1.1	3.0
WEST GERMANY				
Household and Noncorporate	7.0	7.7	7.3	6.2
Government	0.5	-3.0	-2.9	-2.3
Corporate	-7.0	7.7	7.3	6.2
Foreign	0.6	0.9	-2.1	3.6
ITALY				
Household and Noncorporate	11.2	14.5	9.6	12.2
Government	-5.8	-9.2	-8.0	-10.2
Corporate	-4.8	-5.6	-4.1	-2.0
Foreign	0.7	-0.2	-2.4	0.0
UNITED KINGDOM				
Household and Noncorporate	1.7	4.2	6.4	-0.3
Government	-0.4	-4.1	-3.5	-1.0
Corporate	-0.7	-2.0	-0.7	1.3
Foreign	0.1	-1.3	1.5	-2.2

[a]Pre-1973 estimates are 1960-1973 averages for the United States and West Germany; 1969-1973 averages for Japan; 1968-1973 averages for the United Kingdom; and 1970-1973 averages for Italy.

Source: OECD.

A Soft or Hard Landing?

It appears that the current conventional wisdom among leading econometricians is that the United States will be in for a soft landing when the current expansion ends.[4] The logic behind the soft-landing school of thought is as follows:

1. Despite some recent increases in the rate of growth of inflation and labor costs, both price and wage hikes are moderate compared to the levels

Table 10.7 Net Household Savings as a Percentage of Disposable Household Income

	1980	1985	1987
United States	7.3%	4.6%	3.9%
Japan	17.9	16.0	16.6
West Germany	12.8	11.5	12.2
France	17.6	13.8	13.0
United Kingdom	14.2	9.3	5.6
Italy	28.0	24.2	23.5
Canada	13.6	14.1	9.4
G7 Aggregate	12.6	10.1	9.3

Source: OECD.

generated in the late 1970s. Thus, it will not take a so-called hard landing to unwind the U.S. economy. A short and mild recession is all that is needed to restore the conditions required for a new economic expansion.

2. U.S. corporations recently have done a much better job in the management of inventories than in the past. Under newer "just-in-time" methods of inventory management, inventory-to-sales ratios can be kept quite low. For example, in the 1982 recession, the U.S. inventory-to-sales ratio in U.S. manufacturing and trade sectors was close to 1.75. However, by mid-1989, the U.S. inventory-to-sales ratio was less than 1.55.[5] Thus, if a recession hits, it would not have to be a long and hard slump to work down inventories.

3. So-called "New Wave" economic theories also point to a soft landing. New Wave economists point out that the structure of the U.S. economy has experienced a vast change since, say, the 1960s. Not only does manufacturing employment represent less than 20 percent of the U.S. labor force (and service-sector employment represent more than 75 percent of the U.S. labor force), but the U.S. economy has become "regionalized." Many service-sector industries do not tend to have the same inventory problems as manufacturing industries. Thus, many service-sector firms may not experience deep business cycle slumps, New Wave economists argue. Also, in a more regionalized economy, one section of the country can be down on its luck while other sections are booming. The net result could be a "rolling" regionalized slump instead of one large nationwide slump, New Wave thinkers assert.

4. In 1979–1983 there was a strong political coalition backing tight monetary policy that gave up on management of interest rates. This same type of coalition may not develop in the early 1990s. Thus, the Federal

Reserve may not have the political backing to keep monetary policy very tight for, say, three years in a row.

5. Meanwhile, many U.S. financial institutions have been able to brace themselves for possible loan defaults from Third World nations. Loan loss reserves have been raised at many banks, and the Brady Plan of the Bush administration has recognized the need to write off some Third World debt. For all of these reasons, a recession might not have as hard an impact on the debt situation as it would have had in the early 1980s. This would help generate the "soft-landing" case.

Despite the above logic, there are other arguments that point to a hard landing, including the following.

1. U.S. public policymakers and their economic advisers have generally been unable to create "mild" recessions in the post–World War II era. Recessions often have been deeper and longer than "intended" by political and economic decision makers. Wishing for a mild recession does not make it so. In fact, a more globalized recession could move with a force that individual national leaders might find quite difficult to reverse.

2. Corrective U.S. fiscal and monetary policy might be much more difficult to apply in the next recession than they were in the business slumps of the recent past. The U.S. budget deficit is already quite large, even in an economic expansion. Thus, public policymakers may find it difficult to expand the relative size of the deficit to, say, 6 or 7 percent of GNP in a recession. Monetary policymakers also face difficult choices. Tight monetary policies could reduce inflation and induce higher interest rates, which would attract foreign capital to U.S. shores. But the price could be a serious recession. Expansionary monetary policy might keep the current business expansion going, but it would also generate higher inflation rates and reduce the inflows of foreign capital. Hence, all monetary policy choices will have serious side effects and trade-offs. Macroeconomic management could be difficult if one hopes to depend on monetary and fiscal policy adjustments.

3. Corporate debt levels have increased to a point where many firms could find it very difficult to stay out of bankruptcy in a recession. For example, interest payments as a percentage of corporate cash flow have increased from less than 10 percent in 1977 to almost 19 percent in 1987.[6] Beyond the quantity of corporate debt, there is also the matter of "quality" of corporate debt. It is possible to construct economic theories in which financial factors have no impact on the real economy. However, I believe that one would not be acting on rational expectations if one were to put much faith in these theories. Recent financial shifts can have a significant impact on the real economy in the short run (and even in the intermediate run).

4. While the Brady Plan has garnered much press, many of its specific details are a long way from being finalized. If a recession were to come today, the Brady Plan would not help prevent a "hard landing." Moreover, Third World debt could work to make any slump quite deep and sustained.

For all of the above reasons, I think it would be unwise to rule out a hard and painful landing in the early 1990s. It is also important to remember that, within many U.S. corporations, what was unthinkable only a few years ago is now often standard company policy. What also should be noted is that the U.S. social safety net is not as strong now as it was in the 1970s. A hard landing could inflict a great deal of pain on many individual Americans as well as many U.S. corporations.

Burdensharing and Cooperation

As indicated above, it makes more sense to think of U.S. international economic policies as being driven by domestic considerations than the reverse condition. Current U.S. macroeconomic results point to the need to "unwind" from current conditions. While many experts see a soft landing in the cards, I see many signs that point to a hard landing instead.

I am also of the opinion that, although one can point to some commercial, economic, and military policies that have been "unfair" to the United States, the vast majority of recent U.S. problems have been created by our own public and private sectors. To put it in simple English: We Americans recently have shown a real propensity to shoot ourselves in the foot.

In terms of public-sector policies, unwise U.S. economic and social policies in the 1980s have created the vast bulk of U.S. fiscal, monetary, and social problems. In terms of private-sector policies, unwise positions have led us to take a very short-run view of economic and social life.

To say that we Americans are the cause of most of our problems is, in the final analysis, an optimistic view of what can be done in the future. Just as we created many of these problems, we can take steps to get our house in order as well. In some cases we might need some changes to be made on the part of foreign governments and business concerns. However, most of the required changes entail shifts in American public- and private-sector behavior. The United States—despite recent global changes—still has the ability to be the master of its fate as long as it is willing to stay within realistic bounds. If this view is correct, then our primary goal should be to examine and correct those American-generated problems that have gotten us into trouble.

I do not, however, expect any realistic self-inventory and self-adjustment process on the part of most Americans. Instead, I think we will all too often blame "foreigners" for our various problems. Super 301 activity will continue.

Table 10.8 Indicators in the Burdensharing Debate[a]

	National Income as a Percent of Total	Defense Spending as Percent of Total	Ratio of Defense Spending to National Income
Income and Defense Spending			
United States	48%	70%	1.47
Other NATO Members	36	27	0.74
Japan	17	4	0.21

	Population as a Percent of Total	Ratio of Defense Manpower to Population	Ratio of Naval Tonnage to National Income
Population and Defense Manpower			
United States	32%	1.22	1.35
Other NATO Members	53	1.13	0.92
Japan	16	0.14	0.19

[a]1985 data.

Source: Richard Brandon, "Budget Discussion Paper," Working Paper for a Council on Foreign Relations study group on the Economic Choices Confronting the Next President, New York, June 7, 1988, p. 14.

As Michael Aho of the Council on Foreign Relations noted, the United States has recently been spending $1.04 for every $1.00 it produces. Restoring equilibrium would require the United States to spend 99 cents for every $1.00 it produces for the next few years.[7] In the worldwide picture, this is a "double" adjustment (in theory) and not that large a shift compared to what has happened in many other countries. But given promises to read a president's lips, adjustments that are easy to make on a college blackboard in a macroeconomics class will be almost impossible to make in political reality.

Given a U.S. domestic impasse, it will prove much easier to blame "foreigners" for our difficulties. This is not to say that the United States should not seek to adjust its relationships with friends and foes. But these shifts will not solve basic U.S. problems unless domestic adjustments are made as well.

One key area of foreign adjustment will be the issue of burdensharing. As indicated in Table 10.8, the United States currently contributes to

Western defense (both in terms of money, manpower, and in areas like naval tonnage) much more in relative terms than the other NATO members or Japan. In the United States, calls for burdensharing will increase in the near future.[8]

Japan has taken dramatic strides in recent years to increase its aid to Third World countries. Given Japan's military past, this added aid to the Third World could be seen as an alternative form of total burdensharing.[9] However, a good portion of this aid has been "tied aid," or aid that must be spent on Japanese goods and services. This situation has raised new tensions among various interest groups in the United States. Is Japan using increased aid to improve the Japanese hold on various markets? some U.S. trade experts have been asking. Of course, the U.S. record on "tied aid" has not been 100 percent clean. Nevertheless, this issue has been raised to show the types of tensions that can arise even as one nation feels it is taking on more social burdens (or responsibilities).

Also, it will be quite difficult for Americans to get used to new realities if burdensharing "wins the day." With reduced "burdens" or "responsibilities" comes reduced "power" or "influence." It is not unrealistic to think that the United States will go through a period in which it will want to have its cake and eat it too. Americans may want reduced financial responsibilities, but will Americans like reduced influence over the Western Alliance nations? Serious tensions could arise in this area between U.S., European, and Japanese leaders in the 1990s.

The other area of serious tension centers on the United States's so-called "J" curve, which in reality has been more of an "L" curve. As the value of the dollar has declined, the U.S. trade deficit in theory should have shown dramatic improvement. Instead, the trade deficit has been closer to an L curve than a J curve. In an "L" curve, the deficit remains very large despite changes in the value of the dollar. Although many economists might think it unwise to look at deficits on a country-by-country basis, many political leaders cannot resist looking at country-by-country figures.

Table 10.9 shows that the U.S. trade deficit with Japan and the NIEs has remained strong. These trends are bound to increase debate in the U.S. Congress over proposals designed to produce a "level playing field." These proposals will include renewed efforts to "open" certain foreign markets. In the conflict between "national" treatment and "reciprocity," U.S. lawmakers may be much more interested in "reciprocity." This approach would only increase U.S.-Japanese and U.S.-NIE tensions.

The issues of foreign direct ownership in the United States will also come up. Recent survey research indicates that many Americans wish to change the "rules of the road" in this area.[10]

Table 10.9 U.S. Merchandise Trade Deficits[a] (in billions of U.S. dollars)

Japan	$55.8
Canada	9.8
Western Europe	7.4
NIEs	21.2

[a]Estimate based on February 1989 annualized rates.

Source: U.S. Department of Commerce.

Regional Trading Blocs?

The analysis so far points to a difficult macroeconomic period for the United States combined with the propensity to "blame others" for our problems. Combined with these factors should be key shifts in the international trading system.

GATT has served as the main system of trade in the post–World War II era. However, research done by the National Planning Association indicates that this multinational trading system may be on thin ice in the eyes of the U.S. business and labor communities. The NPA recently surveyed many executives and labor leaders at Fortune 500 companies and in top unions. These senior executives are leaders in the international aspects of their organizations.

The NPA asked these business and labor leaders if they felt that the world economy is shifting more in the direction of regional trading blocs (e.g., the United States and Canada, the European Community, Japan and Asia, and so forth). As indicated by the estimates presented in Table 10.10, 89 percent of the executives agreed that the international economy is moving in the direction of regional trading blocs. Meanwhile, 76 percent felt that the shift to regional trading blocs would hurt the U.S. economy; 64 percent said they felt this shift would hurt the world economy.

Three-quarters of the surveyed executives said they felt that the trend toward regional trading blocs would hurt the current round of GATT talks. Also, 64 percent said they felt U.S. workers would be hurt by these trends.

About 66 percent of the surveyed U.S. executives said they felt most of the NIEs would rather form a regional trading bloc with the United States than with Japan. At the same time, the survey results showed strong U.S. interests in signing free-trade agreements with other countries.

Table 10.10 The Role of Regional Trading Blocs in the World Economy

1.	Percent of surveyed U.S. executives who believe that the world economy is shifting in the direction of regional trading blocs.	89%
2.	Percent of surveyed U.S. executives who believe that regional trading blocs would hurt the GATT talks.	75%
3.	Percent of surveyed U.S. executives who believe that the NIEs would rather form a trading bloc with the United States than with Japan.	66%
4.	Percent of surveyed U.S. executives who believe that the United States should sign free-trade agreements with the following nations:	
	Mexico	66%
	One or all of the NIEs	41%
	The European Community	55%
	Japan	41%

Source: Estimates based on 1989 NPA survey data.

These NPA survey data point to several trends within the U.S. business and labor communities, including the following:

1. A lack of great faith in the GATT to reform itself;
2. A feeling that regional trading blocs will increase in importance;
3. A concern that the United States should give primary concern to the formation of free-trade agreements that favor U.S. interests; and
4. A feeling that the United States could interest the NIEs in casting their lots with the United States instead of Japan.

If U.S. business, labor, and government interests act on the above-stated views in the next few years, then the international trading system could be in for a period of real turbulence. It may prove to be quite difficult to improve international cooperation in this type of environment.

As indicated by Table 10.10, 41 percent of the surveyed executives said they would be interested in a free-trade agreement with Japan. The Japanese Finance Ministry and the Ministry of International Trade and Industry are looking at potential agreements with the United States. Meanwhile, the U.S. Federal Trade Commission is looking at agreements with Japan. Former

U.S. Ambassador to Japan Mike Mansfield and Senator Max Baucus have advocated such agreements.

While a U.S.-Japanese Free-Trade Agreement could lower tensions in this area, many would agree with the Secretary of Agriculture (and former U.S. Trade Representative) Clayton Yeutter: "As a practical matter, it seems to me that a decision is a long way off."[11] These types of agreements will not be in place soon.

The Implications for Asia-Pacific Cooperation

The trends that have been noted in this chapter have serious implications for economic cooperation in the Asia-Pacific region. The key points are as follows:

1. It will be much harder for the Asia-Pacific region to fashion an institutional system that promotes economic cooperation similar to those that have already been formed in North America and Western Europe. It could be very difficult, in fact, to create lasting Asia-Pacific region agreements. Meanwhile, the United States-Canadian Free Trade Agreement and European plans to form a unified internal market by 1992 are moving forward.

2. Japan may wish to play the role of the hegemonic leader in this part of the world. However, memories from the era of World War II will hurt Japan if it tries to play the role of an overt hegemonic leader. Also, survey data from the National Planning Association indicate that the majority of leading U.S. business executives believe that Asia-Pacific nations would rather enter a regional trading bloc with the United States than form one with Japan. This means that many private- and public-sector leaders in the United States are not prepared to see Japan become the hegemonic leader in this part of the world.

3. Thus, the leaders of many Asian and Pacific nations face a very difficult choice in the near future. For many Asian and Pacific nations, their economic relationship with Japan is growing. Nevertheless, the United States still represents the largest open market for many of their products. Thus, it is not unrealistic to expect that leaders in many Asian and Pacific nations will look to the United States—and not Japan—for leadership in the area of regional cooperation.

4. However, the United States—faced with difficult trade and budget deficit problems—often will find it easier to blame other nations for U.S. problems than to see the behavior of the United States as the main source of these problems. It could prove to be very difficult for the United States to lead cooperation in the Asia-Pacific region when it starts programs such as the recent Super 301 campaign.

5. The tensions mentioned in points one through four will appear in a world without an economic slump but with slow economic growth. If

the world economy enters a recession in the next few years, tensions in the Asia-Pacific region will be even stronger.

All of these trends point to the conclusion that the next few years may not see a flowering of cooperation in this region of the world; rather, the key issue could be one of damage control.

Notes

Richard S. Belous is vice president, International Affairs, and a senior economist at the National Planning Association. This chapter represents his personal views and does not necessarily represent the views of NPA.

1. Audrey Freedman, *The New Look in Wage Policy and Employee Relations* (The Conference Board, 1985), pp. 1–14.

2. Richard S. Belous, *The Contingent Economy: The Growth of the Temporary, Part-Time, and Subcontracted Workforce* (Washington, D.C.: National Planning Association, 1989).

3. Thomas A. Kochan, et al., *The Transformation of American Industrial Relations* (New York: Basic Books, Inc., 1986), pp. 21–46.

4. David Wessel, "If a Recession Hits Is U.S. Prepared for It?" *The Wall Street Journal*, April 17, 1989, p. 1; and Lindley H. Clark, Jr., "Will Low Inventories Soften a Slump?" *The Wall Street Journal*, April 10, 1989, p. 1.

5. Ibid.; and *The Wall Street Journal*, July 24, 1989, p. 1.

6. Thomas Courchene, *Savings and Global Imbalances*, National Planning Association Background Paper, 1989.

7. C. Michael Aho and Marc Levinson, *After Reagan: Confronting the Changed World Economy* (New York: Council on Foreign Relations, 1988), pp. 12–30 .

8. British North American Committee on Preserving Shared Values, "A Statement on the Occasion of the 40th Anniversary of the Signing of the North Atlantic Treaty," (London: British North American Research Association, 1989).

9. Rebecca Hartley, "Burden-Sharing Is Only the Beginning," *Looking Ahead*, vol. 11, no. 2, 1989, pp. 6–13.

10. Howard Muson, "Gift Horse or Trojan Horse," *Across the Board*, April 1988, pp. 42–43.

11. *The New York Times*, May 20, 1988, p. A2.

11

Technology Transfer in the Pacific Basin: Issues and Policies

Charles T. Stewart, Jr.

The future performance of all economies depends on the availability of new technology and the effectiveness with which it is employed. Nations must either develop their own technology or import it from elsewhere. In fact, the developed countries and the Newly Industrializing Countries (NICs) must do both. The Less Developed Countries (LDCs) cannot yet generate their own technology and have limited ability to import it.

International technology transfer is an important complement of domestic technological development. For most countries, it is an essential complement. A study by Jong-Bum Kim found a strong positive correlation between domestic research expenditures and technology imports for all countries observed except the United States.[1] Even in Japan, which has become a major technology exporter, much domestic research and development is still built around a core of imported technology. Japan's technology imports, as well as those of the United States, continue to increase. Kim found no country in which technology imports were a substitute for, hence a deterrent to, domestic technological development. The view held in some countries that imported technology displaces domestic research is unfounded. The export of technology, on the other hand, is part of the compensation for technology development, particularly for firms in countries with small domestic markets.

The international transfer of technology presents three kinds of problems: (1) finding access to the desired technology; (2) using the technology developed or imported, that is, absorptive capacity; and (3) coping with the consequences of successful transfer of technology.

The Pacific Basin includes nations at very different stages of development. Countries can be classified on the basis of (1) their ability to export technology, and (2) their ability to import technology. The first group is led by Japan and the United States, which because of their large size and advanced stage of development are major exporters of technology as well as importers. The second group—the NICs—includes Taiwan, South Korea, Singapore, and Hong Kong, all of which have a well-developed ability to absorb foreign technology, all of which have reached intermediate levels of development, and all of which are beginning to develop their own technology and to transfer technology to LDCs. The third group—the LDCs—although diverse, is a step behind in development and industrialization and lags in technological level and absorptive capacity. The People's Republic of China is a special case, because in the midst of a backward and traditional economic structure it has a technologically advanced sector which concentrates on military research and production and has little interaction with the rest of the economy.

For the industrial nations, and especially for the NICs, future growth depends on continued access to new imported technology—on technology transfer. Even the United States, which in the 1950s and 1960s conducted a disproportionate share of world research and activities, is becoming more dependent on imported technology as other countries expand their technological development efforts and their share of global research and development. For the LDCs, the issue is not access so much as ability to absorb. Most of the technology from which they could benefit in the years ahead is not proprietary but there is limited ability to make effective use of it. It is a problem not of transfer of technology from proprietary sources, but diffusion of technology that is the common property of all who know how to use it.

I will distinguish three sets of problems and policies: first, those involving technology relations among the developed nations, in particular between Japan and the United States; second, relations between the advanced countries and the NICs, especially Taiwan and South Korea; third, relations between the advanced industrial countries and the LDCs. Some countries in the third group, such as Thailand, may be in the process of crossing over to the second group.

The usual discussion of technology transfer focuses on patents, licensing, trade restrictions (access to technology), protection of property rights, and markets. These issues are important for technology transfer within group one, and from group one to group two—to Taiwan and South Korea in particular. It is not yet important, in my opinion, for technology transfer to group three. For all but group one, absorptive capacity is an issue, although for different types and levels of technology as one moves from group two to group three. Finally, the problems engendered by successful absorption of imported technology—unemployment, urbanization—have been dealt with rather successfully by group two but are enormous and threatening to group three.

The Industrial Nations

Among the industrial countries there are concerns and disputes about transfer that involve political and military issues, primarily between Japan and the United States.[2] There are also problems of protecting indigenous technology in order to attain or preserve competitive trade advantages. These are primarily business concerns but have become politicized.

Most of the really advanced technology is transferred within and between firms, only incidentally between nations. Much of this technology is developed by multinational firms, and more and more of it has no nationality. It obtains nationality only by virtue of seeking and obtaining patent protection. Most multinational firms will conduct research and production wherever the resources are found and the price is right. There are national differences, however. R&D in the United States has never been a cooperative venture; until recently such a venture might have been considered illegal, and even now cooperation is only tolerated. In Japan, cooperation is the norm and is encouraged by the government; thus domestic technology transfer is very rapid. And Japanese firms have not multinationalized their research activities, nor even the production of sophisticated new products, nearly to the same extent as the multinationals of other industrial nations. The result is that new Japanese technology is less accessible to other countries than new technology of other industrial nations. This asymmetry is embedded in culture, institutions, and laws.

So far as the advanced nations are concerned—Japan and the United States in particular—the issue is not only transfer of technology but in which country will it be implemented in new and better products and to which countries these products will be exported. The old issue of technology transfer is becoming an investment and trade issue as technology is becoming internationalized through several developments: (1) the convergence of advanced countries in their ability to absorb new technologies; (2) the convergence of basic and applied research and development in many industries; and (3) the dominance of multinational firms in the development of new technology.

Research and Secrecy

New technology is the product of applied research conducted by firms and basic research largely conducted by universities, other nonprofits, and government laboratories. But the linkage is becoming closer between basic research, which is mainly open, largely international in character, and usually unpatentable, and important commercial applications. The recent award of a Nobel Prize to two IBM employees for their contributions to superconductivity is a case in point. Neither is American, and their work was done in Switzerland; already scientists in many countries have made further advances based upon their initial discoveries; and practical applications may be implemented without benefit of, need for, or possibility of a legal patent monopoly. This is the situation prevailing among the advanced industrial countries. More and more of the recently developed technology has no nationality, and transfer between advanced nations is not the issue.[3] The issue instead involves the property rights of corporations in innovations whose development they financed.

The convergence of basic and applied research means that basic research, once the exclusive domain of universities and other nonprofit institutions and Bell Labs, is more and more being financed and sometimes conducted by business firms. The spirit of openness traditionally surrounding basic research is becoming endangered, as firms financing or conducting it naturally are seeking a head start in the resulting applied research. But we are talking about the competitive advantage of firms, not nations. There is one exception. Whereas major firms in North America and Western Europe are substantially internationalized, this has not been true of Japanese firms. But a combination of increased protection in Japan's major markets, the export of capital from Japan, and the rise in the value of the yen is compelling the internationalization of Japanese business as a necessary condition of preserving existing overseas markets and entering new ones.

To what extent are governments likely to restrict the transfer of valuable technology to other nations? In the past such restrictions have usually been applied only in cases involving national security interests. The Patent Secrecy Act provides a legal means for such protections. At times it appears that this cloak of secrecy has been stretched to cover commercially valuable technology developed in government laboratories. Recently, cases have arisen, notably in superconductivity, of attempts to restrict the freedom of scientific information for purely commercial reasons.[4] This issue will become more important as the close linkage of science to technology spreads to more and more industries. Product and process life is much shorter in some science-based industries than in more traditional industries, hence patents are of limited value, even if obtainable and enforced; the head start and industrial secrecy become the main concerns. In the future, the issue of secrecy may become more important than patent issues.

Policies Among Industrial Countries

What should the advanced countries do to promote the development and transfer of new technology? As more and more industries move toward the frontiers of technology, they must marry technology to science in order to progress. The occasions multiply for "general" research, which is of more than purely scientific interest but aims at commercial applications only indirectly and in the long run. It aims instead at creating the preconditions for applied research and development. More and more of it is being done by industry and through university-industry collaboration; more could and should be done via research consortia and other cooperative arrangements. Human resources for such research are scarce, and funding is limited. Rescher offered evidence that there are diminishing returns to invention and that the costs of scientific progress are rising exponentially.[5] Duplication is not only wasteful, it reduces the output of general and precompetitive research, which is the input for commercially oriented research and innovation.

Among the industrial countries, appropriate policies include the free exchange of scientific information and participation in collaborative research activities. There are comparative advantages in research. Furthermore, smaller industrial countries cannot mount an across-the-board research effort effectively and must instead specialize in particular areas and rely on cooperation in others.

What kind of collaborative research should be encouraged? First, noncompetitive research, the type of research that is basic, that may or may not eventuate in commercial innovations but that is so far removed from such innovations in time and approach that proprietary concerns do not arise. Japan is contributing to basic research projects being conducted in the United States, not only financially but also by sending research workers. For example, it has endowed twelve chairs at MIT, financed a spectrometer at Brookhaven, and greatly increased the number of Japanese researchers at the National Institutes of Health.[6] Much of basic research is still done by government organizations, universities, and nonprofit foundations and institutes, and cooperation among such organizations should be encouraged.

Second is research, whether basic or applied, whose product is a public good, that cannot be appropriated by any one supplier. One may mention here collaboration in weather research, oceanographic research, geological research leading to better earthquake predictions and mineral exploration, research on environmental hazards, and much public health and medical research. This type of research too is typically carried out by government laboratories and nonprofits.

A problem with the above types of research is the one-sided nature of the collaboration. Many researchers from Japan and other Asian nations come to work in the United States, but few American researchers go to Asia. In part this is the inevitable consequence of differences in research facilities and opportunities, which should be reduced in time, but in part it is due to the reluctance of Americans to take advantage of foreign opportunities. Japan has increased the number of fellowships for American scientists and engineers to study in Japan, but many fellowships go begging.[7]

Third is precompetitive research. This is the area that is most difficult to delineate and earmark for cooperative effort, in part because much of this research is conducted by business firms and business organizations. Fears persist in the United States about the antitrust implications of cooperation, despite passage of the National Cooperative Research Act in 1984 to encourage joint research. Time and a few test court cases are needed to allay such fears. Japan has shown us that it is possible for firms that compete vigorously in production and distribution to cooperate in research. Another problem is the prospect that such research may result in immediately applicable findings that individual firms may wish to monopolize. Hence many large firms may choose to go their own way rather than collaborating in such research.

The NICs

The NICs import nearly all their technology, although they are able to adapt it and are beginning to develop their own. They have the capability to license technology across a wide range of industries. In order to facilitate technology transfer, the NICs first of all will need to obtain advanced graduate education and experience in industrial countries; they also would benefit from assistance in developing their own research and development facilities and capabilities, including related advanced scientific and technical education. The main barriers to technology transfer from advanced nations to the NICs are the lack of protection for industrial property rights, which discourages licensing and technical assistance, and the emigration of some of their best technical and entrepreneurial people. These barriers are, of course, interconnected.

Technology Development Strategy

A nation's level of development should be associated with appropriate technology development strategies, recognizing the role of technology imports. As countries advance, their technology imports keep on rising (see Table 11.1). However, as domestic research and development grows, at some point the ratio of technology import payments to domestic R&D expenditures begins to decline. It has been declining for some time in Japan and has begun to drop in South Korea. In the United States, it rose during the 1970s, mainly because the rest of the advanced world was doing much more research than it had done in the past; opportunities for technology import improved. More recently, it has dropped (see Table 11.2). The relation between technology imports and domestic research in Japan and South Korea has been highly complementary. Their development strategies have been imitative, with domestic research built around imported technology.

Table 11.1 U.S. Technology Trade with Pacific Nations (in millions of U.S. dollars)

	1987		1988	
Country	Receipts	Payments	Receipts	Payments
Canada	87	9	59	12
Japan	723	88	886	92
Australia	30	3	30	2
New Zealand	13	*	12	0
Singapore	30	*	13	0
Hong Kong	4	1	6	*
South Korea	34	*	70	*
Taiwan	31	*	44	*
Indonesia	5	0	4	*
Malaysia	*	0	*	0
Thailand	2	0	4	0
People's Republic of China	37	*	33	*

* Less than US$500,000.

Source: U.S. Department of Commerce, Bureau of Economic Analysis, Form BE-93.
Data refer to royalties and license fees received and paid for use of industrial processes.

Japan is now following defensive or even aggressive strategies in most areas. Japan is now depending more on its own research and relatively less on technology imports; South Korea plans to move in the same direction and aims to increase its research and development expenditures from 2 percent of its GNP today to 5 percent by the beginning of the next century. In the United States, which follows primarily an aggressive development strategy, technology imports and domestic research and development are mainly

Table 11.2 Ratio of Technology Imports to Domestic Research and Development, Selected Pacific Basin Nations

Country	1960	1970	1975	1980	1985
United States	.003	.009	.013	.012	.007
Japan	.20	.11	.07	.057	.063
South Korea	NA	.071	.300	.334	.205

Sources: Republic of Korea Ministry of Science and Technology and Japan Management and Coordination Agency, cited in Jong-Bum Kim, Technology Development Strategy and the Relationship Between Technology Import and Domestic Research and Development (R&D), unpublished doctoral dissertation, The George Washington University, Washington, D.C., 1989.

independent, in some cases substitutive.[8] Technology development policies of other Pacific nations are imitative, hence technology imports are highly complementary to their development.

An imitative strategy is best implemented by licensing technology and through foreign direct investment. Defensive and, in particular, aggressive strategies rely much more on indigenous research and development capabilities.

Protection of Industrial Property Rights

The traditional concerns about technology transfer involve the protection of industrial and intellectual property, adequate compensation for transferring technology, and safeguards to protect the owner of technology from competition with companies and nations to which his technology has been transferred. The issues are quite different for the NICs and the LDCs than they are for industrial nations.

The NICs usually have no interest in honoring patent rights. Why should they? Patent laws are intended primarily to reward domestic inventors by protecting inventions in the home country, not to reward foreign inventors by protecting foreign inventions. Until a country has enough inventors and inventions of its own to make them worth protecting, its leaders may not think that it is really in their nation's interest to protect intellectual and industrial property rights. The NICs (and the LDCs) are interested in gaining access to the existing stock of technology as quickly and as cheaply as possible, with no concern for the future flow of new technology. Firms owning technology are concerned with obtaining a return on their investment. The industrial nations, on the other hand, are concerned with adequate rewards for invention and innovation in order to provide incentives for future inventive and innovative activities.[9] All benefit by a large continuing flow of new technology.

This is a policy research issue. What ratio between domestically generated technology and imported technology "justifies" respect for patent rights? The ratio would be lower for a nation that is also exporting domestically generated technology than for those which are not. The exporter would have to consider the impact of disregard for such property rights on its ability to import technology. This is itself a complex issue encompassing opposite effects: copying permits import of technology on the cheap in some cases; but the prospect of copying dissuades some technology transfer. Lack of protection for intellectual property rights may also discourage domestic invention and innovation and encourage scientific and technical "brain drain."

The protection of industrial and intellectual property rights is a much bigger issue for the NICs than with either industrial nations or LDCs.

Complaints about patent infringement go on year after year. Existing international agreements are too limited in scope; the number of signatories is too small; and there are no effective enforcement powers or means of settling disputes.[10] The interests of industrial nations are in conflict with those of LDCs and NICs as they see them.

When a small country gains through protection at the expense of open markets everywhere else, the losses to others are too small and too diffuse to have noticeable consequences. When large countries follow the same policy, the losses are too big to be ignored. The same reasoning applies to losses to firms that develop new technology at high cost when they are injured by violation of their patents and other intellectual property rights. How large must the losses be before the losers decide that investment in new technology is not worth the cost? Before they decide that licensing technology to countries where it is not protected is not worth the risk? That investing in productive facilities in countries that do not protect its property rights is counter-productive? That trade with such countries is not in their interest?[11] How long will it be before they decide to rely on secrecy rather than patent rights, and to invest less in new technology and more in making new technology burglar-proof? Before the nations adversely affected decide to reciprocate, making patent violation costly to the firm, and to the nation that tolerates it?

All of the above are the consequences of disregard for intellectual property rights, and these problems inevitably slow the development of new technology as well as the international flow of technology. There are other effects that have a more direct impact on nations that do not protect intellectual property: First, lack of protection discourages domestic inventive activity; second, domestic inventors seek protection for their property elsewhere, in countries that do afford them protection, and third, as a result, there is a tendency for inventors to emigrate. The United States may not have suffered much damage in this regard because it is the world's largest free market and because its protection of new technology has attracted many inventors from abroad, particularly from countries that neglect the interests of their own inventors. I know of no study on this topic; it should be researched. Some noted inventors from Taiwan, for instance, now reside in the United States, but neither the numbers nor the factors inducing them to come here are known. Taiwanese nationals received more patents in the United States in the period from 1983 to 1988 than inventors from any other developing country (and more than several small industrial countries); South Korea was number two.[12] Moreover, both countries have greatly increased the number of their U.S. patents since then. (See Table 11.3.)

The issue of protection for industrial property rights is a problem only for the NICs: the four dragons, which may soon be joined by a fifth or

Table 11.3 U.S. Patents Awarded, by Nationality of the Inventor

Country	1983-1985	1986-1988
United States	110,790	122,137
Japan	32,671	45,924
Canada	3,548	4,397
Australia	874	1,179
Taiwan	338	1,008
New Zealand	123	175
South Korea	94	224
Hong Kong	65	106
Singapore	18	NA
Philippines	13	NA
Malaysia	8	NA
People's Republic of China	7	NA
Thailand	4	NA
North Korea	4	NA
Indonesia	2	NA

Source: U.S. Patent and Trademark Office, "Technology Assessment and Forecasting Special Report--All Technologies 1/63 - 12/88," April 1989.

sixth. The advanced industrial nations all have laws for the protection of intellectual property rights, and the institutions to implement these laws. It is the NICs that have the capacity to violate valuable patent rights and licensing agreements and that lack the national will to enforce them even when they have the appropriate legal structure. Unlike the industrial nations, they question whether it is in their interest to protect what are seen to be mainly foreign property rights. (Among the industrial nations, there are far more complaints about Japan's inadequate protection of industrial property rights than about any other industrial nation, but the complaints are few compared to those about some of the NICs.)

A recent study on national commitment to the protection of intellectual property rights identifies eight countries with the lowest commitment, four of which are in Pacific Asia: Taiwan, South Korea, Indonesia, and the Philippines.[13] Runners-up include Singapore and Thailand.

In time, when a country becomes an advanced industrial nation, as in the case of Japan, it finds that it is more in its interest to afford protection for industrial and intellectual property rights. This shift occurs because the country's relations with other advanced nations becomes a reciprocal one, not the one-sided relationship experienced between advanced and developing countries. Problems of violation remain, but they are no longer different in kind from those found within other industrial nations; most of them are legal rather than political problems.

Patent infringements are not the only issue. Even when countries have an interest in protecting such rights, there are differences among countries in what is patentable (products vs. processes, life forms, chip designs, software); in terms of patent awards, there are differences in duration, scope, and licensing provisions as well as in enforcement procedures and their effectiveness. These variations, of course, are all subject to mutual accommodation or, if not, remain as clear differences that business can and must take into account.

Is there anything the United States, and now Japan, can do to make it in the NICs' interests to respect patent rights? (All the countries except Indonesia have patent laws, but enforcement is too uncertain, too little, and too late, so that there is no effective patent protection in the eyes of the foreign firm.)

Persuasion alone does not appear to be very effective. Even if there is agreement on the desirability of a system of property rights that rewards the inventor and investor and serves as an incentive for innovation, the NICs see short-run advantages in violating such rights and discount long-run costs. After all, most of the rights pertain to foreigners. Taiwan is the worst offender in terms of costs to owners of industrial property rights. Taiwan is a small country. Forty percent of its exports go to the United States. Singapore and South Korea are also major violators. The direct losses to industrial countries in 1986 were estimated at $23 billion, half of which was borne by the United States.[14] Probably over half of these losses were inflicted by firms in Pacific nations.

Other, larger countries will follow Taiwan's example as they increase their ability to violate patent rights, which will happen long before they develop an interest in protecting them. Their combined impact cannot be ignored by the industrial countries, in particular by the United States, which is both by far the largest loser and the largest export market for every current and prospective major violator of industrial property rights. The connection between property rights and market access will not be overlooked much longer.

If the infringement is only in domestic markets, the industrial countries have little leverage. By the time the problem becomes serious, the country involved has outgrown eligibility for foreign aid. The industrial country may link credit policies, access to its domestic markets, and other policies to compliance with patent agreements, but the linkage is indirect and unlikely to be believed or accomplished.

If, on the other hand, the infringement is in the production of a good that is exported, and the country directly affected is the main or a major export market for the product, then there is potential leverage: Access to its market may be denied. This, however, is rarely done, and only in extreme cases. No matter how justified such action may be, its political costs are high in terms of relations with the government and peoples of the country whose products are banned. The threat of closing export markets has not been very credible for these reasons. The United States is the largest export market for most of the leading infringers, who happen to be in East and Southeast Asia; therefore it does have the potential leverage. But it has not been willing to use it. For instance, the United States requires consideration of intellectual property right protection before renewal of generalized system of preferences (GSP) privileges. There are negotiations, and agreements are reached, but the problem remains. The persistence of the United States trade deficit may, however, overcome U.S. reluctance to use its trade leverage. There is no shortage of protectionist and retaliatory bills before Congress. Linkage will be legislated at some point.

The LDCs

The LDCs lack the capacity to absorb most new technologies. They lack the capacity to benefit by stealing valuable new technology; their pirating of trademarks and copyrights may be costly to the owners but does not involve much valuable new technology. (However, copying of software is an important exception. The People's Republic of China is reported to be one of the worst offenders, costing U.S. business from $100 to $400 million a year. Some U.S. companies are reportedly unwilling to sell on the Chinese market for fear that the software will be pirated.)[15] However, countries that do not respect copyrights are not expected to respect patents. And pirating diverts their enterprise and expertise from more growth-inducing activities. Shakespeare had something to say on this topic:

> Good name in man, and woman, dear lord,
> Is the immediate jewel of our souls.
> Who steals my purse steals trash . . .
> But he that filches from me my good name
> Robs me of that which not enriches him,
> And makes me poor indeed.
> (*Othello*, Act III, Scene iii, lines 155ff)

LDCs lack the highly trained human resources, and the supporting technological and industrial infrastructure, for successful reverse engineering. Except for old established technology, import through licensing is premature. And for most such technology, licensing is not needed because it is no longer proprietary. Licensing provides know-how and training more than access to technology.

For the LDCs in Pacific Asia, the dominant constraint on technology transfer is the lack of absorptive capacity. The principal means of reducing this bottleneck is direct investment by foreign firms that provide training and experience for nationals, and by overseas education and experience for nationals, enabling them to master and manage technology. The relevant issues, therefore, refer to domestic policies that inhibit foreign investment. Access to overseas education is not a problem, but opportunities for overseas work experience are diminishing.

Such nations may not be in a position to select technologies for importation or to bargain knowledgeably on licensing terms. They should rely heavily on foreign firms to make decisions and import technology through direct investment and joint ventures. The foreign firm that makes the choices also takes the risks and incurs the cost of training workers and investing in supporting infrastructure. Industrial countries supplement the efforts of foreign firms by providing education, supplying the LDC with needed skills or with the capability of acquiring them.

A major vehicle for technology transfer, the U.S. multinational firm in the Pacific Rim countries, has diminished in importance. Direct investment by high-technology multinational firms is down, and the expected further decline in the value of the dollar relative to some Pacific Rim currencies is likely to keep investment down. New investment is required for continued hiring of local nationals; as they gain the experience, this results in both greater absorptive capacity and increased technology transfer and technology. This approach is the main vehicle for technology transfer to the LDCs. I stress U.S. overseas investment, although in most countries Japanese investment is larger, for two reasons. The first is that, until recently, much Japanese investment was in traditional industries with limited technology transfer potential. The second is the great reluctance of Japanese firms to hire local nationals for senior managerial and technical positions in order to give them the opportunity to acquire the experience helpful in enhancing the nation's absorptive capacity and the transfer of technology. A related difference is the greater tendency of U.S. firms to source from domestic firms in LDCs versus the Japanese preference for establishing subsidiaries or to source from other Japanese firms with local plants.

The main obstacles to technology transfer are barriers imposed by LDCs to foreign investment, which at their stage of development is or should be the main vehicle for technology transfer. Host country policies limit technology transfer indirectly.[16] Requirements for local majority ownership deter investment by some firms with valuable proprietary technology—U.S. firms in particular—who fear loss of managerial control and technology "seepage." Other barriers include exclusion of foreign investment from certain industries, undue limitations on the number of expatriates allowed work permits, and undue local content requirements.

Local content requirements, intended to force-feed technology, can do this for some firms that consider themselves captive, but they can drive out other firms and deter yet other firms from coming in. More often than not such requirements are poorly disguised subsidies to host country nationals. Only nations with a large actual or potential domestic market can afford to use the leverage of that market to coerce uneconomic (premature) technology transfer.

Limits on the employment of expatriates, justified as a lever to force training of nationals, can paradoxically raise costs, particularly for advanced technologies. Most foreign firms, with the exception of the Japanese, are eager to replace expensive expatriates with nationals as rapidly as is feasible.

The exclusion of foreign investors from certain industries (banking and insurance being common examples) limits technology transfer. Restrictions on licensing—short maximum duration of licensing agreements, low ceilings on allowable fees (intended to prevent exploitation of domestic firms lacking the knowledge or the market position to bargain effectively)—can preclude the transfer of valuable technology via this route altogether. Only Malaysia, Singapore, and Thailand leave the terms of royalties and fees up to negotiation between licensor and licensee. It is also a matter of contract enforcement. Firms would be more willing to license valuable technology if they were confident that contract violations would be promptly and effectively prosecuted. Licensing to domestic producers as a vehicle for technology transfer is of little consequence for the LDCs but grows progressively more important relative to direct investment with the growth of absorptive capacity.[17]

In larger countries, whose domestic market is the principal attraction for foreign investors or licensors, the possibility of "unfair" competition from public firms creates uncertainty about sales and profitability.

For the LDCs, protection of patent rights and the like is a small issue; copyrights and trademarks, involving very little technology transfer, are the main concern. Firms from advanced nations have no reason to transfer advanced, proprietary technology to such nations: The countries lack the absorptive capacity; costs of transfer would be very high; and the host country unwilling if not unable to pay. The issue for the LDCs is developing absorptive capacity for open, readily available technology, not speeding up transfer of proprietary technology.

An issue raised by some LDCs is the decoupling of technology transfer from direct investment and/or from trade. In this case, the nation wants the technology but does not wish to buy it embodied in imported products. Or it may not wish to obtain the technology via a foreign presence, which raises nationalistic hackles and also raises questions about whether technology is actually transferred or remains in a foreign enclave—a transplant, not a transfer. This issue is premature for the LDCs and, in some cases, even in the NICs. It is Japan and North America that are able in most cases to import technology without the need for intermediation. For nations with less absorptive capacity, the technologies that can be decoupled and effectively transferred are the open technologies readily available through engineering consulting firms. These technologies raise no transfer issues. They are free for the taking, for anyone who can implement them.

Some LDCs are facing an enormous problem of growing unemployment and underemployment as technologies readily available in agriculture and in traditional industries permit very large and rapid increases in productivity.[18] The Asian NICs succeeded in exporting their unemployment; the Latin American NICs failed. As additional Pacific Basin nations accelerate productivity gains and structural change, they are likely to face growing unemployment problems. The prospects of employing workers displaced from agriculture and traditional industries in export industries are much less favorable than they were for Japan and the first generation of NICs.[19] But that is another topic.

Education and Training

The most important form of technology transfer offered by the United States to Pacific Basin countries is subsidized higher education. This aid is not provided by the federal government but by hundreds of state and city universities and colleges and private nonprofit institutions. In all, especially the former, the price (tuition) is far below actual costs, so that the average foreign student receives several thousand dollars of subsidies per year. The annual subsidy to Pacific Basin countries alone is very crudely estimated to run a half billion dollars per year.

Hundreds of thousands of Pacific Rim nationals (the number could exceed a million by now) have earned college degrees in the United States. A large proportion of them have earned postgraduate degrees. Some idea of the continuing dimension of the "export" of educational services is provided in Table 11.4. An estimated 145,000 students from ten East and Southeast Asian nations were enrolled in U.S. colleges and universities in the 1987-1988 academic year, just over one-half of whom were graduate students. In addition to students, thousands of exchange visitors and research scholars from Asian countries are in the United States (their presence helps explain the discrepancy between the figure in Table 11.4 of 25,000 Chinese and the Chinese Embassy report of 40,000). Many of them contribute to the host nation, but most also derive benefits from their experience that are of value to their home countries.

A high proportion of these students, graduate students in particular, are in specialties relevant for technology transfer, utilization, and development. This is well known. What is less appreciated is the fact that many of those obtaining scientific and engineering degrees go on to work for U.S. firms

Table 11.4 Foreign Students in the United States, 1987-1988

Country	Number	Graduate (%)	Undergraduate (%)	Other (%)
People's Republic of China	25,170	81.0	14.9	4.1
Hong Kong	10,650	29.7	68.1	2.2
Indonesia	9,010	28.7	66.9	4.4
Japan	18,050	23.6	58.2	18.2
South Korea	20,520	72.8	23.9	3.3
Malaysia	19,480	21.3	77.1	1.6
Philippines	4,420	41.0	53.1	5.9
Singapore	4,870	21.6	76.8	1.3
Taiwan (ROC)	26,660	78.3	18.1	3.6
Thailand	6,430	56.3	38.0	5.7

Source: Institute of International Education, Open Doors, 1987-88, New York, 1987.

in the United States and in overseas branches, acquiring experience vital to mastering the technologies involved and giving them the capability of transferring these technologies to their own countries. Those who return home directly after completing their education contribute to their home countries' capacities to absorb advanced technologies. Those who first gain experience abroad and then return home prove to be important agents for the transfer of technology. The Korean computer industry owes much to Koreans and Korean Americans educated in the United States with experience in U.S. firms. Some who did not return to their home countries nevertheless were instrumental in facilitating technology transfer, given their contacts and their knowledge of the language and customs of their home country. This is not to suggest that attrition is not a problem, in particular for the PRC, many of whose nationals studying in the United States have not returned.

In fact, the desire of many of the students to remain in the United States is a major problem with educational aid. In engineering and the sciences, many students have succeeded in staying. Opportunities in the United States may explain most of the attrition. For some, their home countries do not offer them the opportunity to make use of their higher education, hence their emigration should not be considered a loss. Others may eventually return home when conditions are suitable, or they may play a role as intermediaries in facilitating technology transfer. But many who stay make no further contribution to their home countries related to their advanced training. They raise policy conflicts between nations, reflecting differences in both interests and values.

Other advanced nations have also contributed to the export of educational services to Pacific Rim countries. Of foreign students from Asia in 1986, 57.5 percent were in the United States, 6.4 percent in the UK, 6.2 percent in Canada, 4.4 percent in the Federal Republic of Germany, and 2.4 percent in France. But most who went abroad for scientific or technical education went to the United States.

The United States, with its huge and diverse industry of higher education, can and does leave the acceptance of foreign students up to individual universities. Smaller advanced nations may have to plan for foreign admissions in the light of domestic needs and capacities. LDCs and NICs that subsidize students' education abroad usually do exercise some controls. For them, sending students abroad for training is a step toward developing domestic educational institutions and capabilities as well as domestic research facilities and activities. The cooperation of advanced nations is needed for developing LDC and NIC national and regional capabilities. Although many U.S. universities and some nonprofit foundations (Ford, Rockefeller) have taken the initiative in assisting selected universities and research institutes, their disaggregated approach cannot do the job alone. Some multinational firms have taken the lead in establishing regional training facilities for their own employees. Concerted planning is needed by the host countries to establish priorities, and among advanced nations on how resources should be allocated.

Small nations, developed or not, will always remain dependent on other nations, or on regional and international institutions—such as the Asian Institute of Technology in Thailand and the International Rice Research Institute in the Philippines—for some specialized training and research.

As a nation advances from LDC to NIC status, its domestic educational capabilities grow. At the same time, its needs for overseas education change from, say, undergraduate training of engineers to specialized postgraduate training only, particularly in those specialties that its own educational system does not provide. Its needs for overseas training of scientific and technical graduates also changes: The training is for more advanced professionals and in the more technologically sophisticated industries not yet well established domestically. Whatever the strategy and stage of development, overseas training and experience play a role. But for LDCs it could be undergraduate education and industrial work experience; for the advanced nations it could be fellowships in leading research institutes.

Overseas education as an avenue for technology transfer is not closing, but it is narrowing. The doors of foreign universities are still open. The U.S. Department of Defense has suggested restricting foreign access to advanced education in highly technical fields. Nothing has come of this suggestion, however, and it is not likely that anything will come of it. Other suggestions for restricting access to advanced education, research fellowships, and the like have been aimed primarily at Japan because of its highly competitive position in some technical fields, but such a policy could affect citizens of other countries as well. There are also grumbles about foreign visitors working in U.S. research institutes.[20] Nothing is likely to come of this either. What is a concern is the decline in opportunities for valuable work experience after completion of professional education. This decline is resulting from a combination of factors: the increasing reluctance of the Department of Labor and of immigration authorities to allow foreigners to work, and employer reluctance to employ aliens as a spillover effect of new and much stricter legislation on employment of illegal aliens. A third deterrent to hiring aliens in many fields is the great increase in the number of Americans with advanced education, resulting in an excess supply of qualified candidates in many managerial, professional, and technical areas. The People's Republic of China, a latecomer in sending large numbers of its citizens for advanced study in the United States, will not find the opportunities to gain experience in U.S. firms which were available to the Koreans and Taiwanese. In some scientific and engineering specialties there is a shortage of U.S. graduates (from past experience, a temporary shortage). But the opportunities for foreigners in the immediate future are more likely to result in permanent residence in the United States than in a few years of valuable work experience followed by return home.

Developments in Science and Technology and Some Implications

Lack of adequate patent protection has resulted in greater stress on industrial secrecy, which inhibits the flow of technology. But many older technologies had "natural" protection: They could not be easily copied or reverse engineered. Pharmaceuticals were an exception, and drug companies have been major victims of patent violators and trademark counterfeiting. Some important new technologies, however, are easily and cheaply copied or reverse engineered. We are referring to software, to microchip designs, and to biotechnology. There is no international consensus on whether there should be property rights in these areas, and if so, how these property rights ought to be protected. What is clear is that under existing policies and procedures, there is no way they can be effectively protected. Secrecy is impossible. Perhaps there is no way to protect these rights that is politically acceptable in free countries. That leaves "retaliation" via official trade restrictions as the only feasible response. The link between trade and technology transfer has always existed; it is simply becoming more explicit as it grows in importance.

An immediate concern for international trade is the new process patent law in the United States making it illegal to import products made by unauthorized use of protected processes. Japan already has such a law. Process patents are particularly important in pharmaceuticals and biotechnology. Generic drug manufacturers in the United States depend heavily on imports. It is very difficult, if not impossible, to determine in advance that there has been no violation, and the cautious policy is to switch to domestic producers.[21]

The problem is a domestic one in the industrialized countries, as well as an international issue. If a legal monopoly is not enforceable, and the technologies are so easily copied that the inventor has little lead time in which to recover his development costs, then we need to consider other ways of providing rewards for inventive activities. Otherwise, our ability to copy could reduce our willingness to invent.

The industries affected are diverting resources to render their inventions as copy-proof as possible, on the one hand; on the other, they are introducing frequent noncompatible changes and unduly accelerating product obsolescence, to the loss of consumers, in order to reduce the profits from pirating. This may not be in the long-term interest of any nation, but the prospects of obtaining the cooperation of nations currently benefiting from such practices appear poor.

Conclusions and Policy Recommendations

The main vehicles for transfer of technology to LDCs are foreign direct investment and economic growth–related education and training to increase absorptive capacity. Instituting the appropriate policies for generating a good business climate attractive to foreign investment is the responsibility of the LDC government; advanced countries can and do contribute to education and training. The export promotion path toward growth will probably be much rougher than it has been, and this prospect should influence priorities for technology import.

The NICs developed their absorptive capacity in a trade climate more favorable than today's. In such a climate, absorbing workers displaced from agriculture into export industries until such time as domestic demand could help pick up the slack was more easily accomplished than it is today. The technologies the NICs of today need are new, in modern industries, and are largely proprietary. The two main technology transfer issues are really one: access to proprietary technology developed in the industrial countries, and protection of the industrial property rights of foreign firms, as the NICs exploit their capacity to reverse engineer, copy, and counterfeit, as well as to compete with the firms from which they obtained start-up technology.

At present the perceived interests of the NICs and the industrial nations are in conflict. The United States has placed intellectual property rights on the agenda of GATT and is also working through the World Intellectual Property Organization. But for the industrial nations, the only available effective means of persuading the NICs (and the LDCs, in the case of copyright and trademark violations) to offer some protection to industrial property that is costly to develop appears to be to create a trade-off: reduced access to the markets of industrial nations. This is particularly the case for the United States, the largest market for most of the Pacific Asian nations. Since new technologies in computers, communications, and biotechnology are very easily copied and cannot be held secret, the credible threat of retaliation may be the only way of slowing down the industry of theft. Since involuntary, uncompensated technology transfer replaces exports, import restrictions may even seem fair.

The industrial nations must soon confront a new issue: the growing linkage between basic research, traditionally available to all, and industrial applications, appropriated via patents or industrial secrecy. Attempts to stretch the cloak of secrecy over some basic research can only hinder the capacity for technological progress everywhere. And diversion of investment from better products at lower cost to defensive ends—secrecy, reducing the feasibility of copying or reverse engineering—is also damaging to technological progress. Yet these are the likely outcomes of the failure of international agreements on reasonable protection for industrial and intellectual property.

But the marriage of basic science and industrial technology in industry after industry offers opportunities for collaboration in noncompetitive research, in research in "public goods," and in precompetitive research. The escalating costs of research and the scarcity of resources recommend more cooperation, less wasteful duplication. Policies need to be developed that encourage cooperation—not just in financing, but also in performance of research.

What policies can be recommended to encourage the international flow of technology?

First, basic and general research conducted in universities, other nonprofits, and government laboratories in the industrial countries must remain open, through the free flow of information, exchange of research personnel, and more shared financing.

Second, cooperative and joint precompetitive research conducted by or financed by business firms and organizations should be encouraged. International cooperation would make much better use of scarce resources and would accelerate technology implementation and transfer. It can only be encouraged if proprietary rights in ensuing commercial applications can be assured.

Third, all nations must be urged to enact or enforce laws protecting industrial property rights; to facilitate cooperative research among industrial nations; to induce technology transfer from them to NICs and LDCs; and to forestall the closing of industrial nations' markets to the exports of those NICs that violate these rights.

Fourth, LDCs should reduce the obstacles to foreign investment that are the main deterrent to technology transfer. They should also consider which technologies are most suitable in an international environment less favorable to growth via export promotion than it was for Japan and the current NICs.

Fifth, the advanced industrial nations contributing to the technology absorption capacity of LDCs and NICs via advanced education for their nationals should further assist these nations in developing their own national and regional educational and research institutions.

Sixth, international agreement is needed on measures for the protection of new technologies not adequately protected by traditional measures, particularly in software, computers, and biotechnology. Since effective global agreements may be far in the future, bilateral agreements should be sought between industrial nations as well as between them and the NICs, which both need their markets and threaten the rewards of invention in non-traditional products. Without such agreements, little progress can be made on freer trade in technology.

Notes

1. Jong-Bum Kim, "Technology Development Strategy and the Relationship Between Technology Import and Domestic Research and Development (R&D)," unpublished doctoral dissertation, George Washington University, Washington, D.C., 1989.

2. Harold Brown, *U.S.-Japan Relations: Technology, Economics, and Security*, (New York: Carnegie Council on Ethics and International Affairs, 1987).

3. Mark Crawford, "Japan's U.S. R&D Role Widens, Begs Attention," *Science*, July 18, 1986, pp. 270-272; Justin Bloom, "A New Era for U.S.-Japan Technical Relations? Problems and Prospects," *Journal of Northeast Asian Studies*, Summer 1987.

4. Robert L. Park, "The Superconductor Follies," *The Washington Post*, August 2, 1987, p. C5.

5. Nicholas Rescher, *Scientific Progress*, (Pittsburgh: University of Pittsburgh Press, 1978), Chapters 11-14.

6. Mark Crawford, "Japan's U.S. R&D Role Widens, Begs Attention," pp. 270-272.

7. Marjorie Sun, "Japan Lays Out Welcome Mat for U.S. Scientists," *Science*, March 24, 1989, pp. 1546-1547.

8. Jong-Bum Kim, "Technology Development Strategy."

9. H. Peter Gray, "North-South Technology Transfer: Two Neglected Problems," *Journal of Economic Development*, July 1986, pp 27-45.

10. Robert Benko, *Protecting Intellectual Property Rights*, (Washington, D.C.: American Enterprise Institute, 1987), pp. 26f.

11. "Whose Idea Is It Anyway?" *The Economist*, November 12, 1988, pp. 73-74, states that "businessmen simply will not trade in areas where their wares might be stolen."

12. U.S. Patent and Trademark Office, "Technology Assessment and Forecasting Special Report—All Technologies 1/63-12/88," April 1989.

13. J. Davidson Frame, "National Commitment to Intellectual Property Protection: An Empirical Investigation," *Law and Technology*, Summer 1987, pp. 5, 6.

14. International Trade Commission (ITC), *Foreign Protection of Intellectual Property Rights and the Effect on U.S. Industry and Trade*, USITC Publication 2065, February 1988.

15. Daniel Southerland, "U.S. Businesses Urge Trade Sanctions to Stop Piracy of Software in China," *Washington Post*, April 11, 1989, p. E7.

16. Chas T. Stewart, Jr., and Yasumitsu Nihei, *Technology Transfer and Human Factors*, (Lexington, Mass.: Lexington Books, 1987), Chapter 1.

17. Linsu Kim, "Stages of Development of Industrial Technology in a Developing Country: A Model," *Research Policy* 9 (1980), pp. 254-277.

18. S. K. Jayasuriya and R. T. Shand, "Technical Change and Labor Absorption in Asian Agriculture: Some Emerging Trends," *World Development*, March 1986, pp. 415-428.

19. Harry Oshima, "Issues in Heavy Industry Development in Asia," *Ekonomi Dan Keuangan Indonesia* [Indonesian Economy and Finance], March 1984. Harry Oshima, *The Significance of Off-Farm Employment and Incomes in Post-War East Asian Development*, Asian Development Bank Economics Staff Paper No. 21, Manila, January 1984.

20. Bloom, "A New Era," pp. 28, 34.

21. Daniel Moskowitz, "New Process Patent Law Could Create Headaches for Importers," *Washington Post*, March 6, 1989, p. 16.

12

The European Community: A Looming Challenge

William H. Lewis

Implications for the United States and Asia

The twelve member states that make up the European Community (EC) are seeking to reform much of Western Europe's internal market by 1992. Their decisions will have a decisive influence on the political and economic landscape of the continent. All are pledged to remove all internal barriers to trade in goods and services, as well as movements of capital and labor, by December 1992. Most regional specialists agree that formidable issues of national sovereignty—for example, taxation, subsidies to industry, and immigration—will impede full implementation of this agreement. Nevertheless, the underlying momentum toward economic integration is likely to be sustained well beyond 1992.

The Single Europe Act, signed in February 1986 and subsequently ratified by the national parliaments of the member states, was the first major reform of the EC since the founding Treaty of Rome in 1957. The Single Act represents an effort to establish an effective tariff zone; it also symbolizes a desire to establish the foundations for unified monetary, foreign, and national security policies. The EC today comprises a dual executive, the European Commission, which initiates and implements EC policy, and the Council of Ministers, which is the EC's principal decision-making body; the European Parliament, the only multinational European entity directly elected by the European people; the Court of Justice; and the Economic and Social Committee, which represents employers and unions as well as consumers and farmers.

The aim of EC officials is to use the momentum of economic reform to establish a more coordinated and assertive community role in international affairs. The strongest impulse behind the reform movement is the Europeans' belief that they must compete more vigorously with the United States and

Table 12.1 Membership in the EC, Council of Europe, NATO, and WEU

	EC	CDE	NATO	WEU
Belgium	X	X	X	X
Denmark	X	X	X	
France	X	X	X[a]	X
Greece	X	X	X	
Ireland	X	X		
Italy	X	X	X	X
Luxemburg	X	X	X	X
Netherlands	X	X	X	X
Portugal	X	X	X	b
Spain	X	X	X[a]	b
United Kingdom	X	X	X	X
West Germany	X	X	X	X

[a]Not a member of the integrated military command.
[b]Negotiations on membership began in 1988.

Japan if they are to be assured of significant economic growth over the next several decades. EC leaders view Japan and the United States as having a distinct advantage in the international marketplace. The smaller individual national markets within Europe do not afford European corporations opportunities to achieve the economies of scale and production levels often encountered in the United States and Japan. They anticipate that a single European market embracing 320 million consumers—one-third as large as the U.S. market—will greatly diminish, if not cancel out, this disadvantage.

In U.S. circles, "Europe 1992" is perceived as part of a historical process signaling the end of U.S. hegemony in world affairs and a not unanticipated drift toward greater freedom of choice on the part of Europeans in the economic, political, and military realms. The mounting assertiveness of the EC in all three sectors is reinforced by the overlapping membership of the twelve states in other multilateral (and regional) organizations. Table 12.1 outlines the extent of this overlapping membership. The Western European Union (WEU), established in 1955 following failed efforts to form a European Defense Community, has been resurrected in recent years for the purpose of fashioning a common defense policy among member states and to promote armaments cooperation. While the WEU remains an embryonic organization, it is viewed by some EC officials as a potential appendage of the European Community—or, in the common coinage of contemporary European officials, a budding "second pillar" for the defense of Western Europe.

The Official U.S. Position

The official response to Europe 1992 by the U.S. government is heavily influenced by three considerations. Since the conclusion of World War II, security has served as a leitmotif of successive U.S. administrations, traditionally anchored in Cold War imperatives and the North Atlantic Treaty Organization (NATO). The deployment of more than 300,000 U.S. service personnel in Western Europe, Greece, and Turkey serves as testimony to U.S. support for the protection of Western democracies. Second, and consonant with the concept of an Atlantic community, are the historical ties that link most Americans with their familial and cultural roots in Europe. These ties serve as an enduring bond that sustains the United States and its allies in the face of frequent transatlantic disputes.

Of comparable significance are common economic interests, which are both enormous and complex. The members of the EC collectively constitute the largest trading partner of the United States. In 1988, commerce and trade between the two exceeded $160 billion. In addition, investments in each other's economies are estimated at $750 billion and, in the case of recent U.S. investments in Europe, are growing dramatically. Not surprisingly, the U.S. government has publicly supported Western Europe's economic integration. President Bush, in a May 1989 speech, averred that a strong, united Europe is in the best interest of the United States. His view has been further elaborated by officials who suggest that a "purposeful Europe is critical to addressing the Soviet threat." One senior State Department officer, in a recent public address, offered the following plaudit:

> [I]n our view, 1992 is primarily a deregulatory exercise. We accept at face value the European Community's statements that they are trying to build a more economically efficient community, and we do not see a more economically efficient European Community as a threat. Rather, we see it as good for the United States and the world. The European Community will become: A better market for U.S. products; a competitor that helps drive U.S. enterprises to excellence; and we believe that the efficiency gains that the EC achieves will, in one form or another, be available to the rest of the world.[1]

The State Department's assistant secretary for business and economic affairs hastened to offer the following cautionary note, however:

> [W]hile we are optimistic about 1992, we are also wary about 1992. . . . Our wariness is that the single market will be less than open, either as a result of discriminatory directives or regulations, narrow application of existing trade regulations, or through the failure of the Uruguay Round of GATT

(General Agreement on Tariffs and Trade) negotiations to develop worldwide rules for new areas, such as financial services.[2]

The United States itself has moved toward regional economic integration in recent years. We have recently entered into a far-reaching free-trade agreement with Canada that covers intellectual property, investment, and services. These efforts have been paralleled in Southeast Asia, within the European Free Trade Association (Sweden, Switzerland, Austria, Norway, Finland, and Iceland), in North Africa, and in the Persian Gulf. These embryonic arrangements suggest that the international community, including the United States and the EC, is entering a new era in global economic relations, the configuration of which is difficult to predict.

Whatever the future configuration, Europe 1992 will be a centerpiece of U.S. economic and security concerns for the next several years at least. The U.S. defense community has followed the evolution of the single market closely, and members of the legislative branch whose purview is U.S. defense preparedness have evidenced mounting concern over the possible consequences of the single market for alliance defense cooperation.

On May 3, 1989, a delegation from the House Armed Services Investigations Subcommittee transmitted a memorandum to Secretary of Defense Richard B. Cheney raising serious reservations about Europe 1992. The delegation had just recently returned from a visit to Western Europe where it had discussed Europe 1992 with British and French counterparts. The subcommittee's concerns were expressed to Secretary Cheney clearly and concisely:

> Europe 1992 is an important step in the continuing evolution of the European pillar. However, we are deeply concerned that not enough attention is being extended to the political and security implications for the United States resulting from this historic step. Specifically, in the defense sphere, any effort that moves away from the present level of . . . cooperation could degrade the . . . quality of NATO weapons and equipment. It could also lead to a serious deterioration of long-term efforts to field systems that meet the NATO requirements for rationalization, standardization, and interoperability.

The delegation had ample reason to ventilate its concerns. Europe 1992 is evolving at a time when the transatlantic relationship that has been so laboriously constructed over the past four decades is undergoing severe strain. Several factors contribute to existing stresses, including:

- The Uncertain Economic Environment—The United States has entered an economic period characterized by an unsatisfactory balance of trade,

high budget deficits, low productivity, and inadequate savings by a public addicted to "consumerism";
- The Maldistribution of Defense Responsibility—As perceived by a host of U.S. legislators, the United States is shouldering a disproportionate share of the NATO defense burden, one that enhances European security and economic well-being at the expense of the United States; and
- Growing Competition in the Arms Market—Despite intermittent pledges of arms production cooperation, West European military plans are directed toward a reduction of dependence on U.S. sources of supply, a situation that will be exacerbated when EC reforms are implemented.

The emergence of Mikhail Gorbachev in 1985 as the Soviet leader has added to the existing malaise in the transatlantic relationship. Through a well-orchestrated diplomatic and public relations initiative the Soviet president has generated widening belief in the Western world that Moscow's reform efforts (glasnost and perestroika) are emblematic of the termination of the Cold War. Among Western publics, Gorbachev has succeeded in drastically altering perceptions of the Soviet threat by calling for major reductions in conventional and nuclear forces, for the opening of European frontiers to cultural and economic exchanges, and for reliance on the United Nations and associated bodies for the resolution of international disputes. The advent of Mikhail Gorbachev has ended Moscow's traditional role—for the moment at least—as a reliable adversary. In the process, Gorbachev has shifted the agenda of post–Cold War issues from military preparedness to arms control and economic security.

The U.S. Senate, impatient with NATO allies and with Japan, issued a challenge to both on August 2, 1989. Contending that the United States bears a disproportionate share of the cost of mutual defense, the Senate Committee on Armed Services fashioned a "comprehensive initiative" on burdensharing that was incorporated into the defense authorization bill for fiscal year 1990. Among its salient provisions are the following: (1) a call to Japan to strengthen its security and foreign aid programs; (2) a requirement that the president negotiate an agreement with Japan to reimburse the United States for monies spent to maintain U.S. forces deployed in the defense of Japan; and (3) a ceiling on the percentage of Americans among NATO troops in Europe. The latter provision is the direct consequence of reports received in Washington that some NATO allies are contemplating substantial reductions in active duty forces earmarked for the defense of Western Europe, no matter what the outcome of current arms control negotiations with the Warsaw Treaty Organization. In the Senate's view, such unilateral drawdowns in military manpower would severely weaken the arms control negotiating position of the rest of NATO. Senators Sam Nunn and John McCain have staked out a bipartisan position on the issue:

> Some might say that the United States must show leadership, and that we should not cut our troops just because our allies cut. But we believe that if our allies began to make significant unilateral cuts in their deployed active-duty forces in Europe without waiting for the talks on Conventional Forces in Europe, it tells us they are not serious about conventional defense. It tells us that they are content to rely on the NATO threat of an early first use of nuclear weapons—a threat that is gradually eroding—to deal with a large-scale Warsaw Pact attack on Western Europe.[3]

In seeking what it regards as a stable, secure, and fair balance of military commitments in the free world, the U.S. Senate will not be unmindful of EC efforts to create a single integrated market. While applauding these efforts with official rhetoric, most legislators will scrutinize Europe 1991 for indications of European protectionism of a type that redounds to the disadvantage of U.S. interests, both in the defense and nondefense sectors.

Areas of Potential Disagreement

The touchstone for the current effort to establish a common internal market is a proposal made by Lord Cockfield released in June 1985.[4] The proposal provided firm direction and fresh momentum to an EC that had been becalmed for many years. The report requires that approximately 300 decisions, directives, and regulations be issued before January 1, 1993, in three clearly identified sectors—physical, technical, and fiscal barriers.

The first, physical barriers, involves removal of impediments to trade, as well as to the movement of "factors of production"—e.g., passport and immigration controls, payments of border taxes on farm products, and the like. It is of more than passing interest that EC-wide arrangements for combating drug smuggling and terrorism are to be accorded priority treatment. The second sector, technical barriers, calls for adoption of production and manufacturing standards in each member state to ensure that products lawfully made and sold in one member state may be freely traded within the EC as a whole. Finally, with respect to fiscal barriers, the members are encouraged to secure agreement on goods subjected to value-added tax (VAT) rates for commodities imported.

Concomitantly, the twelve member states have signaled their intention to forge common foreign policies in an effort to enhance the EC role in international affairs. The justification for this effort, European Political Cooperation (EPC), is outlined in Title III, Article 30, of the Single Europe Act, which stipulates that:

- EC members will endeavor to formulate and implement a joint foreign policy;
- Members will try to avoid any action or position that impairs their effectiveness as a cohesive force in international relations;
- Consultations at the foreign minister level will take place at least four times a year in the EPC framework;
- A political dialogue with third countries and regional groups may be organized when necessary; and
- The parties will coordinate their positions more closely on the political and economic aspects of security. Such coordination is not intended to impede cooperation within the framework of the Western European Union or NATO.

The Community has allocated substantial financial and technical resources to the EPC, whose influence and scope of activity have been greatly expanded over the past several years. Transatlantic friction could result. A key area in which EPC and U.S. positions are likely to diverge involves security approaches to evolving East-West relations. While no NATO ally wishes to decouple the United States from its security commitments in Europe, the prevalent sentiment in many EC capitals is that their positions on salient security questions should be expressed more aggressively vis-à-vis the United States. The U.S. government has expressed its displeasure from time to time regarding EPC actions that have been at variance with or outside the framework of established NATO policy.

The Bush administration can expect to be confronted with unpalatable EPC positions on a host of other foreign policy and related security matters. These will likely be most pronounced on questions relating to the Middle East and Latin America. On the sensitive Palestine and Arab-Israeli questions, for example, the EC is already on record as supporting the right of self-determination for Arabs living in Israeli-occupied territories; it has also called for an international conference, under United Nations auspices, to deal with the problems attending exercise of this right. The EC foreign ministers have issued a statement condemning the Israeli policy of creating new settlements on the West Bank and in Gaza as being in violation of international law.

The habit of consultation and coordination between the United States and EC allies in the economic realm also is undergoing erosion in European precincts. This erosion is particularly noteworthy in such sensitive areas as financial and economic assistance to hard-pressed East European regimes, ties with the Council for Mutual Economic Assistance (CMEA), and technology transfers to the Soviet Union. Moscow has recently established diplomatic relations with EC headquarters and in July 1989 communicated a desire to be accorded a special relation with the Community.

On a more narrow front, that of transatlantic trade and investment, senior officials in Washington have expressed reservations concerning recent EC directives and actions. As Michael Calingaert, a foreign service officer with far-reaching expertise in the subject field, has observed:

> The key question for U.S. business interests is whether, and if so to what extent, completion of the internal market will be accompanied by measures that limit opportunities for U.S. firms. The areas where U.S. interests will be vitally affected are regulation of services, regulations and standards, and public procurement. . . . Pressures exist in the EC both for and against a measure of protection or at least extracting concessions from other countries in return for the benefits their firms will derive from the single market. The outcome of that debate will be affected not only by a balancing of interests within the EC, but also by the economic climate, the state of U.S.-EC relations, and the extent to which the EC considers it necessary to protect itself against perceived unequal treatment by the Japanese.[5]

The EC clearly intends its reform program to accord European corporations a competitive advantage in forming regional ties and exploiting and expanding the regional market. In anticipation, several U.S. and Japanese firms have repositioned themselves by initiating local investments, seeking takeovers, and proposing joint ventures in order to position themselves to participate fully in the emerging single market. The EC Commission would prefer a slowdown in such non-European interventions in order to permit European enterprise an opportunity to develop stronger internal positions before establishing ties with U.S. and Japanese firms.

In the interim, the U.S. government has adopted a defensive posture on EC regulations that is predicated on the following principles:

- Reciprocity—Indications that the EC will insist on equivalent access to the U.S. market will be ill-received in Washington. The United States seeks to accept the standard of national treatment because of states' rights factors in this country. The U.S.-EC dialogue is directed primarily toward the EC banking directive; the EC, for its part, insists that European banks be afforded an opportunity to participate in the U.S. market.
- Rule of Origin—The principal here involves EC regulations to define the national origins of a product in dumping cases. The United States is "looking very closely at the possible interaction of rules of origins and other trade measures . . . that might create a systemic bias in favor of locating in Europe, rather than exporting to Europe."
- Local Content Requirements—Quotas or local content requirements could serve to exclude U.S. products from duty-free measures. The

impact of strict measures would be to compel U.S. business entities to invest heavily in joint ventures in Europe. Such an impulse, inter alia, could adversely affect U.S. defense mobilization capabilities.
- Standards—The U.S. government has expressed its interest in the standards, certification, and testing processes to be established by the EC. There is a very real potential for discrimination that excludes differing U.S. technologies, requires costly U.S. design adjustments, or generates noncompetitive testing.

The U.S. perspective is that Europe 1992 is a potential challenge to all the partners of the transatlantic alliance. The sorting-out process will involve an overlap of economic, foreign policy, and security interests on the part of all participants. The test of Western cohesion involves all three dimensions. Frequently neglected is the question of how the disagreements within the EC itself over the application of the newly coined regulations will affect the cohesion and solidarity of the Community.

The European Perspective

Sponsors of Europe 1992 believe that they are in a position to fashion a new strategic environment in Europe in which the EC and ancillary organizations can serve as key variables to U.S. predominance in the existing alliance system. Using Jean Monnet's original theory of European integration as a point of departure, they contend that the unification of economic functions contemplated in the 1992 program will be accompanied (or followed) by a "great leap forward" when the EC assumes responsibility for setting guidelines in the sphere of regional security policy. Ultimately, they envisage an as yet vaguely defined form of political confederation involving a loose amalgam of member states.

What precisely is the basis for these "great expectations"? While the timing may be inopportune, the year 1992 is to become the annus mirabilis of the Community. Before it emerges full-blown as a rival to the United States and Japan, however, a number of delicate issues will have to be addressed, including the following:

- Economic Implications—Integration threatens the viability of many small European firms that depend on state subsidies for their existence. The elimination or reduction of protectionist regulations and subsidies would rule out inefficient companies in European-wide competition—thus raising the specter of unemployment and rising social welfare costs in some member states.
- Social Implications—Labor unions in several of these states have expressed fears that the program will eliminate several hundred thousand

jobs in the short term as competition leads to the demise of inefficient firms. They are skeptical that, by "stripping away regulation," company costs will be reduced, economic growth will be stimulated, and millions of new jobs created. They also observe that the proposed elimination of border checks will open their countries to a flood tide of unskilled, "undocumented" migratory workers competing with their nationals for available jobs.
- Welfare Implications—The adoption of standard regulations governing welfare benefits poses serious problems given the considerable void that exists between the most prosperous member states of the north and their southern counterparts. A sensitive issue of downward versus upward leveling—with attendant EC and human costs—remains to be addressed.

Other issues of equally serious moment also need to be negotiated. For example:

- Future Members—The core EC membership is also a part of NATO. Its leaders frequently adopt the public posture that Europe's economic integration ultimately enhances its burdensharing contribution to NATO. However, Ireland is not a NATO member state, nor does its government offer any indication of wanting to alter its existing neutral status. Paradoxically, Turkey, a member of NATO, is not included in the EC— and current indications are that the EC does not wish to make an early decision on Turkish application. Even more paradoxical is the unofficially expressed willingness of the EC's leadership to contemplate an application from Austria, much to the consternation of Ankara.
- Moscow and Eastern Europe—Moscow has finally recognized the EC, and talks have been launched between Brussels and the Communist Council for Mutual Economic Assistance (CMEA). At the same time, Hungary and Poland are seeking direct bilateral contact with the community.

One might envisage a situation in which Hungary and Poland petition for associate status within the Community. Gorbachev might well approve their initiative on the grounds that it promised to foster a restructuring of European relationships—i.e., it would auger the extension of a united "economic Europe" eastward while offering impetus to the weakening of the cement of NATO. Under such circumstances, a Europe stretching from the coasts of France to the Urals and sharing common economic interests would be transformed from a flight of Gorbachev's fancy into a feasible reality in the decade ahead.

Even the Gorbachev "vision" might not be sufficiently alluring to help resolve several disputes that have arisen within EC precincts. Among the more noteworthy are the following:

- Common Currency—Eight EC countries have linked their countries to one another within the European monetary system.[6] Brussels's headquarters is urging consideration of a "monetary union" in which one common currency would prevail as the unit of pricing and exchange. This approach is stoutly resisted by British Prime Minister Margaret Thatcher.
- Valued-Added Taxes (VATs)—Proposals to "harmonize" value-added taxes amongst the twelve member states also have raised a fire storm of controversy. At present, VATs vary from zero to 38 percent from country to country. Ireland and Denmark, which derive substantial revenue from VATs, would fare badly if forced to lower their high rates.
- A Federalized Europe—Particularly contentious have been statements by high-level EC officials that Europe 1992 is intended to serve as a forerunner to "common sovereignty over foreign policy, defense and security, monetary, economic, environmental, and social policy."

The redoubtable Margaret Thatcher has taken firm, vociferous issue with this view. Her target in recent months has been European Commission President Jacques Delors. Thatcher has contended that she had "not successfully rolled back the frontiers of the state in Britain, only to see them at a European level, with a European superstate exercising a new dominance from Brussels." The issue here is over long-term objectives rather than substantive questions relating to the 1992 deadline. We should not lose sight of the fact that the most dedicated "Europhiles" are prepared to be patient and to outlast the stewardship of Britain's "iron lady."

Meanwhile, the stakes for the United States are high. Europe is our principal foreign customer, buying almost one-quarter of U.S. exports. This includes almost one-half of U.S. computers and computer parts, a significant portion of electrical machinery (including semi-conductors), and approximately one-third of all overseas sales of U.S.-made aircraft and scientific equipment.

The Reagan administration generally supported an integrated European market. On defense, President Reagan underscored this position in February of 1988. In his words: "We in America welcome multilateral and bilateral defense cooperation among our European partners of the sort that the Western European Union, and the Germans and the French, and other governments have demonstrated within the overall framework of our alliance. Such cooperation and coordination are essential to strengthening the

European Pillar of the Alliance and thereby the Alliance as a whole."[7] Slightly more than one year later, senior members of the Bush administration and of Congress are raising warning flags about the consequences of the single-integrated European market for U.S. defense interests. We are not clear at present what U.S. policy has been developed on this central question.

Within some official circles, strategists are calling for increased U.S.-Pacific Basin cooperation as a counterpoise to Europe 1992. They note that, in 1980, U.S. trade with Pacific nations was higher in total dollar value than with our NATO partners. In 1988, the ratio was 7:5 in favor of the former ($273 billion with Asia as compared to $189 billion with Western Europe). Taking cognizance of this fact, then-Secretary of State George Shultz proposed the establishment of an intergovernmental forum in July 1988 to discuss Asia-Pacific regional cooperation in the realms of education, communications, and energy. Other U.S. officials are urging the creation of a regional economic forum, in part to examine the implications of the EC program for trade and commerce with Asian and North American members of the Pacific "Community." Most view greater Asia-Pacific economic cooperation as an unavoidable imperative for the decade of the 1990s. They also believe that such cooperation is an important hedge against future forms of European protectionism. The Bush administration would prefer to avoid making unpalatable choices of this nature. But, as yet, it has failed to fashion a promising strategy to cope with forces that could unravel relations with traditional friends and allies in Asia *and* in Europe.

Notes

1. Eugene J. McAllister, "U.S. Views on the EC Single Market Exercise," address before The American Association of Exporters and Importers, New York City, May 18, 1989.

2. Ibid.

3. Sam Nunn and John McCain, "U.S. Allies: No More Free Rides," *The Washington Post*, August 14, 1989, p. B-7.

4. Lord John Cockfield, "Completing the Internal Market," European Community White Paper, June 1985.

5. Michael Calingaert, *The 1992 Challenge from Europe: Development of the European Community's Internal Market* (Washington, D.C.: National Planning Association, 1988), p. XIV.

6. Only Britain, Spain, Portugal, and Greece retain separate currencies at the present time.

7. Address by President Ronald Reagan on the U.S. Information Agency's International Service, "Worldnet," February 23, 1988.

About the Editors and Contributors

Anthony C. Albrecht is president of Albrecht Incorporated. As the former deputy assistant secretary of state in charge of U.S. economic relations with the Asian region, Secretary Albrecht was the leader and coordinator of the U.S. delegation to the ASEAN-U.S. Economic Dialogue meetings in Washington and Manila. He currently works as a consultant with multinational companies and various business groups, such as the U.S.-ASEAN Council. He also serves as chairman of corporate programs at The Asia Society/Washington Center.

Richard S. Belous is vice president of international affairs and a senior economist at the National Planning Association. He is also North American director of the British–North American Committee, of which the National Planning Association is the U.S. sponsoring organization. Dr. Belous has been an adviser to several presidential commissions. His most recent book is *The Contingent Economy*.

John P. Hardt is associate director for research coordination and senior specialist in Soviet economics at the Congressional Research Service, Library of Congress. He is also an adjunct professor in economics at The George Washington University and Georgetown University. Dr. Hardt has traveled extensively in the Soviet Union, Eastern Europe, and elsewhere on congressional business and has written numerous books and articles for commercial, government, and academic publications.

Young C. Kim is professor of political science and international affairs at The George Washington University and coeditor of the *Journal of Northeast Asian Studies*. He is also chairman of The American Council on Asian and Pacific Affairs, Inc. His many publications include *Japanese and U.S. Policy in Asia*, coedited with Gaston J. Sigur, and *Soviet Strategy Toward Japan*.

Bon Ho Koo is president of the Korea Development Institute of Seoul, Korea. He is also chairman of the Financial Reform Commission, a member of the Foreign Capital Inducement Deliberation Committee, and a member of the Coordinating Committee for Fourth, Fifth, and Sixth Five-Year Economic Planning of the Economic Planning Board. His publications include *The World Economy in the 1980s*, *A Study on the Internationalization of Korea Venture Capital*, and *Exchange Rate Policy in Korea*.

Paul W. Kuznets is a professor in the Economics Department at Indiana University and author of *Economic Growth and Structure in the Republic of Korea* as well as many articles on the South Korean economy. He is currently writing a book on contemporary economic development in South Korea. Professor Kuznets serves as a member of the Advisory Council of the Korea Economic Institute of America.

Nicholas R. Lardy is professor of international studies in the Jackson School of International Studies at the University of Washington. His books include *Economic Growth and Distribution in China* and *Agriculture in China's Modern Economic Development*.

William H. Lewis is the director of the Security Policy Studies Program and professor of political science and international affairs at The George Washington University. A former foreign service officer, Dr. Lewis has served as office director in the Bureau of Political-Military Affairs and in the Bureau of African Affairs.

Edward J. Lincoln is a senior fellow in the Foreign Policy Studies Program at The Brookings Institution. He also has taught at the Johns Hopkins University School of Advanced International Studies. His most recent publication is *Japan's Unequal Trade*.

Dick K. Nanto is head of the Japan Task Force of the Congressional Research Service, Library of Congress. Dr. Nanto has published many articles on international trade issues, the economy of Japan, and economic management.

Charles T. Stewart, Jr., is professor of economics at The George Washington University. His most recent book is *Technology Transfer and Human Factors*, which he coauthored with Yasumitsu Nihei.

Yuan-li Wu has been a senior consultant to the Hoover Institution on War, Revolution, and Peace at Stanford University since 1960 and is professor of economics emeritus at the University of San Francisco. He formerly served in the U.S. Department of Defense as a deputy assistant secretary for policy plans and in the National Security Council in the Office of the Assistant Secretary for International Security Affairs. Dr. Wu's latest book is *Human Rights in the People's Republic of China*.

Index

Absorptive capacity. *See under* Technology
Accountability, 5
ADB. *See* Asian Development Bank
Afghanistan. *See under* Soviet Union
Africa, 19, 202
Agricultural cooperatives, 8
Agricultural exporting countries, 59
Aho, C. Michael, 171
Ajiken. *See* Institute of Developing Economies
American Soybean Association, 110, 112, 113, 114
Antidumping, 55, 75
APEC. *See* Asia Pacific Economic Cooperation conference
Apparel, 71, 72(table), 111, 130, 143
 import quotas, 52, 75
Arabs, 205
Arms control, 8, 11, 19, 204
ASEAN. *See* Association of Southeast Asian Nations
ASEAN-U.S. Initiative (AUI), 116-117, 119
Asian Development Bank (ADB), 34, 38, 43, 44(n6), 64, 120, 131, 133
Asian Institute of Technology (Thailand), 193
Asia Pacific Economic Cooperation conference (APEC) (1989), 58-61, 62, 63, 64, 65
Asia-Pacific region
 competition, 93
 cooperation and development, 41-43, 46, 48, 58-65, 85-86, 89, 94, 96-98, 100, 102-105, 115-122, 210
 diversity in, 22, 97
 economic growth, 1-2, 46, 89, 90, 93
 education abroad, 191-194
 exports, 22, 49
 GDP, 90, 91(table)
 geography, 22, 103
 and global economic system, 9, 41, 53-54, 176
 industries, vertical integration of, 90
 instability, 2
 market-oriented economies, 1, 9, 13, 93, 102, 141
 military, 1, 18-19
 population, 97
 trade, 22-30, 38, 49-52, 90, 91(tables), 94
 trade imbalance, 93
 trade surplus, 48
 See also Association of Southeast Asian Nations; Japan, and regional *subentries;* Newly Industrializing Countries; Soviet Union, Asia policy; Technology; *individual countries; under* United States; Canada
Association of Southeast Asian Nations (ASEAN), 19
 direct investment abroad, 92(table)
 direct investment in, 30, 92(table), 114, 115
 economies, 90, 113-115
 exports, 113
 foreign aid to, 31, 32-33(tables), 110, 114, 120
 and FTA, 55
 and global economic integration, 115, 116, 122
 and Japan, 109, 110, 113, 114, 115
 labor, 118
 and OECD, 116
 and PECC, 61, 120
 Post-Ministerial meetings, 120, 121, 122
 and PRC, 109, 111, 115, 118
 protectionism, 110, 115
 raw materials, 115
 and regional cooperation, 115-122
 and regional economy, 58, 60, 62, 115, 137
 and regional security, 117-118
 and South Korea, 121
 and Soviet Union, 109, 110-111, 115, 117
 trade, 50(fig.), 91(table), 97, 110, 113, 116-117
 and U.S., 109, 110, 111, 113-114, 116-117, 119, 121
 and Vietnam, 111, 117-118
 See also Indonesia; Malaysia; Philippines; Singapore; Thailand
AUI. *See* ASEAN-U.S. Initiative
Australia, 41, 43, 63
 direct investment in, 92(table)
 and Japan, 59, 92(table)
 and PECC, 61
 and PRC, 102
 and regional economy, 58, 59

213

regional trade, 22, 23(tables), 59(fig.), 64, 91(table)
technology, 183(table), 186(table)
trade deficits, 93
and U.S., 29, 92(table), 183(table)
Australia–New Zealand Closer Economic Relations (CER) agreement, 60
Austria, 12, 202, 208
Automation, 31
Automobiles, 52, 79, 85

Baikal-Amur Magistral (BAM), 9, 10
Baker, James, 54, 58
Balance of payments, 14, 16(table), 70
BAM. *See* Baikal-Amur Magistral
Bankruptcy, 169
Baucus, Max, 54, 175
Beef, 47, 84
Beijing Review, 104
Belgium, 200(table)
Bell Labs (company), 180
Bentsen, Lloyd, 54
Bilateralism, 89, 93, 120
Biotechnology, 194, 196, 197
Blogoveshchensk (Soviet Union), 15
Bonn Summit (1989), 12
Bradley, Bill, 59
Brady Plan, 4, 19, 169, 170
Brain drain, 157, 184
Bretton Woods institutions, 9
Brezhnev, Leonid, 10, 13
British commonwealth, 22–23, 144(table)
Burdensharing. *See under* United States
Burma, 33(table), 34
Bush, George, 76, 101, 205, 210
Byrd, Robert, 54

CAFA. *See* Conventional Forces Asia
CAFE. *See* Conventional Forces Europe
Cairns Group, 59
Calingaert, Michael, 206
Cambodia. *See* Kampuchea
Canada, 9
  and Asia-Pacific economy, 58, 59
  and Asia-Pacific trade, 23–29(tables), 50(fig.), 91(table)
  direct investment in, 92(table)
  foreign students in, 193
  and Japan, 50(fig.), 92(table)
  labor costs, 165(table)
  and PECC, 61
  savings, 168(table)
  technology, 183(table), 186(table), 190
  and U.S., 50(fig.), 92(table), 173(table), 183(table)
  and U.S. Free Trade Agreement, 41, 47, 60, 65, 75, 104, 175, 202

Capital, 14
  equipment, 51
  flight, 150, 157, 159
  flow, 54, 57, 62, 63, 141, 169
  formation, 79
  markets, 96
Carter, Jimmy, 83
CDE, 200(table)
Central America, 8
CER. *See* Australia–New Zealand Closer Economic Relations agreement
Cheney, Richard B., 202
Chevron (oil company), 14
Chiang Ching-kuo, 131, 132, 133, 135
Chile, 61
China International Trust and Investment Corporation (CITIC), 102
Chinese communities overseas, 137, 145, 148
Chun Doo-hwan, 70
CICP. *See* Japan Federation of Economic Organizations, Committee on International Cooperation Projects
CITIC. *See* China International Trust and Investment Corporation
Citrus products, 47
CMEA. *See* Council for Mutual Economic Assistance
Coal, 29, 72(table)
Cockfield, John, 204
Coconut oil. *See* Tropical oils
Cold War, 201, 203
Commerce, U.S. Department of, 75, 112, 118
Communist economies, 2. *See also* Eastern Europe; People's Republic of China; Soviet Union
Comparative advantage, 5, 70, 72, 79, 80, 85, 90
Competition, 5, 80, 85, 93, 118, 127. *See also* Japan, economic competition
Congressional Research Service, 61–62
Consultation mechanisms, 120–121, 152, 205
Contingent workers, 164
Conventional Forces Asia (CAFA), 12
Conventional Forces Europe (CAFE), 8, 12
Cooperatives, 6, 8
Copyright, 85, 188
Corporate debt, 169, 170
Council for Mutual Economic Assistance (CMEA), 205, 208
Council on Foreign Relations (U.S.), 171
Countertrade, 15
Countervailing duties, 55, 75
Crane, Philip, 54
Cranston, Alan, 59
Credit, 14, 15, 36, 78, 80, 93
Cuba, 8

Index

Current account. See *subentries* trade deficits; trade surplus *under individual countries*

DAC. See Development Assistance Committee
Daiyawan (PRC) nuclear power plant, 143
Damage control, 162, 176
Debt, 4, 9, 14, 16(table), 47, 48, 53, 59, 69, 80, 96, 101, 169, 170
Defense, U.S. Department of, 193
Defense spending, 171(table), 172
Defensive reasonable sufficiency, 19
Delors, Jacques, 209
Democratic Progressive Party (DPP) (Taiwan), 134
Democratization, 19, 89, 95
Deng Xiaoping, 107, 134, 136, 137, 145, 146, 147, 150, 157
Denmark, 200(table), 209
Deposit-taking companies (DTCs), 150
Deregulation, 164
Development Assistance Committee (DAC), 34
Development investment, 3, 14, 98, 100
Direct investment, 14, 17, 18, 19, 30-31, 36, 90, 92(table), 94
 and technology, 190-191, 195, 197
 See also Japan, regional direct investment; United States, and Asia-Pacific direct investment; *individual countries*, direct investment abroad; *individual countries*, direct investment in
Dispute settlement mechanisms, 56
Division of labor, 90, 94, 95, 98
Dollar (Hong Kong), 125-127(table), 147, 153
 collapse (1983), 150
Dollar (Singapore), 125-127(table)
Dollar (U.S.), 38, 46, 127, 129(table), 150, 165, 166
 devaluation of, 76, 80, 161, 172
DPP. See Democratic Progressive Party
Drug trade, 63, 204
DTCs. See Deposit-taking companies
Dumping, 206. See also Antidumping

East Asian Newly Industrializing Economies (NIEs), 51, 52, 56, 71, 158, 159(n1), 161, 162
 balance of payments, 76
 exports, 101
 trade deficit, 56
 and U.S., 172, 173, 174
 See also Hong Kong; South Korea; Taiwan
Eastern Europe, 2, 12, 19, 128, 205
 and EC, 2, 205, 208
East-West relations, 1, 46. See also Cold War; United States, and Soviet Union
EC. See European Community
Econometrics, 48, 167

Economic growth, 47, 69, 80, 89, 90, 94
 global, 1
 See also *individual countries*, economy; *under* Asia-Pacific region
Economic integration, 9, 10-11, 12, 46, 84, 95-96, 101. See also *individual countries*, and global economic integration
Economic statistics, 60, 63
Economic Summit (seven-nation), 115, 116, 121
Economies of scale, 90, 200
Educational exchange, 63, 191. See also Technology, and education
Efficiency, 5, 14, 80, 90
EFTA. See European Free Trade Area
Electronics, 79, 130
Emigrant (journal), 152
Emigration, 63, 151-152, 156-157, 159, 192
Entrepôt development, 15, 142. See also Hong Kong, as entrepôt
Environment, 8, 41, 58, 63, 133
EPC. See European Political Cooperation
Equity, 5
European Common Market, 9
European Community (EC), 1, 12, 46, 47, 49, 57, 59, 65, 84, 97, 104, 115, 118, 120, 121, 204-205, 209
 banking directive, 206
 Council of Ministers, 199, 205
 Court of Justice, 199
 Economic and Social Committee, 199
 European Commission, 199, 206, 209
 GDP, 91(table)
 and Japan, 200, 206, 207
 marketing techniques, 8
 membership, 200(table), 208
 1992, 1, 116, 122, 124, 175, 199, 200, 201, 202, 207-208, 209, 210. See also Single Europe Act
 and security, 205, 207, 210
 and Soviet Union, 205, 208
 trade, 91(table), 116, 124, 127, 128, 137, 144(table), 174(table)
 and U.S., 199, 200, 201-204, 205, 206-207, 209-210
European Defense Community, 200
European Free Trade Area (EFTA), 12, 202
"European House," 11
European monetary system, 209
European Parliament, 199
European Political Cooperation (EPC), 204-205
Exchange rates, 35, 54, 59, 78, 79, 93, 96, 125-127(table)
 convertible, 5, 12, 15, 17, 105, 106, 147
 flexible, 3
 floating, 147
Export-oriented Asian models, 13, 69

Factor endowments, 80
Factor proportions, 79, 87(n13)
"Far Eastern Comprehensive Economic Development Plan to the Year 2000" (Soviet Union), 10
FDA. *See* Food and Drug Adminstration
FDI (foreign direct investment). *See* Direct investment
Federal Republic of Germany (FRG), 76, 128(table), 144(table), 166, 167–168(tables), 193, 200(table). *See also under* Soviet Union
Federal Reserve (U.S.), 47, 168–169
Federal Trade Commission, U.S., 174
Finland, 202
Food and Drug Administration (FDA) (U.S.), 114
Footwear. *See* Apparel
Ford Foundation, 193
Foreign aid, 4, 11, 19. *See also* Grants; Japan, foreign aid from; Official development assistance; South Korea, foreign aid from; United States, foreign aid from; *individual countries*, foreign aid to
Foreign commerce zones, 14
Foreign direct investment (FDI). *See* Direct investment
Foreign exchange. *See* Exchange rates
Foreign Exchange Fund, 147, 150, 153
Fortress Europe, 93
France, 128(table), 168(table), 193, 200(table)
Free market mechanism, 60, 123
Free-trade area (FTA), 53, 56, 57, 64, 84–85, 174–175. *See also* Canada, and U.S. Free Trade Agreement; European Free Trade Area; Pacific Free Trade Area proposal
Free trade zone, 41. *See also* Free-trade area
FRG. *See* Federal Republic of Germany
FSX (Japanese fighter plane) debate, 112
FTA. *See* Free-trade area

GATT. *See* General Agreement on Tariffs and Trade
GDP. *See* Gross domestic product
General Agreement on Tariffs and Trade (GATT), 9, 43, 52, 53, 56, 74, 75, 77, 78, 84, 85, 93, 117, 120, 130, 131, 162, 173, 174, 196
 Article XXIII, 83
 liberalization process, 52, 58
 Multilateral Trade Negotiations, 55, 59, 64, 118. *See also* Uruguay Round of Multilateral Trade Negotiations
Generalized system of preferences (GSP), 39, 40, 56, 82, 109, 114, 188
Glasnost, 203

Global economy, 3. *See also under* Soviet Union
Globalism, 3, 8
Global market structures, 2, 4, 164
GNP. *See* Gross national product
Gold, 16(table), 20(n17)
Goodpaster, Andrew, 9
Gorbachev, Mikhail S., 8, 9, 10, 134, 203, 208–209
Gostev, Boris, 5
Gramm-Rudman Act (U.S.), 162
Grants, 34
Great Britain, 65, 128(table), 144(table), 148, 149, 156, 200(table), 209
 foreign students in, 193
 and PRC, 145, 146, 147, 149. *See also* Hong Kong, and PRC sovereignty
 savings, 167–168(tables)
Greater East Asia Co-Prosperity Sphere, 61
Greece, 200(table), 201
Grenada. *See under* People's Republic of China
Gross domestic product (GDP), 29, 79, 90, 91(table), 142
Gross national product (GNP), 69, 96, 133, 162, 163, 166, 169, 183
G-7 countries, 54, 166, 168(table)
GSP. *See* Generalized system of preferences

Hallstein Doctrine (Taiwan), 130
Hard currency, 14, 16(table), 147
Hawke, Robert, 43, 58, 118, 119, 121
Heihe (Heilongjiang province, PRC), 15
Hong Kong, 62, 64
 and ASEAN, 118–119
 banking, 148–149, 150, 157
 Basic Law (1988, 1989), 152, 153–156, 157
 currency. *See* Dollar (Hong Kong)
 direct investment abroad, 156
 direct investment in, 30(table), 51
 and EC, 144(table)
 economy, 1, 46, 69, 141–142, 147, 148, 149, 150, 153, 157, 159
 emigrants, 151–152, 156–157, 159
 as entrepôt, 142, 148, 149
 exports, 101, 142, 143–144(tables), 148
 GDP, 142, 143(table)
 and global economic integration, 9, 148
 imports, 142, 143, 144(table)
 industry, 142, 143, 148
 and Japan, 49–51, 144(table)
 labor, 143(table)
 land development, 149, 150
 population, 143(table), 145, 149, 159(n2)
 and PRC, 102, 118, 137, 142, 143–147, 148, 149, 157, 158
 and PRC sovereignty (1997), 145, 146–147, 149–150, 152–157

Index

reexports, 142, 143(table), 160(n19)
and regional economy, 148
regional trade, 23-28(tables), 29, 50(fig.), 141, 144(table), 158
and South Korea, 144(table), 158, 160(n19)
stock market, 150
and Taiwan, 144(table), 158, 160(n19)
technology, 141, 145, 178, 183(table), 186(table)
and U.S., 183(table), 192(table)
and U.S. trade, 129(table), 143, 144(table)
"Hong Kong formula," 11
House Armed Services Investigations Subcommittee (U.S.), 202
Housing, 4, 13, 79
Hsinchu Science Park (Taiwan), 128, 130
Huang Xiang, 102
Human capital, 79, 90, 138, 151
Human rights, 63, 149
Hungary, 12, 208

IBM (company), 179
Iceland, 202
IMF. See International Monetary Fund
Import-liberalization ratios, 71-72
Import substitution, 13, 78, 80
Income
distribution, 95, 124, 135
household and savings, 168(table)
national, 171(table)
per capita, 22, 69
real, 106
Indochina, 34. See also Burma; Kampuchea; Laos; Vietnam
Indonesia, 59
direct investment in, 30, 51
foreign aid to, 32(table), 33
and PRC, 101, 139(n6), 158
raw materials exports, 29
and regional economy, 59
regional trade, 23-28(tables), 29
technology, 183(table), 186, 187
and U.S., 110, 183(table), 192(table)
Inflation, 7, 8, 36, 106, 124
Information flows, 63
Institute for International Economics, 55
Institute of Developing Economies (MITI), 35
Institute of Science and Technology project, 145
Intellectual property rights, 15, 55, 56, 60, 63, 114, 180, 182, 184-188, 195-196
Interdependence, 8, 22, 57, 89, 90, 120, 122
Interest-group politics, 77, 78, 83, 84, 96, 111, 112, 113-114
Interest rates, 48, 49, 73, 80, 93, 169
Internationalists, 40, 112

Internationalization, 95-96. See also Economic integration
International Monetary Fund (IMF), 9, 17, 43, 64, 85, 130
Article VIII, 96
International Rice Research Institute (Philippines), 193
International Studies Center (PRC State Council), 102
Investment, 56, 58, 63. See also Development investment; Direct investment; Manufacturing investment; subentry domestic investment under South Korea; Soviet Union; Taiwan; United States
Ireland, 200(table), 209
Iron ore, 29
Israel, 205
Italy, 166, 167-168(tables), 200(table)

JAIDO. See Japan International Development Organization, Ltd.
Japan
agricultural market, 3
Asian factories, 37, 138
balance of payments, 76
budget, 76
bureaucracy, 34-35
consumer goods, 36
as creditor nation, 47, 48, 62
defense, 49, 117, 171(table), 172, 203
economic competition, 1-2, 21, 39-40, 46, 56, 138, 193
economy, 2, 13, 40, 42, 46, 47, 48-49, 57, 61, 90, 104
emperor's funeral (1989), 35, 38
foreign aid from 4, 11, 19, 31-35, 37, 40, 41, 42, 49, 51, 110
foreign exchange reserves, 51
and foreign students, 193-194
GDP, 29, 142
and global economic integration, 9, 19, 43, 47, 122
imports, 29, 30, 35-36, 42, 47, 51, 56, 113
imports and development needs, 14, 29, 177, 182-183
industry, 31, 36, 37
inflation, 36
investible funds, 2, 18, 21, 48
labor, 191
labor costs, 31, 165(table)
manufactured imports, 29, 35-36, 38, 51
militarism (1930s-1940s), 35, 61, 110
Ministry of Foreign Affairs, 60
Ministry of International Trade and Industry (MITI), 14, 35, 40, 41, 59, 60, 174
overseas subsidiaries, 49, 57, 189

political parties, 47
protectionism, 35, 41, 65
regional direct investment, 30-31, 35, 36-38, 39, 40, 41, 51, 62, 91, 92(table), 110, 189
 and regional economy, 1, 3, 4, 21, 22, 37, 38, 39, 40, 41, 42-43, 58, 59-62, 64, 65, 103, 116
 and regional energy policy, 40, 41
 and regional security, 18-19, 37
regional trade, 23, 24-29(tables), 30, 48, 49, 50(fig.), 51, 56-57, 64, 91(table), 113, 124, 162, 175
savings, 166, 167-168(tables)
stock market, 49
technology, 18, 31, 35, 177, 178, 179, 180, 181, 182, 183(table), 186, 190, 195, 197
trade surplus, 2, 42, 49, 51, 93
trading companies, 34
and U.S., 3, 38-39, 40, 41, 43, 109, 112, 113, 117, 118, 122, 127, 161, 162, 172, 179, 181, 183(table), 192(table), 203
 and U.S., direct investment in, 36, 51
 and U.S. trade, 31, 46-47, 48, 50(fig.), 52-53, 54-58, 73, 80, 84, 85, 112, 129(table), 172, 173(table), 174-175
 and Vietnam, 111, 118
 See also under ASEAN; European Community; individual countries
Japanese Export-Import Bank, 11
Japan Federation of Economic Organizations (Keidanren), 37
 Committee on International Cooperation Projects (CICP), 37
Japan International Cooperation Agency (JICA), 34
Japan International Development Organization, Ltd. (JAIDO), 37, 38, 40, 41
Japan-U.S. economic charter proposal, 56
J curve, 172
Jiang Zemin, 107
JICA. See Japan International Cooperation Agency
Johnson, Chalmers, 85
Joint ventures, 11, 13, 14, 15, 17, 18, 206, 207

Kampuchea, 11, 63, 109, 110, 111
 foreign aid to, 33(table), 34
 political-military instability, 2, 12
Kanghua affair (1988) (PRC), 157
Keidanren. See Japan Federation of Economic Organizations
Khabarovsk (Soviet Union), 15
Khazan district (Soviet Union), 15
Khmer Rouge, 111
Khrushchev, Nikita, 6
Kim, Jong-Bum, 177
Kimura, Hiroshi, 11

KMT. See Nationalist party
Korean peninsula, 2
 independence (1948), 70
 See also North Korea; South Korea
Korean War (1950-1953), 148
Korea Trade Promotion Corporation (KOTRA), 78
KOTRA. See Korea Trade Promotion Corporation
Kowloon Peninsula, 145
Kuo, Shirley W.Y., 133
Kuomintang. See Nationalist party
Kurile Islands, 9

Labor, U.S. Department of, 194
LADA (Soviet Fiat model car), 13
Laos, 33(table), 34, 63
Latin America, 19, 63, 191
L curve, 172
LDCs. See Less Developed Countries
Lease law, 18
Lee Huan, 132
Lee Teng-hui, 132, 133
Lenin, V. I., 8
Leningrad. See Vyborg Special Economic Zone
Less Developed Countries (LDCs), 9
 and technology transfer, 177, 178, 184, 185, 188-191, 193, 195, 196, 197
Levine, Mel, 59
Liberal Democratic Party (Japan), 47
Liberalization, 74, 76, 77, 81, 82, 83, 95-96, 98, 116, 117, 131
Liberal world economic order, 3, 4, 9
Li Peng, 134, 136
Living standards, 3, 5, 106
Luxembourg, 200(table)

Machinery, 72(table), 73, 79, 209
Macroeconomic policies, 35, 42, 48, 54, 57, 59, 74, 77, 78, 79, 84, 94(table), 115-116, 161, 162, 169, 173
Malaysia
 direct investment in, 30, 36, 137
 foreign aid to, 32-33(tables)
 and Japan, 36
 and OECD, 116
 raw materials exports, 29
 regional trade, 22, 23-29(tables)
 technology, 183(table), 186(table), 190
 and U.S., 110, 183(table), 192(table)
Managed trade, 52-53, 54, 85
Management schools and exchanges, 17, 98, 145
Mansfield, Mike, 41, 54, 175
Manufacturing investment, 30-31, 51
Market sharing, 75

Index

Massachusetts Institute of Technology (MIT), 181
Mexico, 8, 50(fig.), 57, 59, 61, 174(table)
MFN. *See* Most-favored-nation status
Microchips, 194
Middle East, 205
Military conflicts, 1, 2
MIT. *See* Massachusetts Institute of Technology
MITI. *See* Japan, Ministry of International Trade and Industry
Modernization, 1, 2, 14
Moiseyev, Nikolai, 10
Monnet, Jean, 207
Most-favored-nation (MFN) status, 56, 60, 64, 82
Multifibre Arrangement (1973), 52, 75
Multilateral aid agencies, 31, 32-33(tables), 34
Multilateralism, 74, 76, 77, 81, 83, 120
Multinational corporations, 17, 150-151, 179, 189, 193

Nakasone, Yasuhiro, 59
Nakhodka Special Economic Zone, 11, 13, 14, 15, 18
Nanto, Dick K., 21
National Committee for Pacific Economic Cooperation (PRC), 102-103
National Cooperation Research Act (1984) (U.S.), 182
National Institutes of Health (U.S.), 181
Nationalist party (KMT) (Taiwan), 131, 132, 134, 135
National Planning Association (NPA), 161, 173-174, 175
National Security Directive No. 185 (1985), 62
NATO. *See* North Atlantic Treaty Organization
Natural gas, 29
Natural resources, 8, 63. *See also* Raw material-exporting countries
Netherlands, 128(table), 138, 200(table)
Newly Industrializing Countries (NICs), Asian, 1, 142
  balance-of-payments policy, 14
  direct investment abroad, 91, 92(table)
  direct investment in, 30, 37, 92(table)
  domestic priorities, 4
  economies, 40, 90
  education abroad, 192-193
  export-oriented, 13, 90
  and global economic integration, 9, 18, 19, 40, 42-43
  and GSP, 39, 40
  labor abroad, 191
  labor costs, 165
  technology, 90, 93, 177, 178, 182, 184, 185-187, 195, 196, 197
  trade, 49-52, 90, 91(table), 97(table), 137
  See also Hong Kong; Singapore; South Korea; Taiwan
New Taiwan (N.T.) dollar, 76, 124, 125-127(table)
  appreciation, 127
New Territories, 145, 146
New Thinking, 8-9, 11, 19
New Wave economies, 168
New Zealand, 41
  direct investment in, 92(table)
  and Japan, 92(table)
  and PECC, 61
  and regional economy, 58, 60
  regional trade, 22, 23-29(tables), 50(fig.), 91(table)
  technology, 183(table), 186(table)
  trade deficits, 93
  and U.S., 92(table), 183(table)
NICs. *See* Newly Industrializing Countries, Asian
NIEs. *See* East Asian Newly Industrializing Economies
Nobel Prize, 179
Nonequity financing, 36
Nontariff trade barriers, 63
North Africa, 202
North America. *See* Canada; United States
North American Free Trade Zone, 1
North Atlantic Treaty Organization (NATO), 9, 171(table), 172, 201, 202, 203-204, 205, 208, 210
  European members, 200(table)
Northeast Asia, 8
Northern Territories, 2, 8, 9, 11
North Korea, 2, 8, 9, 63, 98, 186(table)
Norway, 202
NPA. *See* National Planning Association
NPC. *See* People's Republic of China, National People's Congress

ODA. *See* Official development assistance
OECD. *See* Organization for Economic Cooperation and Development
OECF. *See* Overseas Economic Cooperation Fund
Official development assistance (ODA), 31-35, 41
Oil, 15, 29
  prices, 73
  revenues, 13, 14
  shocks (1970s), 49, 69
Omnibus Trade and Competitiveness Act (U.S. P.L. 100-418) (1988), 48, 49, 52, 75

Super 301 provisions, 48, 52, 76, 93, 112, 161, 170, 175
Opium War (1839-1842), 146
OPTAD. *See* Organization for Pacific Trade and Development proposal
Organization for Economic Cooperation and Development (OECD), 31, 34, 61, 64
  and Asian NICs, 40, 42-43, 116, 120, 121
  labor costs, 165(table)
  statistics, 63
Organization for Pacific Trade and Development (OPTAD) proposal, 96
Ota, Seizo, 14
Overseas Economic Cooperation Fund (OECF) (Japan), 34, 37

Pac-8, 59
Pacific Basin Economic Council (PBEC), 64, 96, 100, 119
Pacific Basin forum, 107
"Pacific century," 142
Pacific Economic Cooperation Conference (PECC) (1980), 60-61, 62, 63, 96, 100, 102, 120
  funding, 64
Pacific Forum for Economic and Cultural Cooperation proposal, 59-60
Pacific Free Trade Area (PAFTA) proposal, 41, 51, 54-58, 59, 85, 100, 121
Pacific Islands, 61, 63
PAFTA. *See* Pacific Free Trade Area proposal
Palestinian question, 205
Palm oil. *See* Tropical oils
Park Chung-hee, 70, 78
Patents, 184, 185, 186(table), 187, 188, 194-195
Patent Security Act, 180
Patrizansk district (Soviet Union), 15
PBEC. *See* Pacific Basin Economic Council
Peace Corps, 42
Pease, Donald, 55
PECC. *See* Pacific Economic Cooperation Conference
People's Republic of China (PRC), 59, 64
  agricultural exports, 101
  arms trade, 158
  balance of payments, 136
  border forces, 9, 11, 12, 19
  Chinese Communist party, 152
  corruption, 157
  currency. *See* Yuan
  debt, 101
  direct investment abroad, 92(table)
  direct investment in, 92(table), 102, 151
  economy, 103, 104, 105, 107, 111, 135, 136, 145, 158-159
  education abroad, 192(table), 194
  exports, 101, 105, 106, 107
  foreign aid to, 33, 92(table), 104
  and global economic integration, 101, 106
  and Grenada, 134
  imports, 101, 102, 105, 111, 148
  inflation, 106
  and Japan, 4, 11, 32(table), 33, 50(fig.), 92(table), 102, 104
  manufactures exports, 101
  military, 153
  modernization, 1, 2, 145
  National People's Congress (NPC), 152, 154, 155
  nuclear power plant, 143
  and PECC, 61, 102
  population, 1
  prices, 106
  protectionism, 104, 105, 106
  and regional cooperation, 102-105, 107
  regional trade, 23-28(tables), 29, 101, 102, 105, 106, 111
  self-sufficiency, 2
  and Soviet Union, 4, 9, 10, 11, 12, 15, 18, 19, 109, 134
  State Council, 155
  technology, 31, 104, 178, 183(table), 186(table), 188
  trade, 101
  and UN, 131
  and U.S., 33, 92(table), 104, 131, 183(table), 191, 192(table), 194
  and U.S. trade, 129-130(tables), 160(n19)
  See also Tiananmen Square uprising; *under* individual countries
Perestroika, 5, 9, 13, 203. *See also* New Thinking
Persian Gulf region, 8, 202
Peru, 61
Petri, Peter A., 73
Petrochemicals, 14, 72(table)
Petro-dollars, 148
Pharmaceuticals, 194, 195
Philippines
  direct investment in, 30, 137
  foreign aid to, 31, 32(table), 33
  and Japan, 33
  regional trade, 23-29(tables)
  technology, 186, 193
  and U.S., 29, 110, 192(table)
Philips Company (Netherlands), 138
Pogranichny district (Soviet Union), 15
Poland, 12, 14, 17, 208
Population, 97, 143(table), 149
  and defense, 171(table)
  over-, 8
Portugal, 200(table)
PRC. *See* People's Republic of China
Prestowitz, Clyde, 85

Index

Private property rights, 141, 153
Private sector, 60, 115, 120, 141, 166, 170
Process protection 75, 76, 81, 83
Product standards, 54, 63, 80, 204
Protectionism, 53, 74, 84, 86, 89, 93, 96, 98, 204, 210. *See also under* Association of Southeast Asian Nations; Japan; People's Republic of China; South Korea; Soviet Union; United States

Quality control, 14, 136
Quota rents, 75

R&D. *See* Research and development
Rate of return, 5
Raw material-exporting countries, 29, 97, 101
Reagan, Ronald, 62, 74, 82, 83, 209
Reciprocity, 74, 76, 77, 81, 82, 83, 85, 172, 206
Recruit scandal (Japan), 112
Regionalism, 89, 93
Republic of China (ROC). *See* Taiwan
Republic of Korea. *See* South Korea
Rescher, Nicholas, 181
Research and development (R&D), 15, 165, 177, 178. *See also under* Technology
Research Institute on the National Economy (Japan), 40
Resource development projects, 30
Reverse engineering, 188, 196
Rice, 110, 112, 113
ROC (Republic of China). *See* Taiwan
Rockefeller Foundation, 193
Roh Tae Woo, 83
Rong Yiren, 102
Ruble (Soviet currency), 15

SAR. *See* Special Administrative Region
Savings, 124, 165, 166, 167-168(tables), 203
Scandinavian countries, 8
Schott, Jeffrey J., 55
Semiconductors, 52-53, 75, 209
Senate Committee on Armed Services, 203
Services, 56, 75-76, 95, 145, 168
SEZs. *See* Special Economic Zones
Shakespeare, William, 188
Shenzhen (PRC) Special Economic Zone, 145
Shmelev, Nikolai, 5
Showa emperor. *See* Japan, emperor's funeral
Shultz, George, 54, 58, 210
Siberia (Soviet Union), 4, 9-10, 13, 14, 17
Singapore, 9, 62, 142
 currency. *See* Dollar (Singapore)
 direct investment in, 30(table), 51
 economy, 46, 69
 foreign aid to, 32(table), 33
 and OECD, 116, 121
 and PRC, 158

regional direct investment, 30
regional trade, 23-29(tables)
technology, 178, 183(table), 186, 187, 190
and U.S., 114, 183(table), 192(table)
and U.S. trade, 129(table)
Single Europe Act (1986), 93, 199, 204-205. *See also* European Community, 1992
Software, 194, 197
Solomon, Richard H., 121
South Africa, 8
Southeast Asia, 1, 2, 8. *See also* Association of Southeast Asian Nations
South Korea, 8, 9, 59, 61-62
 agricultural imports, 77, 83, 95
 agriculture, 82
 and ASEAN, 121
 balance of payments, 70, 73, 74(table), 76, 79, 80
 currency. *See* Won
 debt, 69, 80, 95
 democratization, 89, 95
 direct investment abroad, 95, 98, 99(table)
 direct investment in, 30, 36, 51
 domestic consumption, 95
 domestic investment, 72, 79, 81
 domestic markets, 70
 economy, 1, 13, 14, 46, 69, 78, 79, 80, 89, 94-96
 exports, 69-70, 71, 72-73, 78-79, 80, 89, 94, 97, 101
 foreign aid from, 95, 98
 foreign exchange earnings, 80, 96
 and FTA, 55
 GDP, 79
 and global economic integration, 9, 70, 95-96
 GNP, 69, 80, 94(table), 96, 183
 imports, 69, 71-72, 74(table), 77, 81, 83, 95, 96, 97
 imports and development needs, 14, 182, 183
 import substitution, 78
 income, 69, 82, 95
 industry, 69, 71, 72-73, 78, 79, 94
 instability, 2, 78, 95
 investible funds, 18
 and Japan, 36, 49-51, 71, 72(table), 73, 74(table), 84, 97
 labor, 78, 79, 82, 95
 labor costs, 76, 78
 and OECD, 121
 and PRC, 98, 158
 price stability, 79, 94
 productivity, 79, 82
 protectionism, 70, 74, 82
 and regional cooperation, 90, 96-98, 100
 and regional economy, 58, 59
 and regional investment, 89

regional trade, 23, 24–29(tables), 50(fig.), 91(table), 97(table), 98, 113
Sixth Five-Year Plan (1987–1991), 70, 79
and Soviet Union, 8, 9, 10, 11, 12, 15, 98
technology, 18, 72, 73, 78, 79, 178, 182, 183, 185, 186, 187, 192
trade deficit, 97
trade policy, 78–81, 83–84
trade surplus, 93, 94(table), 95, 96, 97, 98
and U.S., 70, 185, 192, 194
and U.S. trade, 70, 71, 72(table), 73, 74, 75–76, 77, 80, 81–83, 84, 97, 129(table)
See also under Hong Kong
Soviet Union
and Afghanistan, 8, 11, 12, 19
agriculture, 6, 7, 8, 13
and Asia-Pacific trade, 23(table), 24–29(tables)
Asia policy, 1, 8, 9, 11–15, 18, 19, 61
balance of payments, 5, 6–7
bureaucracy, 5, 6–7
and Central America, 8
consumer goods, 5, 7, 10, 13, 18
cooperatives, 6, 8
debt, 14, 16(table)
and decentralization, 5, 6
domestic investment, 5–6, 9–10, 14
domestic market system, 4, 7, 8, 13, 15, 17, 19
economy, 2, 4–8, 13, 14
exchange rate, 5. *See also* Ruble
and foreign investment, 12, 13, 18
and FRG, 11, 12, 13
and global economy, 4, 9, 10–11, 14, 15, 17–18
grain imports, 13
imports, 13–14
industry, 6, 10, 13, 14, 18
inflation, 7, 8, 9
infrastructure, 7, 8, 10, 18
and Japan, 4, 8, 9, 10, 11, 14–15, 18, 19
military, 2, 4, 5–6, 8, 10, 12, 19
monetization, 4, 5, 6
natural resources, 13, 14, 15, 17, 18
oil, 13, 15
price reform, 4–5, 6, 7, 13
productivity, 5, 6, 7, 14
protectionism, 13
R&D, 15
savings, 5
and South Africa, 8
wages, 5, 7, 8
and Western industrial economies, 2, 4, 11, 12, 13, 15, 17–18, 19, 205, 208
See also Siberia; *under* Association of Southeast Asian Nations; *individual countries*
Soybean oil, 112, 114

Spain, 200(table)
Special Administrative Region (SAR) (PRC), 146, 147, 152, 153, 154, 155, 158
Preparatory Committee, 156
Special Economic Zones (SEZs), 11, 13, 14, 15, 17, 18, 145
Standardized parts and components, 90
State, U.S. Department of, 112, 114, 201
Steel, 56, 72(table), 75, 85, 113
Superconductivity, 179, 180
Supply-side economics, 162
Sweden, 202
Switzerland, 202

TAA. *See* Trade adjustment assistance
Taiwan, 62, 64
and ASEAN, 137
Council on External Trade, 140(n11)
currency. *See* New Taiwan dollar
direct investment abroad, 137
direct investment in, 30(table), 36, 138
domestic investment, 124, 135, 136
and EC, 128, 137
economic policy, 124, 127, 130–131
economy, 1, 46, 69, 124, 131, 133, 135–136
exports, 101, 124, 127, 128, 130, 136, 137, 187
foreign aid program, 137
foreign exchange reserve, 124
and FTA, 55
and global economic integration, 9, 124, 131, 133, 138
GNP, 133
imports, 124, 127, 128(table)
income, 124, 135
industry, 130
inflation, 124
and Japan, 36, 49–51, 124, 127, 128(table), 138
labor costs, 124
and Malaysia, 137
and PECC, 61
and Philippines, 137
political parties, 131, 132, 134
political restructuring, 131–133, 138–139(n5)
and PRC, 101, 124, 128, 131, 134–135, 136–137, 138, 146, 158
press, 132
prices, 124, 127
and regional economy, 123, 137–138
regional trade, 23, 24–29(tables), 50(fig.), 113
savings, 124, 137
and Soviet Union, 128
stock market, 133
technology, 128, 130, 136, 137, 178, 183(table), 185, 186, 187
and Thailand, 137

Index

trade surplus, 93, 124
  and U.S., 124, 127, 128, 137-138, 183(table), 185, 192(table), 194
  and U.S. trade, 56, 81, 124, 127-128, 129(table), 130, 136, 187
  wages, 124, 138
  See also under Hong Kong
Takeshita, Noboru, 39, 60
Targeting, 79, 80
Tariff Act (1930) (U.S.)
  Section 337, 75
Tariff schedule of the U.S. (TSUS), 130
Tariff structure, 5, 57, 95
Technology
  absorptive capacity, 177, 178, 179, 188, 189, 190, 191, 195, 197
  assistance, 17, 18, 182, 189
  availability, 177, 190
  cooperation, 196-197
  and education, 182, 188, 189, 190, 191-194, 195, 197
  imports. *See subentry* transfer
  labor-intensive, 93
  licensing, 79, 184, 188, 190
  problems, 178, 182, 186, 187-188, 191, 192, 194-195, 196
  and R&D, 177, 178, 181-182, 183-184, 186, 194, 196, 197
  secrecy, 180
  transfer, 14, 31, 35, 58, 63, 93, 95, 98, 112, 114, 115, 137, 141, 145, 177-179, 180, 182, 183(tables), 184, 189-191, 194, 195, 196, 197
  turnkey, 13
  See also Intellectual property rights; *under individual countries*
Terrorism, 204
Textiles, 71, 72(table), 109, 110, 111, 113, 130, 143, 145
  import quotas, 52, 56, 75
Thailand, 62
  direct investment in, 30(table), 36, 137
  foreign aid to, 32(table), 33
  and Japan, 36, 39, 51
  and OECD, 116
  and regional economy, 59
  regional trade, 23-29(tables), 30
  technology, 178, 183(table), 186, 190, 193
  and U.S., 110, 112, 118, 183(table), 192(table)
Thatcher, Margaret, 209
Third World, 47, 53, 59, 169, 170
Tiananmen Square (PRC) uprising (1989), 18, 33, 107, 134, 135, 149, 150, 151, 156
Timber, 14, 17, 18
Tin, 29
Tokyo Mutual Life Insurance Company, 14-15
Tokyo Summit precondition, 9

Tourism, 15, 149
Trade Act (1974) (U.S.), 75
  Section 301, 75, 76, 77, 82
Trade Act (1988) (U.S.), 113
Trade adjustment assistance (TAA), 83
Trade Expansion Act (1962) (U.S.), 83
Trade imbalances, 93, 96
Trademarks, 188, 194
Trading blocs, 55, 57, 64, 84, 121, 161, 162, 173-175
Trans Baikal military district (Soviet Union), 9, 10, 119
Treasury, U.S. Department of the, 114
Treaty of Rome (1957), 199
Tropical oils, 110, 112, 113-114
TSUS. *See* Tariff schedule of the U.S.
Turkey, 201, 208

UK-PRC Agreement (1984), 149, 151, 152, 153, 154. *See also* Hong Kong, and PRC sovereignty
Underemployment, 191
Unemployment, 74, 79, 163, 164, 207
  and technology, 178, 191
Unionization, 164
Unions, 207
United Nations, 43, 131, 148, 205
United States
  agricultural cooperatives, 8
  agricultural exports, 81, 109, 112
  arms sales, 203
  and Asia-Pacific direct investment, 30, 38, 91, 92(table), 189
  and Asia-Pacific region, 3-4, 18-19, 21, 22, 40, 41, 42, 58-59, 61, 62, 65, 166, 175-176, 183(tables), 187, 191, 192-193, 210
  and Asia-Pacific security, 42, 46, 62, 110, 114, 117, 119
  Asia-Pacific trade, 23, 24-28(tables), 29, 30, 38, 48, 49, 50(fig.), 52, 53-65, 75, 85, 91(table), 127-128, 129-130(tables), 162, 172, 173(table), 175, 188, 196, 210
  balance of payments, 76
  budget deficit, 3, 38, 43, 47, 48, 64, 76, 84, 110, 124, 161, 162-163, 165, 166, 169, 175, 203
  and burdensharing, 171-172, 203-204
  debtor status, 47, 48
  defense spending, 171(table), 203
  direct investment in, 36, 51, 92(table), 169
  domestic investment, 3, 165, 201
  economic indicators, 163(table)
  economy, 47, 113, 161, 162-165, 168, 169, 170
  economy, regionalized, 168
  exports, 48, 73, 112, 209
  foreign aid from, 4, 31-34, 38, 43, 51
  foreign students in, 191-193, 194

and global economic integration, 9, 162
GNP, 162, 163, 166, 169
industry, 168
inflation, 163, 167, 169
isolationist trend, 114, 115
labor, 163-165, 167, 168
marketing techniques, 8
monetary policy, 168-169
and PECC, 61, 62
productivity, 3, 163(table), 164, 203
protectionism, 31, 48, 49, 75, 76-77, 83, 109, 110, 112, 113, 114
R&D, 165, 178
recessions, 47, 168, 169-170
savings, 165, 166, 167-168(tables), 203
and Soviet Union, 8, 10, 18, 46, 59, 112, 114, 203
technology, 177, 178, 182, 183, 185, 186(table), 187, 190, 194, 195-196, 207
trade deficits, 2, 3, 38, 42, 46, 47, 48, 52, 55, 74, 84, 93, 124, 129-130(tables), 166, 172, 173(table), 175, 188, 202
trade policy, 74-78, 81, 82, 83, 84, 93, 113, 116, 127, 161, 173
and Vietnam, 111
wages, 163, 164, 167
See also under Association of Southeast Asian Nations; European Community; *individual countries*
Urbanization, 178
Urengoi (Soviet Union) gas assessment, 18
Uruguay Round of Multilateral Trade Negotiations (GATT), 9, 43, 52, 55, 59, 84, 98, 109, 121, 122, 201
U.S. International Trade Commission (USITC), 54, 75
USITC. *See* U.S. International Trade Commission

Value-added tax (VAT), 204, 209
VAT. *See* Value-added tax
VERs. *See* Voluntary export restraints
Vietnam, 1, 63, 109, 110, 111, 117-118
 foreign aid to, 33(table), 34
Vladivostok Special Economic Zone (Soviet Union), 14, 15
Voluntary export restraints (VERs), 52, 75, 77, 80, 85
Vyborg Special Economic Zone (Soviet Union), 13, 15

Warsaw Treaty Organization, 203, 204
Welfare and social programs, 79, 133, 149, 170, 208
Western Europe, 8, 12, 109, 165(table), 173(table), 201
Western European Union (WEU), 200, 205, 209
Western industrial economies, 2, 9. *See also under* Soviet Union
West Germany. *See* Federal Republic of Germany
WEU. *See* Western European Union
Won (South Korean currency), 96, 125-127(table)
 appreciation, 95, 96
 devaluation, 79
World Bank, 4, 9, 17, 43, 64, 85, 120, 130
World Intellectual Property Organization, 196

Yang Shangkuen, 134, 136
Yazov, Dimitri, 10
Yen (Japanese currency), 21, 35, 40, 51, 125-127(table)
 appreciation, 49, 57, 73
Yeutter, Clayton, 175
Yuan (PRC currency), 105, 106, 125-127(table)
Yugoslavia, 14
Yu Kuo-hua, 132, 133